CROMWELL'S
EARL

A Life of Edward Mountagu
1st Earl of Sandwich

D0539158

RICHARD OLLARD

This book belongs to
Audrey Guille

HarperCollins*Publishers*

HarperCollins*Publishers*
77–85 Fulham Palace Road,
Hammersmith, London w6 8jb

Published by HarperCollins*Publishers* 1994

1 3 5 7 9 8 6 4 2

A catalogue record for this book is
available from the British Library

ISBN 0 00 255003 2

Photoset in Linotron Ehrhardt by
Rowland Phototypesetting Ltd
Bury St Edmunds, Suffolk

Printed in Great Britain by
HarperCollinsManufacturing Glasgow

To Mary

CONTENTS

LIST OF MAPS

LIST OF ILLUSTRATIONS

LIST OF DRAWINGS IN TEXT

Sir Edward Mountagu
(1532 - 1602)

| Henry (d. in infancy) | Edward 1st Lord Mountagu of Boughton (1562 - 1644) | Walter | Henry (1563 - 1642) cr. Earl of Manchester 1627 = Catherine Spencer |

Edward
2nd Lord Mountagu
of Boughton
member C^tee of Admiralty
and Navy
(1616 - 1684)

Edward
killed at Bergen
(1635 - 1665)

Edward
2nd Earl of Manchester
Parliamentary
General etc
(1602 - 1671)
Numerous progeny
by two out of his five
wives. By his third
wife, Essex, he was
the father of yet
another

Walter
Abbot of Pontoi
(?1603 - 1677)

Edward
(?1645 - ?)
whose designs on
the ward and heiress
Anne Wortley the
subject of this biography
suspected

| Jemima = Philip b. 1646   Carteret (married in 1665) | Edward   = Visc^t. Hinchinbrooke 2nd Earl of Sandwich b. 1648 (married in 1668) | Lady Anne Boyle (ob. 1671) | Paulina (1649 - 166 |

Notes:
1. The marriages and deaths of the Sandwich children are only given if
they occurred in the lifetime of their father.
2. This genealogy makes no pretence to completeness and is intended
simply to enable the reader to take in at a glance the relationship of
people mentioned in the text.

```
ames              Charles        Sir Sydney      = Paulina d. of
)p. of Winchester                (?1571 - 1644)    John Pepys of Cottenham
?1568 - 1618)                                      (ob. 1638)




liza      =   Sir Gilbert        EDWARD          = JEMIMA CREW
620 -         Pickering          1st Earl of       (1625 - 1674)
)arried in    (1613 - 1668)      Sandwich          married Nov. 1642
538)                             (1625 - 1672)





y   Anne  = Sir Richard    John & Oliver     Charles    Catherine   James
)   b. 1653  Edgcumbe       |(twins) |        b. 1658    b. 1661     b. 1664
    (married                |(?b. 1655)|
    in 1671)
                            Master of      KC
                            Trinity College
                            Cambridge,
                            Dean of Durham
```

ACKNOWLEDGMENTS

My debt to John and Caroline Montagu for their encouragement in writing this book and for their kindness in making the first Earl's Journal available to me over a long period is great. It is not often that such total immersion in one's principal source is possible.

Second only to that is my gratitude to the Society of Authors for their generous assistance in the form of a grant.

What I owe to other scholars is everywhere apparent. Besides those whose works are directly acknowledged I should like to thank the following kind people who have answered my questions or otherwise supplied me with information. None of them is in any way responsible for any of the mistakes or misjudgments to be found in these pages. Dr Carlos de Azevedo; Professor C.R. Boxer; Sir Raymond Carr; Dr Eric Christiansen; Professor Sir John Elliott; Mr Frank Fox; General Sir Frank and Lady Kitson; Mr Robert Latham; Mr Alistair Malcolm; Sir Oliver Millar; Dr Malcolm Rogers; and Miss Jayne Shrimpton of the National Portrait Gallery; Mr Philip Saunders of the Cambridgeshire County Record Office; Sir Anthony Wagner, Clarenceux King of Arms; and Miss R. Watson of the Northamptonshire County Record Office.

For permission to quote from manuscripts in their possession I am grateful to the Curators of the Bodleian Library, the Trustees of the British Library and the Controller of H.M. Stationery Office.

The list of illustrations enumerates my obligations to those who have kindly permitted me to reproduce pictures or tapestries in their possession. In this connexion I am particularly grateful to Evelyn Joll, my friend for sixty years, for enabling me to see the newly cleaned portrait of Sandwich in the freshness of youth and for providing me with a photograph of it.

Finally I am grateful to my son William for reading the typescript and to Robert Latham for reading the proofs.

A note on Spanish and Portuguese names

In my text as well as in quotation I have followed Sandwich's usage and spelling. This is not always consistent and certainly differs from that which a modern scholar would employ. But very often the differences are so slight that a correction seemed pedantic.

I

Why Sandwich?

ON THE DAY OF the Japanese attack on the American Fleet at Pearl Harbor, 7th December 1941, the British ambassador at Tehran wrote home to his wife:

> *The Times* complained a few days ago about the slowness of British diplomacy in Tehran ... I wish the editor had had to negotiate a treaty in four languages, the other two parties to the tripartite arrangement being each other's hereditary enemies. However, things do get done gradually.[1]

On the other side of the world the other side of the conduct of affairs was being shatteringly exemplified. The two modes seldom coincide in the experience of one man. The skills required in a situation such as that outlined above by Sir Reader Bullard differ in kind and in manner of application from those needed for command in battle. Yet the man who occupies the central position in this book was called on to display both. As a young colonel in the Parliamentary army during the Civil War, as a General at Sea under Cromwell, as an admiral and Commander-in-Chief under Charles II, he had plenty of experience of command in war. As an ambassador successively to Lisbon and to Madrid he came to know the last resorts of procrastination and evasiveness for which those courts were justly celebrated. Indeed during the interminable months of 1666 and 1667 he found himself exactly in the position described by Sir Reader three centuries later, charged as he was with bringing the long war between Portugal

1. *Letters from Tehran* ed. E.C. Hodgkin, p. 97.

and Spain to an end and securing important interests of our own in the process.

Edward Mountagu, First Earl of Sandwich, has been denied the high place in English and European history to which he is entitled. To a great extent this is his own fault – or should one say his own merit? As his cousin Samuel Pepys regretfully observed when Sandwich came to report on his extremely thorough inquiry into the state of the English garrison in Tangier, he lacked the arts of presentation and self-advertisement in which Pepys himself excelled:

> Which though he had admirable matter for it, and his doings there was good and would have afforded a noble account, yet he did it with a mine [i.e. mien] so low and mean, and delivered in so poor a manner, that it appeared nothing at all, nor anybody seemed to value it; whereas, he might have shown himself to have merited extraordinary thanks, and been held to have done a very great service; whereas now, all the cost the King hath been at [for] his Journey through Spain thither seems to be almost lost.[1]

This is more surprising because the two most obvious qualities possessed by this versatile and effective man are decisiveness, both in action and debate, and the power of engaging, as well as giving, loyalty and affection. There is nothing bumbling or insipid about him, except, apparently, where he might be thought to be praising himself.

Such claims require justification before the reader is swept into the survey of a career remarkable even in that age of remarkable men. Decisiveness for a start. At the mature age of seventeen, on 7th November 1642, with the Civil War already begun, Edward Mountagu married Jemima Crew the daughter of a prominent Parliamentarian neighbour. His own father, Sir Sydney Mountagu, was a staunch Royalist who had twice entertained the King and Queen at Hinchingbrooke, the great house near Huntingdon recently acquired from the Cromwell family. The wisdom of the choice of partner at such an age would have astonished Mr Knightley. 'So early in life – at three-and-twenty – a period when, if a man chuses a wife, he generally chuses ill. At three-and-twenty to have drawn such a prize! What years of felicity that man, in

1. *Diary*, 9th November 1668. The editor, Robert Latham, confirmed my conjecture of 'mine' for 'mind' in a letter of 18th March 1992.

all human calculation, has before him!' My Lady, as she is familiarly known to generations of Pepys's readers, amply supports that prognostication. Her gentleness and tact, her strength of principle and her affectionate heart would have made her a favourite with Mr Knightley's creator.

But Edward went further against his father's wishes by choosing actually to fight for Parliament. At the age of eighteen he had raised a regiment for the Eastern Association commanded by his cousin the Earl of Manchester. Before his nineteenth birthday he had seen his first action at the storming of Hillesden House, had faced fierce fighting at the recapture of Lincoln and found himself in a very tight corner at the siege of York where his regiment had broken through the wall after a mine had partly demolished it and had then been cut off and badly mauled by the defenders. At the decisive battle of Marston Moor a fortnight later he so distinguished himself as to be invited to represent his Commander-in-Chief at the signing of the articles of surrender of York which followed soon after. His quality was marked by Cromwell, whom he already knew and admired. Before he was twenty he was given a regiment in the New Model Army and crowned his career in the Civil War by serving in the rank of Major-General at the taking of Bridgwater and of Bristol. He was still not old enough to vote in a Parliamentary election.

As to the power of attracting and retaining friendship abundant evidence will be provided at every stage of his life. To have enjoyed the confidence and intimacy of men as different as Cromwell and Clarendon, even, it seems, of that far from forthcoming character King Charles II, is a rare, perhaps a unique, distinction. It conveys something of the flavour of this large-minded, large-bodied, vigorous and original man whose ideas and achievements have been obscured as much by their own multiplicity as by his ineptitude for publicity.

The versatility of Pepys's abilities and the range of his tastes have often been remarked. Yet his cousin and patron was at least his equal, perhaps his superior. Even Pepys himself, no undervaluer of his own qualities, appears to have felt this. Amongst his unexecuted literary projects was a biography of 'that unparalleled Lord'. As Pepys recognized Sandwich combined to an unusual degree the gifts and achievements of a man of action with those of a reflective and inquiring mind. 'Lord Sandwich celebrated by Sir E. Sherbourn among the mathematicians.

3

The King, Duke, and he the most mathematick Admirals England ever had.'[1]

What did Pepys mean? The King, Charles II, was never an admiral except in a purely titular sense and the Duke, his brother James, was not what Sir E. Sherbourn in his day or anyone in ours would have understood by the term mathematician. Surely he was using the word in its old Renaissance sense, the sense in which Leonardo forbade anyone to study his works who had not first applied himself to mathematics. The word, in this context, signifies system, order, rationality. Both the Stuart brothers were champions in the great tactical controversy of their day of fighting fleet actions in line, not of scrambling into action pell-mell and the devil take the hindmost. So, most emphatically, was Sandwich. That fine scholar the late Dr R.C. Anderson, the leading authority on seventeenth-century sea warfare, makes claims for him that, coming from so cautious, so exact, a writer, are formidable indeed:

> In the sphere of tactics, his ideas seem to have been almost in advance of his time. There can be little doubt that the adoption of a pre-arranged 'line of battle', in which every ship had her appointed station, was very largely due to his influence; while another suggestion of his, to contract and strengthen the line by leaving out the hired merchantmen, was so revolutionary that he could not secure its adoption. It has been said that 'the accidents of fortune and the sensational manner of his death [lost with his ship at the Battle of Solebay] have perhaps given Sandwich a greater reputation than he deserved.' A study of his career in the light thrown by his Journal has brought me to a somewhat different conclusion. Fortune, no doubt, favoured him in many ways, but it certainly placed him on the stage at a time when it was not easy to outshine the other performers. With Blake, Monck, Rupert, and the Duke of York ahead of him or beside him, it cannot have been easy for him to come to the front; while, with Ruyter and Tromp as adversaries, there was no chance for any English commander to establish a reputation cheaply. It is useless to speculate what he might have done had he lived . . . Even if he had had his chance as commander-in-chief, he would have had, as Rupert had, the difficult task of handling a fleet composed of two nationalities [French and English] against one of the greatest sea commanders in history. Any man

1. *Naval Minutes*, 418.

might fail in such circumstances, and yet Sandwich might well have been the man to succeed.[1]

Dr Anderson weighed his judgments by the milligram and was temperamentally averse from the cult of personality. 'I am far more interested in events than in the people who produce them and, if left alone, would reduce even history to tabular form' he once wrote in a letter to the present author. To find him ascribing the main credit for the greatest and most far-reaching innovation in naval tactics, not only of the seventeenth century but of the whole modern period, to Sandwich and putting him by implication in the same class as de Ruyter is a high distinction.

The belittling estimate he quotes to dissent from it is that of Sir John Knox Laughton, the author of most of the naval entries in the original Dictionary of National Biography. Knox Laughton rarely if ever erred on the side of generosity. The sneering tone of his piece on Sandwich perhaps roused Dr Anderson's scholarly passion for truth, for evidence as against unsupported assertion. Laughton's opinion that Sandwich's 'scientific studies were probably vicarious' will not stand up to the most cursory examination of the volume of Sandwich's journal that Anderson edited or to that of its successors which remain in manuscript. Sandwich took pains to master the practical aspects of the naval profession. He did his own navigation. On shore as well as at sea he took regular stellar and solar observations. He was a most accurate surveyor. His habits of description and mensuration whenever he made a journey during his time as ambassador in Spain are what one would expect of one of the early Fellows of the Royal Society. In short Pepys's judgment of his cousin was well founded.

Yet that is only a part of the man who, for all that he enjoyed the friendship and respect of most of the leading men of an exceptional and fiercely divided era, probably regarded himself as a failure. In spite of successes that surpass those of most of his contemporaries – a leading part in the peaceful restoration of the monarch, in the conduct of the opening stages of the Second Dutch War, in the conclusion of the peace between Spain and Portugal – he never achieved high office or a share of real power. He was always the executant rather than the architect of

1. *The Journal of Edward Mountagu, 1st Earl of Sandwich 1659–1665* ed. R.C. Anderson (henceforth cited as *Journal*) N.R.S. 1929, x–xi.

One of Sandwich's astronomical drawings – in this case, of the lunar eclipse
observed in Madrid in May 1668

policy. Again though generously rewarded with honours, lands, sinecures and posts such as the Wardrobe that skilfully managed should have yielded considerable profit, he was negligent of his own affairs and constantly embarrassed for money. The war in which he lost his life he thought both wrong and foolish: indeed he seems to have had a strong premonition that he would not survive it and that his country was being wantonly exposed to the gravest dangers. It seems, somehow, a curious final balance sheet of a life that had earned the trust of Cromwell and Charles II, the friendship of Clarendon and John Evelyn, the approval of so notably censorious a figure as Milton[1] and even a grudging tolerance from so embittered a veteran of the Good Old Cause as Ludlow.[2]

But Sandwich, for all the openness and straightforwardness of his nature as it reveals itself in his journals and private correspondence, is neither simple nor obvious. Who can forget Pepys's astonishment – Pepys, that acutest of observers, who had unrivalled opportunities of penetrating his patron's secret thoughts – when he discovered that Sandwich had played a major part in bringing back the King? Any biographer, separated by several centuries from his subject, had better take care not to be cocksure when so adroit a batsman was so utterly beaten by the deceptive deliveries of Sandwich's slow bowling. This book will not explain Sandwich. But it may perhaps suggest his attractiveness and show something of what an interesting and original man he was.

Why, it may be asked, is he not better known or more widely discussed? Pepys put his finger on the fundamental cause in the passage already quoted. But histories and biographies dealing with the main characters and events of this most arresting period have poured, are still pouring, from the press. Cromwell alone has been the subject of at least half a dozen major studies in the last four decades and yet another is eagerly awaited. Both the eighteenth and the nineteenth centuries, the latter especially, contributed massively to the elucidation of the policies and personalities, the forces and the institutions, whose interaction must engage the historical curiosity of anyone who knows or cares about the past. Even the seventeenth century itself provided a wealth of memoirs

1. *Defensio Secunda.* I owe this reference to the kindness of Professor Austin Woolrych.
2. *A Voyce from the Watch Tower* ed. Blair Worden (1978) is virulent against Monck for his part in the Restoration but on the whole uncritical of Sandwich.

and histories written by those who had themselves been on the stage or in the audience during the actual performance. How has Sandwich come off in all this?

Clarendon, who had found him easy to work with in the delicate preliminaries of effecting the Restoration and had thereafter formed a firm political alliance with him, assigns him no great eminence in the somewhat hasty and slapdash chapters with which he concludes his great *History of the Rebellion.* These passages were in fact wrenched from their original context in his autobiography, in which a much more considered and subtle portrait is offered. Sandwich's personal attachment to Cromwell and Cromwell's encouragement and promotion of his young neighbour are freely admitted in both the *History* and the *Life written by himself.* Of all Royalists who had borne the burden and heat of the day Clarendon was the readiest to admit Cromwell's high qualities of courage and of leadership and to understand how he could command the loyalty of men of honour and principle. In his eyes Sandwich had nothing to feel ashamed of in having belonged to Cromwell's intimate circle and having been one of those who pressed him hardest to assume the Crown. 'What if a man should take it upon him to be King?' Sandwich had been chosen to carry the Sword of State in front of Oliver in March 1657 when he attended Parliament to receive the Humble Petition and Advice, as well as at his formal installation as Lord Protector in the following June. He had been nominated to the reconstituted House of Peers in the last Protectorate Parliament. In all this he had evinced a spirit of conformity to the established institutions of English political life after Clarendon's own heart. When Richard Cromwell threw in the towel in 1659 and left the country exposed to the power struggles of unidea'd Generals, religious and political visionaries of one kind and another and political operators whose motives were somewhat less elevated, there was no inconsistency, certainly no betrayal of principle, in such a man's adherence to the Stuart cause. Rather it was a homecoming.

Clarendon's leave-taking of him, written only months after his death when the author was himself a lonely exile at Moulins, is, after John Evelyn's, his earliest and best epitome:

He was a gentleman of so excellent a temper and behaviour that he could make himself no enemies; of so many good qualities and so easy to live with, that he marvellously reconciled the minds of all men to him, who had not intimacy enough with him to admire his other parts: yet was in the general inclinations of men upon some disadvantage. They who had constantly followed the King while he as constantly adhered to Cromwell, and knew not how early he had entertained repentance, and with what hazards and dangers he had manifested it, did believe the King had been too prodigal in heaping so many honours upon him. And they who had been familiar with him and of the same party, and thought they had been as active as he in contributing to the revolution, considered him with some anger, as one who had better luck than they without more merit, and who had made early conditions: when in truth no man in the Kingdom had been less guilty of that address; nor did he ever contribute to any advancement to which he arrived, by the least intimation or insinuation that he wished it, or that it would be acceptable to him.[1]

John Evelyn who, unlike Clarendon, knew a great deal about naval affairs both as an administrator and as a historian singles out Sandwich for the highest praise 'being one of the best Men of War, that ever spread canvas on the sea . . . an able and experienced sea-man . . . he allwayes brought of his Majestie's ships, without losse, though not without as many markes of true Courage as the stoutest of them; and I am witnesses, that in the late War, his owne ship was pierced like a Culender.' Evelyn is here alluding to the Battle off Lowestoft in June 1665. Contrasting him with his rivals and denigrators such as Monck he supports Pepys's view of him as a 'Mathematick admiral'. 'My Lord Sandwich was prudent as well as Valiant, and always governed his affairs with sucesse, and little losse, he was for deliberation & reason, they for action & slaughter without either.' In sum he found him 'one of the best accomplish[ed] persons, not onely of this Nation but of any other: He was learned in the Mathematics, in Musique, in Sea affaires, in Political: Had been divers Embassies, was of a sweete obliging temper; Sober, Chast, infinitly ingenious[2] & a true noble man, an ornament to the Court, & his Prince nor has he left any that approch his many Virtues behind him.'[3]

Both Clarendon and Evelyn like Pepys knew Sandwich as a man of

1. *Continuation*, 750.
2. Identical terms of praise with Milton's: '*summo ingenio*'.
3. *Diary* ed. de Beer iii, 617–619.

affairs as well as a personal friend of cultivated tastes and beautiful manners. They had sat on committees with him, read his reports and despatches, observed his judgment and handling of men. What of the historians who did not enjoy this advantage? Bishop Burnet hardly mentions him in his *History of My Own Time* and, when he does, refrains, most uncharacteristically, from passing any judgment on him. Macaulay, who was only minimally concerned with the period, does not mention him at all. S.R. Gardiner, whose vast range of knowledge over the whole landscape of seventeenth-century politics and whose insight into naval affairs displayed in the volumes he edited for the Navy Records Society on the First Dutch War, would have made his considered judgment of Sandwich of particular interest, hardly mentions him and, when he does, dismissively. He seizes gratefully on the report of an unknown Royalist agent and on the gossip of the Venetian ambassador to represent Sandwich as the object of Blake's dislike and resentment when the two were joint-commanders as Generals at Sea. Yet as J.R. Powell, Blake's biographer and the editor of his letters, has pointed out the evidence of the documents points the other way.[1]

No historian can transcend his own context and some cannot transcend their own prejudices. Gardiner's sympathy for, his understanding of, the men about whom he wrote was influenced, dare one say limited, by two personal facts: his pride in his own direct descent from Oliver Cromwell and his membership of the Plymouth Brethren. Sandwich's good-natured, well-bred easiness was antipathetic to him. He found it much easier to understand, indeed to a degree to sympathize with, bigots on the opposite side such as Charles I or Archbishop Laud than peaceable, middle-of-the-road figures such as Clarendon or Ormonde. The righteous fury of a trooper hewing down the Lord's enemies expressed in his eyes a nobler spirit than Clarendon's horror of war and violence. Sandwich's calmness, his rationality, evident from all the first-hand accounts of him, are easily identified as the lukewarmness of the Laodicean whom the author of the Epistle to the Hebrews was so anxious to spue out of his mouth.

Sir Charles Firth, on whom Gardiner's mantle fell as the master of those who know about the Civil War and Interregnum, gave Sandwich

1. *The Letters of Robert Blake* ed. J.R. Powell (1937) 330–1.

much fuller treatment in the two volumes with which he concluded Gardiner's unfinished history of the Commonwealth and Protectorate. His opinion of him is set out at its fullest in the notice he wrote in the *English Historical Review*[1] of the two-volume biography published by F.R. Harris in 1912.[2] Though the author gratefully acknowledges Firth's guidance in writing it Firth himself makes it plain that he thinks Sandwich a minor figure and the book of a calibre suited to its subject.

It is an admirable biography: readable, large-minded and extremely well documented. The amplitude of that liberal age before the sophisters and calculators had knocked the gilt off the leaves of the book trade allowed the printing of much original material and the setting of the footnotes on the page in discrete abundance, not the bran tub of fifty assorted references, any one of which may be the authority for a particular statement in the text. The author has no axe to grind. He consulted the leading authorities of his day, Firth, H.A.L. Fisher, Sir Charles Oman and on naval matters the brilliant Sir Julian Corbett. He had a marvellous, beautifully kept archive hospitably put at his disposal by the eighth Earl of Sandwich and supplemented it by a thorough use of the Public Records. He was fascinated by what he found and communicates his interest to his readers. He is in general a most accurate transcriber of material though Dr R.C. Anderson has pointed out some rare deficiencies.[3]

F.R. Harris for all the assurance and accomplishment of this work was an unusual historian. He came, so to speak, from nowhere and vanished without trace. The biography of Sandwich appears to be his only published work. He was born in the North Riding of Yorkshire, the son of a clergyman, in 1869 and was privately educated. Most unusually at the age of 33 he matriculated at Oxford as a non-collegiate undergraduate and was admitted to New College, where, after failing the preliminary examinations at his first shot, he obtained a First in Final Honours in 1905.[4] H.A.L. Fisher was his tutor and presumably he must have also been a pupil of Firth, then Regius Professor, since it was Firth who suggested him to Lord Sandwich as a suitable biographer for his ancestor.

1. Vol. xxix (1914), 577–9.
2. *Life of Edward Mountagu, 1st Earl of Sandwich.*
3. *Journal* xlviii.
4. Information kindly supplied by Dr Eric Christiansen, Fellow of New College.

Since then no further study of Sandwich has been undertaken, although his papers have been used by a number of scholars, notably Robert Latham in his great edition of Pepys's *Diary* and, most recently, Dr Ronald Hutton in his biography of Charles II. The present work grew out of an idea about Cromwell that took root in my mind some time ago – namely this. Whatever one thinks of Cromwell there are no two opinions on his superlative quality as a head-hunter. No ruler in our history has surpassed him in choosing men for high office or command, often from those who had differed from him in opinion, even to the extent of having fought on the Royalist side in the Civil War.

To take half a dozen of the most brilliant, Blake as a General at Sea and Thurloe as head of Intelligence and Counter-Intelligence are towering figures. Monck, Mountagu (as Sandwich then was), Lord Broghill and Sir William Lockhart all acquitted themselves with distinction in land or sea fighting or both and two of them occupied the chief diplomatic posts of their time, the embassies in Paris and Madrid. Yet of the six only one was, so to speak, a cradle Cromwellian and three had fought for the Royalists. Blake, Thurloe and Monck have all recently had their biographies written by distinguished scholars. It seemed to me that the other three, who all went on to hold high office under Charles II, would make an interesting study.

The three were all well known to each other. Widely as they differed in background, Mountagu a scion of one of the most powerful English landed families, Roger Boyle, Lord Broghill, later first Earl of Orrery, the youngest of the brilliant Anglo-Irish family whose brother Robert was the famous scientist, Lockhart a minor Scottish aristocrat who had run away from home to seek his fortune in Europe, they had three things in common: their selection for high and sudden promotion by Cromwell, their clear and genuine attachment to him and the outstanding performance with which they repaid his confidence. Their quality is eloquently attested by their re-employment under the very different regime of Charles II. They typify a Kiplingesque concern with the practical and the possible, without which revolutions would be even more destructive, and exemplify a political tradition that was once wittily described as the extreme centre.

But writers in their umbratic world are similarly confronted by obstructive realities that so often impose a change of course on the conduct of public affairs. As soon as I began to research for the book I had in mind the disproportion of material began to upset its balance. For Broghill and Lockhart the surviving sources were thin: for Mountagu they were rich beyond the dreams of avarice. The Journal that he kept, mostly in his own beautifully legible hand, though it covers even fewer years than that of his famous cousin and has none of the uninhibited forthright judgments on himself and everybody else that makes Pepys such stimulating company, is in its way not less revealing. The light it sheds comes through cracks in the shutters where Pepys draws the curtains back with a flourish to admit the rising sun. Both have the universal curiosity, the appetite, the zest for life that make the reader ashamed of his own sluggish imperception.

What was to have been 'Cromwell's Men' has become 'Cromwell's Man' though I shall still make use of Broghill and Lockhart where their careers run parallel to, or intersect with, Mountagu's, or illustrate an aspect of the theme which may perhaps be perceived more clearly in one life than in three.

II

Beginnings

FEW FAMILIES have managed to engross more peerages than the Montagus or Mountagus as they generally styled themselves in the seventeenth century. By the time the subject of this book was born on 27th July 1625 they were easily the most important family in the two neighbouring counties of Huntingdon and Northamptonshire. Edward himself was, as we know, destined to add the Earldom of Sandwich to the family honours. His own father Sir Sydney, a mere knight, was the youngest brother of the Earl of Manchester and of Lord Mountagu of Boughton, who was Lord Lieutenant of Northamptonshire, the county in which Edward was born at the family manor of Barnwell. In 1627, Sir Sydney moved to Hinchingbrooke, the splendid house just outside Huntingdon that had originally been a nunnery and had then passed into the possession of the Cromwells, a family who like the Mountagus had been prominent under the Tudors but had overplayed their hand under James I. It was indeed the reckless expenditure of Sir Oliver Cromwell, 'the Golden Knight' that had led directly to the sale of Hinchingbrooke and indirectly to the social displacement of the kinsman who was to make that name echo through English history.

Hinchingbrooke was in fact bought as part of a larger acquisition by the Earl of Manchester, but since he had a perfectly good house of his own a few miles away at Kimbolton he re-sold it to his youngest brother. Barnwell was not a grand house and it had come to have tragic associations for its owner. His eldest son, indeed at the time his only son, was drowned in the moat at the age of three, shortly before Edward was born. A touching inscription in the Church suggests that Sir Sydney, who has left the impression of a cold, withdrawn father, had been cut to the heart. Perhaps the affection he had lavished on his first-born made him reluctant to expose himself again to so deep a wound. At any rate solitariness and self-sufficiency seem to have characterized Edward's childhood. His mother, Paulina Pepys after whom the diarist's sister was named, was never robust and died when he was only twelve. A few weeks later his only sister, Eliza, married a neighbour, Sir Gilbert Pickering, who was to be one of Edward's colleagues on the Protector's Council of State and in his House of Lords. The boy was left even more to himself. Among the family papers there are none of the charming exchanges between father and child that Edward when he became a father so lovingly preserved. Sir Sydney was a grim old thing obsessed with theology, an enemy to enjoyment, a puritan of the most rigid type.

Strictness seems to have been his animating principle. He was certainly strict in his attention to his affairs and to his position in society. Disdaining the pomps and pleasures of this world is not the same thing as disdaining its rewards. An industrious if undistinguished lawyer he obtained through family interest a minor post at court and then a lucrative Mastership of Requests. His assiduous cultivation of royal favour was rewarded by a Knighthood of the Bath and by the honour of no less than three royal visits to Hinchingbrooke, the last in 1639 when Charles I was heading northwards to meet the military threat from Scotland occasioned by his attempt to impose episcopacy. The coming war was already ruffling the smooth surface of life.

Edward was then attending the grammar-school at Huntingdon at which Cromwell had been a pupil a generation earlier. Its severe and puritan character no doubt met with Sir Sydney's approval. Educationally it seems to have been efficient. Edward learnt enough Latin to transcribe – and even correct – some of the documents and inscriptions that he came across in his ambassadorial career. And it is a reasonable supposition that the ease and fluency with which he transcribed documents in Spanish owed something to his grounding in Latin. The mathematics for which he was later to be admired and their derivative use in the study of astronomy, navigation and surveying must also stand to the credit of the school. Clearly he early acquired a taste for music and some skill as an instrumentalist. It is doubtful if this featured in the curriculum. More likely music entered his life from the society of bailiffs, upper servants and those concerned with the management of the estate or even from such visits and entertainments as were possible for a well-connected teenager with a single morose parent. Hunting and hawking must have provided some such occasions. He had plenty of cousins not far away at Kimbolton and Boughton. Not far away by twentieth-century standards but too far to ride there and back in the day. The Pickerings, his sister and brother-in-law, lived at about the same distance at Tichmarsh just outside Thrapston. Was it there perhaps that he met his future wife, Jemima Crew? Her father, another Northamptonshire landowner, was very much of the same political persuasion as Sir Gilbert Pickering, a persuasion to which Edward himself was to adhere.

The retrospect of childhood, so often the most vivid part of a twentieth-century autobiography, is not a common feature in seventeenth-century memoirs. Clarendon, Pepys, Evelyn, though they wrote copiously about themselves, rarely supply a glimpse of their boyhood. Only John Aubrey comes to mind. Like Edward's his was a lonely childhood: like him he attended a local grammar-school whose admitted quality was marred by the savagery of the discipline and the bullying. Was Huntingdon like Blandford? If it was Edward Mountagu seems to have suffered less as a result.

The Law, the profession by which the Mountagus had risen and thrived, was the choice Sir Sydney had made for him. He was entered on the books of the Middle Temple at the age of ten. But by the time he was fifteen the Short Parliament had met and been summarily dissolved and the writs issued for the Long Parliament to meet in the autumn. Old Sir Sydney – he was nearly seventy, a great age for those times – was returned as one of the Knights of the Shire. His uncompromising support of the King (uncongenial as his religious policy must have been) soon landed him in trouble. He refused to lend the Parliament money for the purchase of arms for which he was suspended from, but not deprived of, his Mastership of Requests.[1] In December 1642 he was called on to take the oath, tendered to all Members of Parliament, to live and die with the Earl of Essex. Rising in his place he replied with

1. Years later his son succeeded in claiming the arrears of his father's salary when he was a member of Cromwell's Council of State in 1654, a striking instance of the force of continuity in an age of upheaval. Of course the real value of the place was not the salary but the fees.

courage and wit that he would not. 'For, he said, he would not swear to live with him, because he was an old man, and might dye before him; nor would he swear to dye with him, since the Earle was going with an army against the King, which he did not know how to free from treason; and so he did not know what end that great man might come to.'[1] Warming to his work he drew from his pocket a royal proclamation declaring that such members as had already taken the oath were themselves guilty of treason. This was too much, even coming from the uncle of one of the members whom Charles I had tried to arrest. He was bundled straight off to the Tower. But in those early days of the war before vindictiveness had had time to take hold his punishment was light. Less than a fortnight later he was released on the plea of age and ill-health, disabled from sitting but not expelled from the House, and sent to the country. No doubt the known political affection of his young son and heir helped.

As a family the Mountagus ran counter to Lawrence Stone's finding that on the whole the younger generation tended to Royalism whilst their fathers were more likely to think, as even the King's standard-bearer did, that the Parliament were in the right. Even the old Earl of Manchester, whose son was soon to command the army of the Eastern Association, bewailed to Sir Philip Warwick the political company the young man had been keeping. The same authority tells a story of the eldest of the brothers, Lord Mountagu of Boughton, who as Lord Lieutenant of Northampton had been putting in execution the King's commission of Array, that is, raising the county for the Royalists. The Parliament sent a party of horse to arrest him and bring him to London ... 'and this was just about the time when the Earl of Essex was marching out with his glorious army against the King. This good Lord mett this great Generall about Barnett, upon the highway, and the Lord of Essex stopt his coach, intending to go and salute him; but as soon as my Lord Mountague heard of it, he commanded his Coachman to drive away, and said *this was not a time for complements*: which was a true piece of English bravery and loyalty.'[2]

Lord Mountagu's Deputy, who proved effective in raising forces for

1. Warwick *Memoires* 221.
2. *ibid*, 224–5.

the Parliament was none other than Edward's brother-in-law, Sir Gilbert Pickering. Edward himself had already as good as declared his own allegiance a month before his father's outburst in the House of Commons by marrying Jemima Crew at St Margaret's Westminster on 7th November 1642. John Crew, the member for Brackley, the bride's father, was as staunch to his side of the great quarrel as old Sir Sydney and no less courageous. He had voted against Strafford's attainder and had been in trouble with the Parliamentary managers for refusing to surrender the papers of a Committee of which he was chairman. No doubt Sir Sydney approved of the family's Puritan antecedents and principles even if their expression was so much more liberal and attractive than his own, and he could hardly complain that his son had disparaged his family socially or financially by the match. Deeply as he deplored its political implications he seems to have accepted it, for he moved out of Hinchingbrooke back to his old home at Barnwell leaving Edward to run the estate. Groom and bride had only just turned seventeen when these responsibilities devolved on them.

The war prevented them from discharging them in person. In February 1643 Edward was at Bury St Edmunds taking down the articles of association for the Eastern counties. Early in August his cousin, soon to succeed to the Earldom of Manchester, was put in command and on August 20th Edward himself, only a month past his eighteenth birthday, was given a colonel's commission. In November he marched with his regiment to join Manchester in Lincolnshire. He had been appointed Deputy Lieutenant for the county on June 16th. He saw no action until March of the following year when he was present at the storming of Hillesden House, one of the outposts that protected the Royalist headquarters at Oxford. After that he was in the thick of things, at the recapture of Lincoln in early May and in the hot action within the walls of York in mid-June when the Royalists repulsed a determined Parliamentary assault. Three weeks later he fought at the decisive battle of Marston Moor.

In the months that followed he was probably on what we would now call compassionate leave. His father, who had made a second marriage only a few months earlier, was dying. On 25th September 1644 Edward inherited the estate of which he had been in charge, so far as anyone was, for the past two years. A year later, on 13th October 1645, he succeeded his father as Knight of the Shire. We know next to nothing about his movements in the autumn of 1644 except that he was evidently away from his regiment as it was his Lieutenant-Colonel who accepted the surrender of Sheffield two months after Marston Moor. Militarily this was a period of anti-climax for the Parliament. The humiliation of Essex at Lostwithiel in the south-west and the feebleness of Manchester at the second battle of Newbury that enabled the King to get his artillery safely into Donnington Castle had fatally discredited the two principal commanders. Cromwell brought the general resentment into the open by charging Manchester with half-heartedness and demanding his re-placement. Edward unhesitatingly supported him against his cousin. In late November he was one of the colonels who had served in the Army of the Eastern Association who gave evidence against their old chief. It was not so much a matter of military incompetence as of ideological and religious commitment. Manchester, Essex and Warwick, the highly successful director of the naval war, stood for Presbyterianism in religion (as old Sir Sydney Mountagu had done) and for a political compromise with the King. Cromwell and the men whom he had inspired or with whom he acted stood for a diversity of Protestant beliefs that were united in resenting the imposition of Presbyterianism as much as they resented the Arminianism imposed by the King and were perfectly prepared to con-template, even to welcome, the radical transformations that this necessarily implied in politics and society. What these transformations might turn out to be, or how far they were agreed on their actual acceptance, were of course questions that had not yet presented themselves. 'Well, lads, you have done your work and now you may go play, except you fall out among yourselves.' Old Sir Jacob Astley's good-humoured remark after be had surrendered the last Royalist formation at Stow-on-the-Wold in 1646 remains one of the shrewdest historical judgments on the Civil War.

Edward and his brother-in-law Sir Gilbert Pickering, regimental com-manders who knew what it was to have their men wounded or killed in action, might be expected to prefer the vigour and skill of Cromwell's generalship to the expensive dithering of an amiable relation. But what of Cromwell's religious enthusiasm, the bible-thumping that he encour-aged and on occasion practised? How does that square with the well-bred, unaggressively aristocratic, impression that the Earl of Sandwich seems to have left on those who knew him, let alone the man whom

Pepys 'perceive[d] to be wholly sceptical in Religion ... saying that indeed the Protestants as to the Church of Rome are wholly fanatiques'?[1] The young man, the very young man, who was fighting the Civil War had fifteen years of experience in front of him before he was to have this conversation with his clever young cousin. The rhapsodical style favoured by the Independents, as those who opposed the Presbyterians were called, can be found in his correspondence both inward and outward as late as the middle 1650s. On 30th April 1656, when he was serving with Blake in joint command of the fleet, Cromwell's son-in-law Fleetwood wrote him a long letter urging him to rely on the guidance of the Holy Spirit 'could we lye low in the sense of our own weakness, folly and nothingness.'[2] On September 19th of the same year Mountagu devotes the whole first paragraph of a letter to Thurloe, Cromwell's chief of intelligence, to a thankful expression of his sense of the divine mercies, particularly manifested in giving him an opportunity of writing sooner than he had expected.[3] If we call this cant we should remember Hazlitt's admirable distinction between cant – uncritical assertion of accepted opinions – and hypocrisy – professing beliefs one does not hold. The language of the Cromwellian circle to which Edward was beginning to look in hero worship and of which he was to become an intimate was no doubt a refreshing change from the cold, dry formalities of Sir Sydney and his world.

Edward's adherence to Cromwell's party was soon fortified by personal experience. On 10th January 1645 he was appointed Governor of Henley, where his own regiment was quartered. The garrison was an important one. In view of its proximity to the Royalist headquarters at Oxford, subversion was an obvious danger. The men's pay was, like that of all the Parliament's troops at that stage in the war, badly in arrears. The local people were exasperated by the endless depredations of two neighbouring armies. Taut discipline was essential if serious trouble was to be avoided.[4]

1. *Diary* i, 141.
2. Mapperton MSS. Letters from Ministers i, 5.
3. *Thurloe SP*, v, 433.
4. The situation was already precarious. There had been a mutiny in the garrison in August and the Commanding Officer had narrowly escaped with his life. Whitelocke *Diary* ed. Spalding (1990), 178. Whitelocke supported a Motion for the imposition of martial law on 19 Jan. 1646 'the soldiers being very unruly'. *ibid* 184.

Mountagu's first act on taking up his new command was to dismiss two officers whose past record and present misbehaviour did not warrant his confidence. At the same time he wrote to his cousin, still his superior officer, informing him of his action. Manchester, determined to assert himself in the face of Cromwell's accusations which Edward had supported, overrode him and reinstated them. The result was an immediate mutiny in which this precious pair were clearly active. Mountagu, who happened to have gone to London, laid his own authority on the line before the Committee of Both Kingdoms, the supreme authority in military matters. He was upheld. The mutinous troops were marched out and others took their place.

Fortunately for the future relations between the different branches of the Mountagu family, the attack on Manchester was not pressed home. Cromwell judged that his real objective, the establishment of an efficient, well-found military force with himself in a key position in place of the existing unsatisfactory, underpaid, loosely controlled armies, could be more swiftly and easily obtained by the passage of his and Vane's ordinance to New Model the Army. This would have the advantage of avoiding a time-consuming confrontation with the House of Lords who were certain to cut up rough, indeed had already done so, over a direct censure, possibly even the humiliating punishment, of one of their leading members.

The ordinance sped through the House of Commons in January. By the 21st Fairfax had been appointed Lord General and among the first to be assigned command of a regiment was Edward Mountagu. There were still some difficulties to be overcome with the House of Lords. Recruiting proved at first disappointing. But by May the New Model was a going concern, its soldiers all, for the first time, wearing the redcoats that Mountagu's old regiment had worn since the spring of 1644.[1] As an act of solidarity they changed their facings from white to blue, the colour of Fairfax's own regiment.

On June 14th the New Model fought its first battle at Naseby. For all the numerical inferiority of the Royalists it was a close run thing. Mountagu's regiment was on the left of the main body of foot commanded by Skippon as Major-General. In the hard hand-to-hand fight-

1. Firth *Cromwell's Army* 233.

ing Skippon was wounded and the new regiments facing the assault of the Royalist foot, by common consent the best soldiers of the First Civil War, began to give ground. Cromwell's tight control of his successful cavalry and the dissipation of Rupert's equally successful horse in plunder and pursuit turned the day. The Royalist defeat was total.

Mountagu's regiment had taken a hammering with the rest. Indeed its position on the extreme left, after Rupert had scattered Ireton's cavalry that was supposed to protect its flank, must have been dangerously exposed. Not to have broken was a solid if not a conspicuous contribution to the victory. At any rate Mountagu's conduct seems to have been approved by Fairfax and Cromwell since he was appointed to act as Skippon's substitute in the place of Major-General in the subsequent operations against the Royalists in the south-west. As such he took part in the storming of Bridgwater in late July and of Bristol in September. It was with the three Independents, Mountagu, Pickering and Rainsborough, that Rupert signed the surrender agreement for which Charles I reproached him so bitterly.

The King himself had been engaged in the pointless banditry that was all he could find to do now that he no longer disposed of a force adequate to any serious military operation. At the end of August he had raided Huntingdon. Two accounts say that he slept at Hinchingbrooke, whose hospitality he had enjoyed before the war. Whether he did or not there can be no doubt that the house and estate would have suffered the usual pillage and vandalism. But the war was in effect all but over. When Rupert rode out of Bristol on a splendid black Barbary horse escorted by his own bodyguard and by the three colonels of the New Model who had signed terms with him it was the end of his career as a cavalry commander. Only three years later, in the Second Civil War, he was to embark on that of an admiral, in which yet a few years further on he was to be the rival and ultimately the successor of the youngest of the three Parliamentary colonels riding by his side.

III

Breathing Space

EDWARD, TOO, had come to the end of his active soldiering. On 13th October 1645 he took his seat in the House of Commons and thus, by the provisions of the Self-Denying Ordinance which had been designed to get rid of Essex, Manchester and Waller, was disabled from a command in the army or the navy. His regiment was given to Lambert, next to Cromwell the ablest General thrown up by the Civil War, and Edward himself was immediately made a member of the Committee for the Army.

He seems to have made no mark either in the House or on the Committee, unsurprisingly in view of Pepys's sympathetic but devastating description of his self-deprecating manner. In any case as the pressure of war relaxed it was to the reclamation and restoration of his own house and estate that his energies would naturally turn. Besides the pillage and wanton destruction of Royalist raiders the sluttishness and vandalism of friendly troops left a trail of havoc. Edward's lot was fallen unto him in a fair ground but there must have been a deal of cleaning up to do. Now at last he could enter properly into his inheritance, set up house with his wife and raise a family.

We do not know where Jemima had been living while her husband was away with his regiment but the overwhelming probability is that she had been with her parents either at Stene in Northamptonshire – or in London, since John Crew was a prominent figure in the House of Commons. He was a member of the small committee charged with the direction of the war late in 1644 when the quarrel between Manchester and Cromwell was simmering[1] and in January 1645 was chosen as one of

1. Gardiner *Civil War* i, 357.

the Commissioners to negotiate with the Royalists at the unsuccessful Treaty of Uxbridge. Quite apart from the loose, incoherent character of the fighting, which meant that a cavalry raid from the enemy was always a possibility, the war had broken down the none-too-firm structure of law and order in seventeenth-century England. A woman on her own would hardly be safe unless she was ensconced in a castle like those formidable châtelaines at Corfe or on the Isle of Man. It is noticeable that what evidence survives of Edward being absent from his military duties generally shows him in London. And the exact parallel between his own political evolution and that of his father-in-law can hardly have been coincidental. John Crew supported Cromwell and Vane over the Self-Denying Ordinance, was, like Edward, a moderate Independent as against the Presbyterian party, but, again like him, distanced himself from the army radicals and openly opposed the trial and execution of the King. All this suggests that the Crew household was what Edward had regarded as home during his years of active service.

In the year 1646 there appears to be no record of his doing anything at all. Presumably as one of the clutch of Cromwellians brought into the house about this time, such as Fleetwood and Ireton, Oliver's two future sons-in-law, he must have spent some of his time at Westminster. With the King in the hands of the Scots from July to the end of the year the main stream of politics went underground. But with his return to England things began to move again. And Edward Mountagu makes a few spear-carrying appearances on the stage of events.

His cousins and his in-laws were much more conspicuous. His father-in-law was repeatedly chosen as a commissioner to negotiate with the King following the failure to secure agreement at Uxbridge. He was sent to Newcastle when the King was held prisoner by the Scots and again to Holmby when the Parliament had taken charge of him and he was sent finally to the Isle of Wight in the eleventh hour negotiations that preceded the trial and execution. Edward's cousin, who had succeeded as second Lord Mountagu of Boughton in 1644, played an active part in the House of Lords as did his other Mountagu cousin, the Earl of Manchester. All three had been christened Edward so that it is sometimes easy to be mistaken as to who was doing what. All the easier in the case of Lord Mountagu of Boughton since he is apt to sign himself 'Edw. Mountagu' and his hand is very like that of his younger cousin.

This led Sir Julian Corbett in his *Fighting Instructions 1530–1816* to identify the future Earl of Sandwich as the member of the Parliamentary Committee for the Admiralty and Cinque Ports who signed the instructions for his future colleague William Penn on 2nd May 1648.[1] In fact it was Lord Mountagu of Boughton who had been appointed to the Committee on 4th March 1647.[2] The Earl of Manchester had been on that Committee since it was constituted on 15th April 1645.[3] Neither of them had, or was ever to have, any other experience of naval affairs.

Lord Mountagu of Boughton was also like John Crew, Edward's father-in-law, closely involved in attendance on the King. He had been one of the three peers appointed to receive his person from the Scots in January 1647 and had conducted him to Holmby, remaining thereafter as one of his household.

Both men were therefore in attendance on that memorable afternoon in early summer when Cornet Joyce appeared at the head of a body of cavalry to claim the King as the Army's guarantee against a deal being done behind their backs between their employers and the Scots. Both men accompanied him on his journey towards Newmarket which he had chosen as an alternative to Cambridge, Joyce's original proposal. It was natural that both should think of Hinchingbrooke, their kinsman's great house, as a staging point on the journey. Whether it was on their initiative we do not know. But we do know that the King stayed there on this the last of his many progresses through the rich South Midland country and that this final visit to the house he had first known as a boy when it was still in the possession of the Cromwell family was as notable for its welcoming hospitality as any that had preceded it. Was Edward there to do the honours? Again we do not know. The one first-hand account we have commends the entertainment. 'The King was nobly treated there' but names no names. A later version particularly mentions 'lady Mountagu' (she was not then entitled to that style), but this may simply recognize that it is the hostess, not the host, who orders these matters. Edward had obtained leave of absence from the House of Commons some five weeks earlier but this may well have expired. He certainly was not then close enough to Cromwell to have had any advance knowledge

1. B.L. Sloane 1709 f. 62v.
2. B.L. Add.MS 9305 f. 2.
3. C.J. iv, 111–2.

of this bold and unexpected stroke and would therefore have had no special motive for being at Hinchingbrooke or for taking care not to be there. What is certain however is that the courtesy shewn to the King was entered in the political ledgers, credit and debit, under 'Mountagu, Edward'.

To merge into the background, to break up the outline of one's shape and movements, is a necessary art in an age of confusion. Edward was to shew himself a master of it, indeed to an almost incredible degree in the eighteen months that separate the death of Cromwell from the Restoration of Charles II. Perhaps it was a natural endowment, the counter-part of his inability to project himself on to the broad screen of history. But at that point he was a major figure: at this he was merely a promising young man. In any case political warfare was not his talent, and political warfare of extraordinary rapidity and skill of manoeuvre was raging round him. It is possible to infer from his later actions what some of the guiding principles of his silent inertia may have been. He never lost his personal faith in, his personal admiration for, Cromwell. Even after the Restoration he made this perfectly clear in private conversation with Clarendon. But would he have understood, let alone approved, all that Cromwell thought and did as he felt himself threatened, in turn or simultaneously, by his open enemies in the House of Commons, by the winning openness and the unfathomable duplicity of the King, by the rising tide of resentment and mutiny in the troops he had led to victory? Would he, pro-Cromwellian that he instinctively was, have opposed as he did the trial and execution of the King had he known, as we do, of the King's inveterate double-dealing, his reckless readiness to plunge his subjects once again into the degradation and horror of another civil war? The answers to such questions will make interesting reading at the Day of Judgment as we wait for our own case to be called.

That he never lost faith in Cromwell is evidenced by the fact to which Professor Aylmer has called attention, that he was one of the five members of the Army Committee to sign an order for an advance of £500 to Cromwell on his army pay, thus begging the question whether Cromwell still held, or had forfeited, the commission which had, after a series of votes extending it for a strictly limited period, apparently expired.[1] That he did not go all the way with him is shewn by his

1. *History* lvi, 186–7.

expulsion – or seclusion to use the more decorous phrase – from the House of Commons in Pride's Purge of December 1648. He had taken no part in the Second Civil War in the summer of that year.[1] Indeed as we have seen he had surrendered his commission on succeeding to his father's seat in the Commons. His father-in-law, John Crew, was another of the members secluded in December 1648. The similarity of their political opinions, moderate Cromwellians with a dislike of Presbyterian assertiveness and a strong preference for established social and constitutional forms, has already been remarked.

It is from John Crew that we get the only inkling, and that mysterious, of what men who held such opinions thought of what was going on in the four years that separate the execution of the King in January 1649 and Cromwell's expulsion of the Rump (as the last remnant of the Long Parliament was disrespectfully called) in April 1653. Like the letters exchanged by their Royalist neighbour Sir Justinian Isham and the dispossessed Bishop of Salisbury, Brian Duppa, that written by Crew to Edward on 17th April 1651 makes no bones about the danger of denunciation by informers: 'We must take heed what we write and what we say, you will therefore expect no great newes.' Edward certainly seems to have acted on this principle. That he did not approve of what had been done he made clear by his silence but there is no suggestion that he disputed the authority of the government, still less that he was prepared to act against it. On the contrary he still continued to discharge his duties as a Commissioner for the County and Cromwell even mentioned him by name as one whom he would wish to reconcile to the courses he had felt himself obliged to take.[2] The blacks and whites of hindsight are often not discernible in the perplexities of experience. Edward's brother-in-law Sir Gilbert Pickering occupied a position close to but different from that of John Crew. He had attended two sessions of the Court that tried the King but had then absented himself and had not signed the death-warrant. Nonetheless he was immediately appointed to the Coun-

1. Unless we credit a bitterly hostile witness, Lady Fanshawe (see below pp. 103–4 and 163) *Memoirs* (ed. E.J. Fanshawe, 1907) p. 48 'In the latter end of July [1648] . . . as we passed through the town [St Neots] we saw Colonel Montagu, afterwards Earl of Sandwich, spoiling the town for Parliament and himself'.
2. *Writings and Speeches of Oliver Cromwell* ed. Abbott ii (1939) p. 328 Cromwell to Wharton, Dunbar, 4 September 1650.

cil of State, a position he retained throughout the Commonwealth and Protectorate. He shared Cromwell's instincts for pragmatism and toler- ance, voting against the retention of tithe and speaking against the severe punishment demanded for the Quaker enthusiast James Naylor. He became in time one of the Protector's intimate circle and Chamberlain of his household. Such a link may well have served to keep Edward's name in Cromwell's mind when fresh talent was needed to replace the experienced and capable men who were driven out of public life by the expulsion of the Rump in the spring of 1653.

Meanwhile Edward and Jemima were left to the enjoyment of a happy marriage and the raising of a family in private affection and public peace. Their first child, Jemima, was born to them on 18th February 1646. Edward followed on 3rd January 1648, Paulina on 19th February 1649 and Sydney, the son who was to see most of his father, on 28th July 1650. This was the advance guard of a total of seven sons and four daughters who, unlike most seventeenth-century children, not only sur- vived their infancy but enjoyed the upbringing of a wise and loving mother. The happiness of that household and the easy-going, friendly atmosphere of Hinchingbrooke are rendered for posterity in Pepys's *Diary*.

IV

Entry to the Great World

VICTORY IN the Second Civil War had settled matters for England and Wales. Even so horrendous an act as the trial and execution of the King, that human symbol of the divine order that was generally agreed to underpin the institutions of government and law, did not disturb the peace of the country, much though it may have shocked many consciences.

Outside England this was far from being the case. In Scotland Charles II was immediately proclaimed King in succession to his father. In Ireland the bitter feuds of intolerant religion, of English and Scottish settlers against a native race and culture wholly alien, of hereditary rivalries and cross-currents of a century of divisions, resentments and injustices had produced conditions of life as barbarous as anything the Thirty Years War could show in Europe. On the continent itself both the French royal family and the House of Orange were shocked and affronted by the murder – as they saw of it – of a close relation. And Spain, the ageing super-power of the period, could hardly be expected to approve of such an outrage, perpetrated by declared anti-Catholic fanatics. Even a country such as Russia, which was hardly thought of as belonging to the mainstream of European civilization, was so appalled that every trading agreement was immediately revoked and English merchants were peremptorily ordered to clear out.

Monck, Mountagu's senior partner in bringing about the Restoration in 1660, gave it as his advice that the best means of consolidating an uncertain regime at home was to involve the country in war overseas. Perhaps he drew this wisdom from his observation of the course of affairs in the early days of both the Commonwealth and the Protectorate. In the year of the King's execution Cromwell reduced Ireland to order with a ruthlessness from which his most devoted admirers have generally recoiled. In the following year he beat the Scots at Dunbar, crowning his achievement exactly a year later, on 3rd September 1651, by annihilating at Worcester the ill-equipped, unsupported Scottish invading force which was Charles II's last hope of recovering his throne by military action. All this reconciled men's minds to a government whose constitutional antecedents they might have been inclined to doubt. And it also raised the name of Cromwell, who had by now succeeded Fairfax as Lord General, to heights from which a new view of the political landscape might be obtained.

At sea the navy which Warwick had handled with such skill in the Civil War had recovered from the potentially disastrous revolt of its major units to the exiled Royalists. It had pursued the remnants of this semi-piratical squadron, commanded by Prince Rupert with his usual flair and dash, to Ireland and then to Lisbon and finally into the Mediterranean, accounting for all except a couple of vessels in which Rupert and his brother escaped for a cruise that was to take them down the West African coast and across the Atlantic to the Caribbean. It had then mopped up the remaining Royalist privateering bases in the Scillies and the Channel Islands and given much-needed protection to the Levant trade, at that time of Dutch dominance of the ocean sea routes the most important to the city merchants.

Resentment at Dutch high-handedness and envy of their success in engrossing to themselves almost every profitable maritime activity, most recently manifested in a treaty with Denmark that gave them a uniquely favoured entry into the Baltic, spurred the Commonwealth Government into reprisal and protection. Barely a month after the victory at Worcester Parliament passed the Navigation Act, disabling at a stroke the enormous carrying trade on which the Dutch maritime economy was founded. Unless this measure were to be modified, for which the Dutch would have to make substantial concessions and reparations on their side, war was inevitable. The negotiations that followed were hampered by the independent manoeuvres of the two main factions in the Council of State, one of which favoured an understanding with the French and the Dutch, the other an alliance with England's best customer, Spain. The

Dutch, proud, rich, successful and tenacious, showed little sign of satisfying English requirements. By the early summer of 1652 the two countries were at war.

This incessant military activity, and its unbroken success, inevitably swung the weight of power behind the military men. Even at sea the commanders in chief, Blake, Deane, Monck and Popham were men with a distinguished record of fighting on land, a fact recognized in the rank created for them, that of General at Sea. Not, it must be emphasized, admiral. The greatest of them all, Robert Blake, was chosen by Popham as his colleague on the strength of his magnificent defence first of Lyme and then of Taunton against superior Royalist forces. Cromwell himself evidently shared Popham's opinion since he invited him to become his Major-General in Ireland only a few months after he had taken up his joint command at sea. Popham died of fever before the Dutch War had begun and Deane was killed at the Battle of the Gabbard in June 1653 so that Blake was left as the senior Flag Officer with a string of victories to his credit over the foremost maritime power of the age and against some of the greatest commanders in the history of sea fighting.

By the time this came about the political structure of the English Republic had been transformed. The Rump had become so accustomed to the military successes of its servants that it had perhaps not perceived the cracks and shifts in the reality of power. What exactly brought about their expulsion by Cromwell and his file of musketeers on the morning of 20th April 1653 is still unknown and likely to remain so. As Professor Austin Woolrych points out in his fascinating analysis of the situation *Commonwealth to Protectorate* the House was on the point of passing the long promised, long awaited, Bill for a New Representative which would terminate its own existence and create the framework for its successor. But what was in the Bill that suddenly caused Cromwell to act in so furious and obviously unpremeditated a manner? No one knows. Cromwell, clearly convinced that it contained clauses treacherously aimed at himself and at the Army which he regarded as a sacred trust, carried the Bill off and neither it nor any copy has subsequently come to light. Cynics, of course, and Royalist propagandists, obviously, have seen the whole performance as one more step towards the military dictatorship on which he had from the start been bent. Of all explanations this seems the feeblest:

31

> And *Hampton* shows what part
> He had of wiser Art.
> Where, twining subtile fears with hope
> He wove a Net of such a scope,
> That *Charles* himself might chase
> To *Caresbrooks* narrow case

Whatever estimate one forms of Cromwell there is no gainsaying Clarendon's judgment that '. . . he must have had a wonderful understanding in the natures and humours of men, and as great a dexterity in applying them.' No doubt Clarendon's portrait of his great enemy derives some of its tone and dignity from his conversations with Edward Mountagu, whose devotion to him evidently made a deep impression on him.

Whatever the cause of Cromwell's expulsion of the Rump one of its immediate consequences was the elevation of Edward Mountagu to high rank and responsibility. In the so-called Barebones Parliament consisting of 140 members nominated by the Army, or rather its Council of Officers, Edward was returned as member for Huntingdon. Writs for the election (as it was called) went out early in June and the first meeting, addressed by Cromwell, took place on July 4th. Three days later Edward was granted lodgings in Whitehall (a sure sign of admission to the inner ring) and on the 14th he was made a member of the Council of State. Appointment to two Committees, one to consider the state of the Public Finances and the other for the Advancement of Learning soon followed as did the profitable membership of the Commission for Customs. Finance and foreign trade were to remain among the chief interests of his public life. No doubt his mathematical aptitudes drew him to them.

He was not, as we know, much of a Parliamentary performer and the Barebones Parliament, small though it was and short in duration, was not lacking in those who were. He made no mark there, but seized the opportunity of executive responsibility. The Council of State was only to hold office till the beginning of November when Parliament was to elect its successor. Mountagu was returned comfortably if unenthusiastically with fifty-nine votes. The body of which he found himself a member was overwhelmingly conservative in political complexion and largely drawn from well-known, long-established families. The radical minority who made the running in Parliament claimed only four out of thirty-one seats. Recognizing their impotence in its proceedings, they hardly bothered to attend. But Parliament gave them a forum for pressing schemes for an extreme re-ordering of society such as Cromwell had already declared himself against. To forestall an overt collision between military force and a soi-disant constitutional authority such as had taken place in April Cromwell's friends in the House staged a coup by voting the resignation of their powers to him together with their own immediate dissolution. This took place on December 12th and Mountagu was said to be among the co-ordinators of this manoeuvre.[1]

There can be no question that such a change of course was congenial to him. The world might change round him but he was from first to last an unashamed monarchist: a monarchist by instinct, tradition and observation, unentangled with theories of divine hereditary right. Throughout the Cromwellian period, right up to the point where Richard threw in his hand, he steadily supported the effective monarch of the day, as loyal subjects had done in the Wars of the Roses. He was sneered at in the pamphlet literature of the left as one of the 'Kinglings', the hangers-on of Oliver who consistently pressed him to accept the crown. He would not have denied the charge but might fairly have denied the imputation of hypocrisy and self-interest. If he did well out of his career under the Protector he gave value for money as he did under Charles II. Under neither did he prefer his own interests to those of his country.

The Instrument of Government which was almost certainly the work of Lambert, much the acutest political mind among the army grandees, was at once adopted to form the basis of another attempt at erecting a constitution and guaranteeing the rule of law, two objects that Cromwell seems unfeignedly to have desired. Marvell's insight that

> The same *Arts* that did gain
> A *Pow'r* must it maintain

was to prove the aptest comment on his heroic efforts to reconcile the incompatible. But if the ends were to elude him the means were at least efficiently designed. Cromwell was declared Protector on December 16th and he and his Council of State, reduced from an unwieldy thirty-one to a business-like fifteen, were to have unhampered control of affairs until a

---

1. Woolrych *Commonwealth to Protectorate*, 346 where reasons are given for ascribing the initiative to Lambert, not to Cromwell himself.

new Parliament, in its external form nearer to its traditional predecessors than to the Barebone experiment, was elected in the following summer.

Of this powerful new Council Edward was a prominent member. His special fields of responsibility were to begin with two: Public Finance, of which he already had some experience, and secondly what would now be termed the leader's life-style. He was one of the six councillors nominated in March 1654 to model the Protectoral household, an intimate rather than a ceremonial post. Professor Aylmer's distinction, referring to the pre-war division of such responsibilities, is enlightening: 'Generally speaking the household provided most of the necessities of life, while the chamber regulated the routine and ceremony of a court.'[1] The Protector's Master of Ceremonies was Sir Oliver Fleming, a Cromwell family connexion.[2] Edward was to have his bellyful of protocol as ambassador to Spain, perhaps the most status-obsessed country of that status-obsessed age. Though not directly responsible for such matters in his new appointment he must have been made aware of them by the demands made on the resources of the household. Clearly the Protector wished to involve him in the ceremonial side of government, perhaps, too, in the diplomatic. He was chosen as one of the six councillors to attend at the state reception of the Dutch ambassadors on 20th March 1654 in 'the great banqueting room at Whitehall, where his highness hath never given audience before'.[3] Evidently he was not present as a mere glorified flunkey since he was appointed a month later together with Lord Lisle and Sir Walter Strickland 'to treat with the lord neufville'.[4] Moving into Whitehall palace was one of the outward and visible signs of the regal authority implicit in the Protectorate. Up to this point the Cromwells had lived in the Cockpit next door.[5] On April 27th Oliver entertained the ambassadors to dinner at Whitehall, a function at which Edward's brother-in-law, Pickering, seems to have acted as majordomo.[6] He was later to be appointed Lord Chamberlain, a post he retained till the end of the Protectorate.

1. *The King's Servants* p. 29 quot. Roy Sherwood *The Court of Oliver Cromwell* (1977).
2. Grandson of Sir Henry Cromwell and nephew of the spendthrift Sir Oliver.
3. *Thurloe SP* ii 154.
4. *ibid* 234 'Neufville' is M. de Nieuport, one of the Dutch envoys.
5. Sherwood *The Court of Oliver Cromwell* p. 18.
6. Gardiner. *C & P* iii, 70.

The transition from regulating the household of the Head of State to involvement with official hospitality and thus to diplomacy itself is easy and natural in an age when departmentalism was still in its infancy. Edward had anyway been made a member of the Committee for Foreign Affairs in November 1653 in the old unstreamlined Council of State. His earlier appointment to the Committee for considering Public Debt, Bribery and Fraud led to even closer supervision of government finance in two small, high-powered, *ad hoc* committees appointed in February. Early in August he was made a full-blown Commissioner of the Treasury with a salary of £1000 a year.[1]

He was thus deeply concerned from the start with the practical rather than the ideological aspirations of Oliver's regime. Foreign policy – which in effect meant 'war' – finance, trade, overseas expansion, not the constitutional and religious questions with which his colleagues wrestled, were what sailors call his part of ship. Of course these aspects cannot be entirely isolated from each other. Public finance requires a legal, that is a constitutional, basis for its exaction. Religion, war and foreign policy were enthusiastically associated in the Protector's mind. A grand Protestant crusade culminating in the overthrow of the Papacy was his sublunary version of the beatific vision. Hence the alacrity with which he brought the Dutch War to a close, driving a hard bargain at the same time over the exclusion of the House of Orange, with their strong Stuart connexions and sympathies, from any military or political power in the United Provinces. Hence too his determination to force the French government to allow freedom of worship to its Protestant subjects and to stop sheltering the exiled court of Charles II.

To attempt to disentangle the chimerical from the pragmatic in the Protector's mind is to run the same risks as those attendant on the zealous cleaning of an old picture: one may be left with nothing recognizable. That Cromwell was a formidable realist his bitterest enemies would eagerly agree. That he was also a visionary, a mystic, whose deepest convictions were too powerful for coherent expression, too hostile to formality such as reason and language require, seems obvious. Some of his intimate circle shared the same apparently contradictory mentality: Thurloe, for instance, his brilliantly efficient chief of Intelligence and

1. Harris i, 80–3.

Secretary of State.[1] There seems no evidence that Edward did and much to suggest the contrary.

To take the central question of religious toleration, we have seen that Edward, like the Protector, was averse from pressing conformity on the sectaries. But what about the Church of England, that ark of Royalism, and what about the Papists? Cromwell, though he made oafish fun of Anglican pieties and shared to the full in Puritan vandalism, was not, as so many of his associates were, vindictive against English Churchmen as such. But Roman Catholics were, in a cruelly apt sense, for him outside the pale. Edward, by contrast, on his Madrid embassy, could observe, uncensoriously, extravagances of public devotion which might have taken even a northern Catholic aback and habitually in his journal shows respect towards beliefs and practices that he could not himself accept. He invariably refers to saints by their Catholic style and often employs the term Our Lady. One cannot imagine Cromwell or even a career diplomat like Consul Maynard at Lisbon ever permitting themselves such expressions. He was not in the slightest degree a secret Papist fellow-traveller, such as his chief in those later years, Lord Arlington. He was not, on the evidence of his journal and of his intimate family letters, a sceptic as Pepys asserted. But his cool, good-natured temper preserved him from the fanatical anti-Catholicism that lay so close under the surface of English life in the seventeenth century, breaking out from time to time in horrid acts of cruelty and injustice.

On the other hand the coincidence in foreign policy of a declared anti-Catholicism with an aggressive commercial imperialism enabled him to support the second, of which he was a whole-hearted partisan, without involving himself in the first. The account, written in his own hand, of the debates in the Protector's Council concerning the expedition to the West Indies is one of the clearest insights we have into how these questions were actually discussed at what in our time would be called Cabinet level.[2] The pros and cons of using the formidable, and formidably expensive, military and naval forces against either France or Spain are weighed in a manner that suggests the Staff College rather than a gathered congregation of saints. The economic argument that Spain was the

1. Philip Aubrey *Mr Secretary Thurloe* (1990) *passim*.
2. Printed as Appendix B in *Clarke Papers* ed. C.H. Firth, iii, 203–8. The original is in Sandwich's Journal (henceforward referred to as 'J') i, ff. 49–55.

best export market for England's cloth trade was powerfully urged against the final decision to attack Hispaniola and to seek to revive the freebooting glories of the long Elizabethan war. Would an account of the same proceedings given by one of the more pulpit-frequenting army grandees have been less down to earth? Very likely. But it was Cromwell's combination of both these strains that gave Edward his opportunity.

V

High Command

THE PROTECTOR'S much-praised military talent is not seen to best advantage in the planning and execution of the attack on Hispaniola in the spring of 1655. The staff work was abominable, the logistics amateurish and the command structure designed, one would have thought, to ensure disaster. Neither Penn, the only General at Sea to have served a professional apprenticeship to naval warfare, nor Venables, the undistinguished commander of the land forces, was put in charge of the expedition. Indeed decision was pushed even further out of reach by joining three commissioners with them of whom only one was faintly qualified by some knowledge of colonial life. All things considered the unintended capture of Jamaica after the fiasco at Hispaniola itself was a surprisingly fortunate result. But from the vantage point of Edward Mountagu's later career it was the disgrace of Penn that opened unforeseen possibilities.

Edward had been returned as one of the three county members for Huntingdon, after a fierce contest with Valentine Walton, the Protector's brother-in-law and fellow regicide but one of the stoutest opponents of his constitutional experiments. In spite of the pains that had been taken to re-draw the old constituencies, increasing county representation at the expense of boroughs that the government could not control, the first Protectorate Parliament that met in August 1654 was alive with adroit and articulate opponents of the quasi-monarchical executive powers that Cromwell saw as indispensable. Members of the Council of State who were also members of Parliament were in the position of a modern government front bench, charged with carrying policy through the House of Commons. Edward's position at the Treasury and his previous committee work on government finance made him the obvious choice for fighting through the vast estimates for the army and the navy requisite for Cromwell's various projects of overseas expansion. The Hispaniola venture was by no means his only iron in the fire. He was bent on the acquisition of Dunkirk, partly to secure the channel against the privateers who used it as a base and partly as a continental bastion in the great war against the popish Anti-Christ to which he enthusiastically looked forward. Two months before Penn and Venables set out for the West Indies in December 1654, a much more powerful fleet under Blake and Badiley had been dispatched to the Mediterranean. Whether it was to be used against the French or the Spaniards was an open question. But it was to take advantage of whatever the political and strategic situation there offered to assert the right of English ships to pass there on their lawful occasions and to investigate the possibilities of obtaining a permanent base in or just outside the Western Mediterranean. Obtaining the release of English captives from the Barbary pirates and the payment of the money owed by Portugal in compensation for having sheltered Prince Rupert and his squadron were among the subsidiary objectives.

Public avowal of these aggressive intentions would of course go far to frustrate them. It was therefore in effect necessary that the Protector should be given a free hand over the control of the nation's forces and over the expenditures required to maintain them. This the Protector's Parliament was not at all disposed to accept. On the contrary, Colonel Birch, the chairman of the Revenue Sub-Committee, submitted detailed proposals for disbanding a large part of the military establishment and reducing the pay of such as remained. If the government really needed so many men for the defence of the realm they could better be supplied by raising a militia which would itself be under Parliamentary control. The clock had been put back to 1641 with Cromwell in the position of Charles I. Edward was put up to answer Colonel Birch which he did in a speech which not only set out the financial details of what the government needed but analysed Birch's figures and refuted his conclusions on the basis of his own arguments. How compelling this was we do not know. But if he had not learned to present a financial case by the time Pepys heard him fifteen years later it is hardly likely that he succeeded at the first attempt. When the vote was taken it went against him. Whether this had anything to do with his advocacy is again another question. In the years since 1640 Parliament had become readier to assert than to curtail the scope of its authority. What is certain is that Edward shewed the same energy and determination in mastering his brief as his young cousin Samuel Pepys was to do on many similar occasions. His calculations and the notes for his speech are preserved among his papers in the Carte collection in the Bodleian Library.[1]

The loss of this motion coupled with defeat over the control of the militia was a challenge that the regime could not tolerate. The Parliament was summarily dissolved in January 1655. No doubt Edward, like the Protector himself, was happier in executive action than in argument. The Council of State was an efficient businesslike body whose regular meetings took precedence over everything else. The Treasury Commission had, somehow, to raise the huge sums needed to sustain an unheard of military establishment. The information he had gathered about the organisation and expenditure of the navy in December 1654 had evidently aroused his interest. In October 1655 he was made a member of the Admiralty Committee, the first official appointment in what was to turn out his real career. In another foreshadowing of his later responsibilities under the restored monarchy as a Commissioner for Trade and Plantations he attended, perhaps in his Admiralty capacity, a meeting in December of the Committee of Trade which was addressed by the great city merchant Martin Noell, Thurloe's brother-in-law. The notes he took were clear, workmanlike, factual. Together with the doodles with which he interspersed them they survive in the Bodleian Library.[2]

By that time he must have known the extraordinary promotion that the Protector designed for him. On 2nd January 1656 he was appointed Joint General at Sea with Blake. Here he was, an admiral who, in Sarah Duchess of Marlborough's brilliant phrase 'had never seen water but in a bason', joined with a sea commander with a splendid fighting record who was nearly thirty years his senior. It must have been like finding oneself suddenly perched on top of the Nelson column. The prospect was extensive, the position elevated: but the potentialities of disaster were all too clear. Nerve was the supreme requirement.

1. Summarized in Gardiner *C & P* iii, 236–9.
2. Carte MS 74 ff. 11 and 12.

Edward was never deficient in that quality. And his other great strength was his power of application. No detail of the job in hand was neglected. As ambassador in Madrid he was to make exact drawings and descriptions of methods of shoeing horses, erecting fences, preparing chocolate, even going so far as to draw and measure the cooking utensils employed in the process. Did Pepys perhaps learn these habits, or something of them, from his cousin and employer? Certainly as a young man Pepys had leanings, which he never altogether lost, towards dilettantism. Edward's mind settled at once to the task in hand, less inclined to wonder or to ponder. The first volume of his Journal opens with extracts, not in his own hand, from the records of the Council of State dealing with the main concerns of the navy, pay, manning, stores, squadronal divisions of the fleet, ship-lists with names of captains, from 16 August 1652 to October 9th of that year. The Dutch War was then in its opening phase and Edward himself was still living quietly at Hinchingbrooke. Whether he collected this material on his appointment to the Admiralty Committee in October or when he knew that he was to go to sea we do not know. If he kept a record of his voyage with Blake it has not survived. Some detailed drawings of a lunar eclipse observed in the Mediterranean on 26th April 1656, annotated in his own hand, and some drawings and a description of Gibraltar done about the same time are bound up towards the end of the volume. But it is clear, even from these fragments, that already at this early stage of his new career he was taking his own sights and doing his own navigation.

Cromwell's discernment should never be discounted. He had known Edward from boyhood as a country neighbour, had marked his promise as a young officer and rewarded it with a regiment in the New Model, had appreciated his diligence and effectiveness and straightforwardness on the Council. But was confidence in general abilities and character enough to justify so crucial an appointment? Blake's was not a good life. Even in the Dutch War his health had forced him to come ashore for several months. He had returned from his second Mediterranean cruise early in October 'sick, tired and troubled both in mind and body'.[1] His Vice-Admiral, Richard Badiley, veteran of many years' service in the Mediterranean, was in no better case. Both men evidently had hoped to

1. J.R. Powell *Robert Blake* (1972) 272.

Sandwich's drawing of a dustpan, with measurements in the margin,
made during his embassy in Madrid

enjoy the blessings of the land with the fruits of their labours. Both undertook to serve again only from their high sense of duty. Blake, in view of his enfeebled state, requested a partner to help shoulder his responsibilities. Badiley, had he been ten years younger, would have been an obvious choice. But he was to need all his strength to fulfil once more the functions of a Vice-Admiral.

Who else was there? Penn, far the best qualified of the other Generals-at-Sea, was in disgrace. Monck, the other powerful candidate, was indispensable in Scotland. Lawson, the sea officer *par excellence* who was much liked and admired by the sailors, had ruled himself out by his all but open hostility to the regime. To neutralize him Cromwell had appointed him initially to the Vice-Admiral's post which Badiley was to resume. Such a manoeuvre would at once remove him from his command of the Channel fleet with its attendant dangers of support for any *coup d'état* and would place him under the stern hand and eye of Blake. Sensing this, Lawson had thrown up his commission, claiming that he had not been told of the purpose of the voyage. He was followed a month later by two senior Captains, whose reasons, slightly varied from those given by Lawson, were in effect political.

Mountagu's own appointment was thus itself clearly political in origin. Paradoxically it was political because he was apolitical. He would not rock the boat by conspiring with foreigners to bring in Charles II or with the Fifth Monarchy Men to inaugurate the reign of Christ on earth or, as Cromwell's old companion in arms Sexby was at that moment plotting, an unholy combination of the two. He was trustworthy.

The point is unselfconsciously made in the first letter he wrote to Thurloe in his new capacity aboard the *Naseby* at anchor in Stokes Bay on 2nd March 1656. He and Blake had hoisted their flag aboard her ten days earlier, to be faced with the serious refusal of orders by the two captains. Discontent in the service had already reached danger point from the usual cause of non-payment of wages. If a political match were set to this tinder there might be no checking the blaze:

> ... Today after dinner Captain Lyons being come, we spent half an hour in discourse with him about the grounds of his dissatis-faction, which he said in the first place was the neglect of due care for both commanders, and seamen and their families, in case of death or long absence at sea. I urged to him, that that could not be a sufficient ground, for there was a very plentiful provision in that kind, more than I believed was formerly in this nation (by much) and more than in any other state; and that our superiors did make as much conscience of taking care in that way, as any of us could do; and that we had no reason to distrust it. Yet he insisted upon his experience of great sufferings in that kind. And being pressed for further grounds, he said that he was not satisfied in the design we were about; neither against whom he should go, nor where; which was easily replied to, that the sole enemy in view was the Spaniard, and to infest him was our work; but in what place concerned not him, who was to obey commands, and not to weigh designs, whereof he was not properly cognisable.[1]

This is the classic position of the professional officer. Its statement there and then goes far to explain why Mountagu had been chosen. Lyons flatly contradicted it by conscientious objection to fighting the Spaniard at all. 'He thought that we had received no injury from him

1. *The Letters of Robert Blake* ed. J.R. Powell (1937), 393. The original is Rawl.MS 36 f.17.

43

[in the West Indies], but contrarily had done it to him.' He was ready to defend his country in the channel, should the Spaniards appear there with aggressive intentions. 'He also said, his body was not able to bear the service in hot countries.'

Blake and Mountagu had given him a full hearing and more than one opportunity to retract. The fact that he shifted his ground and gave three quite different reasons for declining to serve confirmed their suspicion of a real and undisclosed political motive. They had in any case no alternative to dismissing an officer who claimed the right to pick and choose where he would go and what action he would undertake. He and the other Captain who took the same line were promptly relieved.

The fleet sailed from St Helens about the middle of March. Shortly before they left Mountagu wrote a short note, the first that has survived, addressed 'For my servant Samuell Pepys at my Lodginges in White-halle.'[1] How long this arrangement had been going on is unknown. Probably from the time that Pepys came down from Cambridge in 1654. Exactly what capacity the future diarist filled is also not clear. His enemies later asserted that it was menial. But if it was it cannot have been strictly defined since even as early as March 1656 he was charged in this note with handling a very large sum of money. In less than a year Pepys's own letters to his employer show him ranging easily over the stewardship of the household and the reporting of political gossip that he was soon to refine into a new art form.

Blake and Mountagu arrived off Cadiz towards the end of April to find little opportunity of the aggressive and profitable action for which they had been sent. The remnants of last year's plate fleet had got safely into port. A powerful squadron had recently sailed for the Caribbean to escort the new one home. Cadiz itself, though full of ships, was strongly defended and the navigable channels leading to the harbour were narrow, difficult and easily obstructed. The admirals therefore entered the Mediterranean to investigate the possibilities of establishing a base from which the straits might be controlled and the returning plate fleets profitably harassed. The Protector himself was keen on seizing Gibraltar, an idea originally propounded by a Scottish mercenary soldier, Sir Henry Bruce, in 1625. Cromwell, it seems, may have had thoughts of cutting through

1. Printed in *Letters and Second Diary of Samuel Pepys* ed. R.G. Howarth (1932).

the neck of land that joins the Rock to the mainland and making it an island.[1]

Mountagu was detached to survey and report. His drawings of the Rock, made in May 1656, are in his journal. His conclusions are best summarized in one of his letters to Thurloe. The best way of taking the place would be to land on the isthmus with a force strong enough to cut communications with the mainland. It was well known that the Spaniards never victualled a fort for more than a month, so that if a few frigates were to prevent relief by sea it could be soon starved into surrender. But he emphasized that the initial military force would have to be substantial '4000 or 5000 men well formed and officered'. The troops of the New Model in fact. Seamen would not do '. . . for land service, unless it be for sudden plunder, and then they are valiant much, but not to be ruled and kept in any government on shore: nor have your sea officers much stomach to fight on shore'. Cromwell accepted this judgment, intending to act on it. But he had too many irons in the fire and too little of life left. That Mountagu still kept the project in mind may be inferred from his later annotation of his 1656 drawing: 'Mr Rolt who was at Gibraltar November 2nd 1661 sais that he paced ye sand close at ye foote of Gibraltar hill betweene both ye seas & that it is 600 of his stepps from sea to sea.'[2]

Needing wood, water and provisions the fleet put in to Tangier, then a Portuguese possession, where they were well received. Four years later when the place was offered as part of Catherine of Braganza's dowry Mountagu was eager for its acceptance. Meanwhile he made drawings of other North African ports within the straits, notably Buzema and Tetuan, the second of which he favoured as a possible alternative. What made the straits so acute a prepossession of English policy was not merely the protection of our Levant trade, important though that was. The new element was that France was suddenly emerging as a major naval power. Like Spain she had great ports and bases both in the Atlantic and the Mediterranean. Only by the passage of the straits could the naval forces of either country be united to exert their full strength.

In a war with Spain, such as Cromwell had embarked on, the most

1. Corbett *England in the Mediterranean 1603–1713* (1917), i, 137, 282 ff.
2. J. i,f.369.

urgent necessity, essential where the possession of an anchorage on the straits was merely desirable, was the use of the Portuguese ports, especially Lisbon with its magnificent harbour and ample facilities for the cleaning and repair of wooden ships. The treaty that had been imposed on Portugal in 1654 by the forceful presence of Blake's fleet had still not been ratified and the £50,000 due under it had not been paid. While an English fleet was again in those waters Cromwell sent a special envoy, Philip Meadowe, to Lisbon to obtain this. Meadowe was more conciliatory than the Protector had intended. He gave an undertaking that the English fleet would not molest the Brazil fleet, then daily expected, on which Portuguese finances largely depended and he also, most unwisely, conceded to the papal authorities the right of deciding whether English deserters had in fact turned Catholic. This was a scarlet rag to the Cromwellian bull. To make matters worse Meadowe was the victim, fortunately not seriously hurt, of an attempt on his life in the streets of the capital. Both Cromwell in London and Mountagu in Cadiz Bay were in favour of Palmerstonian retaliation. But Blake knew from long experience how vulnerable to weather and disease a fleet was that had to keep the sea for months on end. No doubt it would be easy to attack the Portuguese, perhaps even in high swashbuckling style to capture their plate fleet. But what would be the next move if all the Iberian ports were closed to English ships? What he did was to sail at once for Lisbon, standing in with the entrance to the Bay of Oeiras a few days before the plate fleet was due and intimating, courteously but firmly, that the treaty must be ratified and the money paid within five days. It worked. Mountagu, himself like Blake notably averse from unnecessary bloodshed, must have learned a valuable lesson on the economical application of seapower.

By now it was late in June. The fleet sailed south and re-entered the Mediterranean. A small force was detached for a successful attack on Malaga but the two Generals at Sea took the main body along the Barbary coast, partly to survey possible anchorages, partly to see whether they could obtain a treaty with the rulers of Tripoli and Tunis whose depredations were a constant hazard to trade. Nothing came of this, except Edward's pilotage drawings and reports. In July they were back off Cadiz. In August they sailed down the Atlantic coast of Morocco to the corsair stronghold of Sallee. Action and negotiation were both inconclusive. The

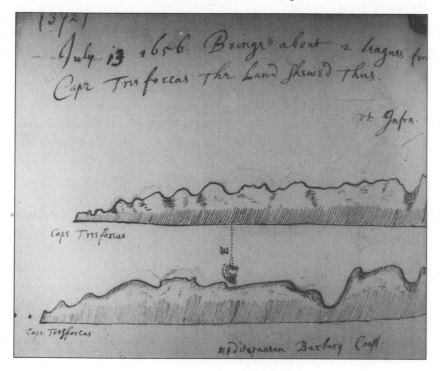

Cape Tresforcas on the Mediterranean coast of Morocco drawn by Sandwich
on his first voyage in 1656

fleet sailed north for Lisbon in September to revictual, leaving a division
of eight ships under the Rear-Admiral, Sir Richard Stayner, to ply off
Cadiz in the hope of catching the Spanish plate fleet.

He was in luck. He caught a detachment that had crossed the Atlantic
without escort when they were within sight of home. Two prizes, both
vastly rich, were taken and three more sunk or burnt. The Governor of
Peru, who was returning to Spain with his wife and children aboard the
Spanish Vice-Admiral, perished in the fire but two of his sons were
saved. They, together with silver variously estimated between £600,000
and £1m, were entrusted to Edward to take home to England in the
Naseby together with three other of the most powerful ships and seven
smaller ones in need of repair. The two boys were soon exchanged for
a nephew of Blake's but Edward it is clear was a kind and affectionate
guardian while they were in his care. The elder who had inherited his

47

father's title of Marquis of Baides charmed everyone, including the Protector. Years later when Edward was appointed to the Madrid embassy they renewed their friendship.

Mountagu arrived back in England during the last week of October and on November 4th received the thanks of the House for the victory. Stayner, who had won it, was hardly mentioned and Waller in the poem he composed to celebrate the occasion ascribes the credit exclusively to Edward. In fact Stayner seems, like other officers and seamen who had taken part in the action, to have made sure of more substantial rewards than the victor's fading leaves. A great proportion of the treasure, well over half, had been embezzled by the time the ammunition wagons laden with silver creaked into the Tower of London. The most stringent inquiry failed to elicit any result. There was no question of Edward having had a hand in the business. Still, having seen for himself the hardships of life at sea and the paucity and irregularity of a sailor's pay he may have felt the force of the Biblical injunction not to muzzle the ox that treadeth out the corn. Perhaps this influenced his own too lax conduct in similar circumstances a decade later.

However that may be he did not neglect the trust Blake, anxious, ill, but indomitable, had put in him to remedy the deficiencies of the ships left behind on the Portuguese station. Even before he came ashore he wrote a long letter to the Admiralty Committee emphasizing their urgent need of victuals, beer in iron-bound cask and canvas for sails.[1] Soon after receiving the plaudits of victory and settling the exchange of his young captives he went down to Hinchingbrooke. He was there till early in the new year, receiving a stream of letters from Pepys, detailing the shopping commissions he was executing in London, reporting the political news, accounting for the disposal of the chests of sugar, tortoiseshell, glass and other valuables brought back from Portugal. He was still a General at Sea and was soon to be employed again in that capacity but this time no longer as a learner driver.

1. *Letters of Blake*, 428.

VI

At Cromwell's Court

ALMOST AT THE SAME TIME as Cromwell had nominated Edward
a General at Sea he had made another appointment hardly less important,
hardly less unexpected, hardly less inspired. He informed Mazarin that
he was sending Sir William Lockhart as his ambassador to Paris.

Lockhart, some four years older than Mountagu, was the eldest son
of a Scottish landed family who had run away from home at the age of
thirteen to a life of adventure on the continent. He took service in a
Dutch regiment and subsequently joined the French army in which he
rose to be a captain of horse. He returned to Scotland to accept a
Colonel's commission in the Covenanting Army to which Charles I surrendered Newark in 1646, on which occasion the King knighted him.
It was the Earl of Lanark, brother to the Duke of Hamilton, who had
invited him to accept the colonelcy of his own regiment so it was natural
that Lockhart should serve in the ill-fated invasion of England that
Hamilton led in the second Civil War. He shewed great courage in
protecting the rear at the disastrous battles of Preston and Wigan but
had at last to surrender to Lambert who sent him prisoner to Newcastle.
He only obtained his liberty by paying a large fine.

The feuds that bedevilled Scottish politics prevented his employment
as General of horse, to which he had at first been appointed, in the army
that asserted Charles II's right to the crown of Scotland in 1650. But
after its defeat at Dunbar he offered to serve as a plain volunteer in the
meagre force with which the King, a year later, went down to final defeat
at Worcester. His offer was rejected, he thought insultingly. Within the
year Cromwell had made him a commissioner for the administration of

justice in Scotland and one of the deputies to negotiate the union of the two kingdoms. In 1653 he was one of the Scottish members of the Barebones Parliament and in 1654 of its successor. In 1655 he was one of the only two Scottish members of the Council set up under Lord Broghill as its President to replace the civil government hitherto directly controlled by Monck, who still remained as Commander in Chief.[1]

Like Monck and Broghill, two of the Protector's ablest lieutenants, Lockhart had fought for the Cavaliers. Like Broghill and Mountagu he was admitted to Cromwell's intimate circle. In 1654 he married the Protector's niece, and sealed his loyalty – could a man do more? – by christening their first son Cromwell. In choosing him ambassador to Paris Cromwell was at the same time intensifying the war against Spain and furthering the project perhaps dearest to his heart, the acquisition of Dunkirk. In the seemingly interminable war between France and Spain the Spaniards, low as they were in the water, had recently met with some unexpected success in Flanders. Mazarin, disliking and fearing the unpredictable and evidently warlike power across the Channel and continuing to encourage the desire for a peace treaty in Madrid, felt it necessary to re-insure by proposing to Cromwell a joint operation in the first place against Mardyke and then perhaps Dunkirk. The bulk of the troops would be provided by England who would acquire either or both of these places should they be taken.

No doubt the Cardinal envisaged a clever manoeuvre by which some of his chestnuts would be pulled out of the fire at little or no real cost. But Cromwell had a quick eye for an opening. To Mazarin's discomfiture he closed before there was time for elegant paltering. Lockhart was sent over with instructions which resulted in a full treaty of alliance between England and France. The Stuart court, hitherto subsidized by a far from lavish pension, was to be bundled out of the country neck and crop. Both powers undertook not to make peace with Spain without giving the other ample warning. Both grudgingly conceded under secret articles consideration to each other's religious scruples. The Protector guaranteed the rights and possessions of the Catholic Church in Dunkirk and Mardyke once they came into his possession and the French government resentfully deferred to his objections to the continued persecution of its

1. For all this see Frances Dow *Cromwellian Scotland 1651–1660* (1979).

Huguenot subjects. To effect the capture of Dunkirk 6000 English troops under their own officers would be provided, supported by a large fleet which would forthwith blockade the two ports of Dunkirk and Ostend from which privateers had been doing far more damage to English trade than any inflicted on Spain by the expensive fleets maintained against her.

Lockhart's success in negotiating with Mazarin is admiringly recorded by Clarendon who, though on the Royalist side of the fence, balanced his contempt for the Spanish government by his detestation of the French. A diplomatic coup brought timely reinforcement to a regime that had still, for all Oliver's heroic efforts, not found firm ground. On the day after voting thanks to Mountagu for Stayner's victory the House had embarked on a long and dangerously unfocused debate arising from the public and provocative blasphemies of James Naylor, the Quaker. Sampling the hideous cruelties of the penalties proposed took up a great deal of time and energy. But had Parliament the right to impose penalties at all, and if so did that right derive from its legislative or its judicial capacity? And what right had the Protector, should he wish, as he did, to mitigate the Pharisaical vindictiveness of its sentence? None, apparently, under the Instrument of Government. This opened questions which neither he nor they could evade. The old constitution of King, Lords and Commons had provided well-known and well-established means for the executive to show mercy and for protecting the rights of the subject. Why not go the whole hog and bring back the institutions now that they had been purged of unworthy persons pursuing undesirable ends? A strong party in the Parliament based on the conservative element that had no particular Cromwellian affiliation favoured this course as the least of evils. The Cromwellians such as Mountagu and Broghill were hot for it. Only a few members of the Protector's council such as Desborough, the Protector's brother-in-law, took violent exception to the revival of what they had intended to bury for ever.

The most important of all opponents was John Lambert, the probable author of the Instrument of Government. It was not, evidently, the monarchical power as such that he objected to, but the danger that kingship might imply the resurrection of the hereditary principle. Lambert was younger and much better preserved than Oliver and might reasonably look forward to succeeding him in the fairly near future. A Lambertian

Protectorate would have pursued a much less adventurous and less expensive foreign policy. There would have been no grand Protestant crusading at the head of a motley body of Swedes, Dutchmen, Lutheran Germans and Calvinist Huguenots, no Elizabethan singeing of the King of Spain's beard. And was it really credible that Richard Cromwell, active only in field sports, should succeed to the control of a military dictatorship? The 'Kinglings', as Mountagu and his associates were called, had not made any such stipulation: but that the danger was implicit was soon to be confirmed by events.

The early months of 1657 were thus taken up for Edward as a prominent officer of both the civil and military departments of government, as a member of the Council of State who had been returned *in absentia* to the second Protectorate Parliament, with a purely political struggle in which the nature of the regime and the future conduct of its foreign policy were at stake. Its resolution had been made more urgent by the uncovering of the latest and most formidable of the plots against the Protector's life. For once the confluence of forces in favour of the government bore Mountagu and his friends to a handsome Parliamentary victory. The Remonstrance, or as it was soon renamed the Humble Petition and Advice, recommending to the Protector the restoration of the Crown and the Upper House and inviting him to occupy the throne was carried on 25th March 1657 by a majority of two to one. Two days later Cromwell was asked to deliver his answer and on March 31st with pomp and magnificence appropriate to the occasion if alien to his own preferences he did so.

That these glorious externals might conceal inner uncertainties was suggested by the fact that it was Edward, not Lambert, the companion of his greatest victories and up to that moment his political heir presumptive, who carried the sword of state before him. When the understudy replaces the principal the audience will want to know why. Lambert made no secret of his continued opposition to the kingship, ostentatiously absenting himself among his tulips at Wimbledon. Cromwell's own strongest political instinct was for social not intellectual coherence. His often proclaimed indifference to forms and names seems to have been perfectly sincere. If he could make the stalled engine fire by assuming the old familiar title he was ready to do so. 'What if a man should take upon him to be King?' he had asked Bulstrode Whitelocke when they were walking together in St James's Park one November day in 1652.[1] Whitelocke had then advised against. Now in 1657 he was in favour: he had acted as Speaker of the House during the indisposition of Sir Thomas Widdrington and had been one of the small group centred on Lord Broghill who had pressed the measure in private on the Protector and in the House itself. As he laconically recorded in his diary on February 22nd 'Whitelocke indeavoured to promote the great buisnes of settlement of the Nation.' That, we may be sure, is exactly how Cromwell saw it. And it was that consideration that led him on March 31st to ask the House for time to reflect and on April 4th to astonish everyone and dismay his friends by refusing.

The Army, that army which had been God's chosen instrument to deliver his people and which was still the best guarantee of order and stability, was the stumbling block. A formidable knot of senior officers were irreversibly opposed and made their feelings known. But so too did a number of their juniors, the plain honest people of God, who, to Cromwell, made palpable the maxim *vox populi, vox Dei*. Clever lawyers like Whitelocke might have come to see the weight of argument for what he had seen from the first simply as cutting the Gordian knot. Clever politicians like Broghill could show that accepting the Crown would both secure the legal provision of revenue for prosecuting the war and bring everyone who served him under the protection of the Treason Statute of Henry VII which legitimated obedience to a *de facto* King. Cleverness was not the well from which Cromwell drew. He had, as Clarendon observed, a wonderful judgment of men. He knew how to make use of them and how to attach them. And the qualities in them to which he responded were his own deepest moral characteristics, loyalty, courage and simplicity. It was these that he recognized in men such as Mountagu and Lockhart. It was these that committed him, against his own pragmatic instincts and his indifference to forms and titles, to rejecting the advice of constitutional experts such as Whitelocke and the pressure of his most trusted servants and friends. He would not be false to his earliest, profoundest loyalty. Once again, to anticipate the final outcome several weeks later, it was while he was taking the air in St James's Park that a frank exchange with a close colleague seems to have been decisive.

1. *The Diary of Bulstrode Whitelocke 1605–1675* ed. Ruth Spalding (1990), 281–2.

Desborough, his brother-in-law, told him that if he took the title of King he would never have anything more to do with him.[1]

Edward and those who thought like him would not take no for an answer. The Humble Petition and Advice had been presented as a totality, take it or leave it, precisely because no one had thought rejection a serious possibility. The first expedient must be to urge Cromwell to think again. But the Republican opposition were cock-a-hoop at the discomfiture of the Kinglings. Once again, as Professor Trevor-Roper has pointed out in his essay on Cromwell and his Parliaments, the Protector had presented his enemies with a Parliamentary opportunity they could not have created for themselves. There would be no two to one majority this time. Edward, who was Teller for the Ayes, was generally thought to have done well to muster a majority of seventy-eight to sixty-five.

To follow the whole course of the negotiations between Oliver and the supporters of the Petition and Advice belongs rather to a biography of Cromwell than of Mountagu. The account given by Firth in *The Last Years of the Protectorate* provides an admirably clear narrative. The reader however would not gather from it the extent of Mountagu's involvement. He was one of the Committee appointed by the House to wait on Cromwell to hear his objections and to suggest how they might be met. He was also one of the intimate circle of Councillors and courtiers to whom the Protector could unburden himself in an easy, even convivial atmosphere. Whitelocke who has recorded some of these occasions entered in his Diary for 11th May 1657: 'a note from the Lord Broghill for Whitelocke to meet this evening at General Mountagues lodging'.

After what must have seemed an interminable series of debates in Parliament and self-questionings by the Protector the Humble Petition and Advice was at last agreed and accepted at the end of May. Its main character was unchanged with the important exception of the kingly title. Its first clause declared Cromwell Protector for life and invited him to appoint his successor. On June 26th he was inaugurated at a kind of laicized Coronation in Westminster Hall. Heralds and trumpeters, ermine robes and richly caparisoned horses, gold maces (but not a crown) showed which way the wind was blowing. The old Earl of Warwick, a

1. C.H. Firth *The Last Years of the Protectorate* i, 190.

shadow now of the triumphant young nobleman painted by Van Dyck, carried the Sword of State but Edward together with Whitelocke and Lord Lisle stood with drawn swords on the steps of what looked like the throne as the Protector mounted to take his seat. The same quartet joined Oliver and his son Richard in the State Coach for the drive back to Whitehall. Mountagu's place in the front rank of the Protectoral government had been publicly asserted. He had long enjoyed the fruits of office, Councillor of State, Commissioner of the Treasury, General at Sea, all of which carried substantial salaries. In September 1655 he had been made a Forester of Waltham Forest. Remodelling the Protector's household doubtless offered useful perquisites. But now he was part of the management, a principal. And all this in only four years. He was not yet thirty-two and, having been out of politics altogether for so great a proportion of his adult life, had no political past of which to be the prisoner. He had made no enemies and seems to have aroused no jealousy. Few courtiers of his time were so happily placed.

VII

Commander in Chief

AT THE END OF MAY, a month before these solemnities in Westminster Hall, news reached London of Blake's annihilating victory at Santa Cruz. Like Trafalgar it closed a supreme naval career at its supreme moment. Blake did not, like Nelson, fall in action but he died as his ship, hardly less battered and worn than he, neared the entrance to Plymouth Sound. In another foreshadowing of Nelson his body lay in state at Greenwich, then a derelict Royal Palace not the great Hospital for old sailors, before being borne up river for burial.

Mountagu was not, as no doubt he would have wished to be, chief mourner at the funeral of his colleague and mentor. On July 17th he had hoisted his flag aboard the *Naseby*, the very ship in which they had sailed together, to take command of the fleet that was supporting operations in Flanders. Vice-Admiral Goodson had been charged with the blockade of Dunkirk and Ostend. Mountagu's task was to protect the supplies of the six thousand redcoats already landed in France and to assist in the reduction of Mardyke by attacking it from sea. The opportunities for successful action depended on the movements of the land forces, which, to the exasperation of the English commanders, were initially away from Mardyke. With their coastal flank protected Mazarin and his great general Turenne took the chance of reducing Spanish strongholds inland. This was not what Cromwell or the commander of his expeditionary force had bargained for. The redcoats had come to fight a battle not to take part in long and intricate siege operations whose moves and counter-moves were the stock in trade of continental generalship. Lockhart in Paris was not slow or timid in representing his master's views to Mazarin. The French alliance was beginning to look another expensive gamble. So inadequate was the provision for paying and supplying the English force that in two or three months desertion and disease had reduced it from 6000 to 4000, and of these hardly half were fit for duty at any one time. The country in which they were quartered was damp and unhealthy. Apart from replacing invalids with fresh drafts from England there was not much that the navy could do.

Lockhart certainly had his hands full. Besides bringing Mazarin to the execution of a project that was more obviously advantageous to England than to France he was also conducting a more delicate negotiation with the emigré Royalist nobleman Lord Fauconberg for a marriage with Cromwell's daughter Mary. By September he had succeeded in both. Turenne marched towards the coast and at the end of the month Mardyke was taken. Mountagu's ships took part in the bombardment of the place but there was not scope for much more. It was simply a large hornwork to protect Dunkirk, three miles away. Dunkirk was the object of the campaign and both Lockhart and the Protector urged an immediate assault. But Turenne wished to secure the besieging force from being taken in the rear by an attack from Gravelines, which as it was lightly held should easily fall. The Spaniards however opened the dykes, making an advance impossible and worsening the already wretched conditions under which the troops were living. It was now too late in the year to attempt so strongly fortified a town as Dunkirk, so the English had to make do with Mardyke, their first continental possession since the loss of Calais a century earlier.

Mardyke was in fact a liability. It was too small to hold enough troops to defend it from the sudden attack from nearby Dunkirk, which might confidently be expected. The sandy treeless terrain offered no possibility of winter quarters, did not indeed afford the timber necessary to house the unfortunate garrison. Bitter recriminations were exchanged between London and Paris. The place was nearly lost to the Spaniards and the frequent encounters between the redcoats and the English and Irish Royalist troops in alliance with Spain led to a stream of desertions and even to an alarmingly friendly meeting between the garrison commander, General Reynolds, and James, Duke of York. Reynolds was promptly recalled to give an account of himself in London but his ship, not a vessel of the State's Navy, was lost with all hands on the Goodwins.

There was indeed little the navy could do. A small squadron cruised off Mardyke but it could have done nothing to repel a land assault. The main fleet had come home when it was clear that there would be no attack on Dunkirk before the spring. Edward was back in Whitehall on October 15th and soon afterwards retired to Hinchingbrooke for the winter. For all the outward signs of success what had he actually achieved? He was now the first man in the navy, and among the handful of men that Cromwell had picked to hold high office. At this very moment he was one of those the Protector was most anxious to see in his revived and highly select House of Lords. Yet as he must have known himself he was not cut out to be a politician. He lacked the instinct to go for the jugular. In his temporary retirement at Hinchingbrooke with his wife and young family he had serious thoughts of retiring altogether. His period of command in the Channel had produced nothing. He had doubts as to how workable the revised constitutional system he had helped to inaugurate would prove to be. Would not the new House of Lords simply cream off the ablest and loyalest of the Protector's supporters from the House of Commons? And if it did how was the government to raise the revenue needed to sustain its military base and carry on a large-scale war? And what would happen if the Protector and the House collided head on? His own loyalty to Oliver and his family was unswerving. Indeed it was to Henry Cromwell, the second and much abler son, to whom, early in December, he expressed his misgivings with an openness that deserves quotation:

'Truly the consequence of that affaire [The issue of writs for the Upper House] is very greate, and what the constitution will prove I cannot imagine, unless my melancholy feares should make mee suspect the worst, because I doubt divers whom I could (and I believe that your Lordship also) wish were of it, will not meddle and noe doubt divers others will readily supply their places; I heartily wish it otherwise. My opportunityes with his Highnesse are not manye, nor is my judgment fitt to advise him, but I have not spared to speake as occasion hath been offered unto mee, and herein only I can boast that I have a heart true to the interest of the publique, and his Highnesse' person and familye, nor shall cease to promote the same to my power.'[1]

1. BL Lansdowne MSS 822 f. 292 printed in Harris, i, 108.

Edward's apprehension that the country was heading down a constitutional blind alley was strengthened by the reactions of his relations. Both his cousins, the Earl of Manchester and Lord Mountagu of Boughton, were invited to sit. The return of Manchester, who had quarrelled so famously with the Protector in the closing years of the Civil War, would have been a powerful reinforcement. But he remained obstinately unresponsive at Kimbolton. He and Edward's father-in-law, John Crew, had been two of the strongest influences on the teen-ager who had defied his father to join the army of the Eastern Association. Now Crew too was refusing Cromwell's writ of summons. These were the men Edward would have liked to find sitting beside him. The house wanted weight. Richard Cromwell and John Claypole, the husband of the Protector's favourite daughter, exemplified its gimcrack character.

When Parliament met in January 1658 Edward's forebodings were soon justified. Disregarding the caution counselled by Bulstrode Whitelocke[1] the infuriated Protector sent them packing. Mountagu had little time, even if he had had the inclination, to involve himself in the question of what constitutional experiment should be tried next. Within a few weeks he was issuing orders as General at Sea for the naval side of the forthcoming assault on Dunkirk. On June 1st he again hoisted his flag in the *Naseby*. Among other consequent advantages his presence with the fleet excused his attendance at the High Court of Justice to which he had been nominated to try the two Royalists, Sir Henry Slingsby and Dr Hewitt, who were convicted of plotting a rising and immediately beheaded. The affair left an unpleasant taste. Slingsby was the most honourable, upright type of old Royalist who had consistently and openly refused to recognize the legitimacy of the usurping regime. He had been entrapped by methods smacking of the *agent provocateur*. The case against Hewitt was at least respectable. But he was a clergyman who had also made no secret of his allegiance and had continued to use the Book of Common Prayer in his ministrations at St Gregory's hard by St Paul's. Such a man could hardly be considered a serious threat as a plotter. It was widely felt that the failure to find an acceptable basis for constitutional government had led to an assertion of power by instilling fear. Would Edward, who had ostentatiously dissociated himself from the trial of the

1. *Diary* 485.

King, have consented to these proceedings which, like the Court that tried the King, had no foundation in Common Law? It certainly made things easier at the Restoration that he had not been involved in them.

Lockhart was the mainspring of the English effort against Dunkirk. He had bombarded the government at home with demands that the garrison at Mardyke, diminished by sickness, be brought up to strength. Of the original 6000 troops only 2000 were now effective. The navy was busy bringing in reinforcements and preventing the enemy from doing the same. Lockhart, though far from well, crowned his endeavours by obtaining leave from the Paris embassy to assume the command of the English army vacant by the drowning of Reynolds in December. He and Mountagu collaborated easily and both enjoyed good relations with Turenne.

Turenne was the first of the great European commanders whom Mountagu was to meet in his crowded career. Both men were too well bred to stand on the dignity of their position and vie for the superiority of status that seventeenth-century states expected of their military and diplomatic representatives. Edward was later to find himself in serious trouble through his failure to exert himself over such trifles. He was, as we can see from his *Journal*, much more interested in the people he met than he was in his effect on them. He reports their conversation, their views, much more fully than his own. As his letter to Henry Cromwell shows he was not in the least self-important. No doubt that is one of the reasons why people of high intelligence liked him and respected him.

The dunes round Dunkirk were crowded with military talent. Apart from Turenne, Schomberg, the great soldier with whom Edward was to have a series of interesting conversations ten years later in Lisbon comparing the notable captains of their time, was present on the French side. The most brilliant commander among the Spanish and their allies was also a Frenchman: the great Condé, whose feud with Mazarin placed his services at the disposal of Philip IV. James, Duke of York, whom Turenne had been reluctant to lose from the French army as required by the treaty with Cromwell, was hardly in the same class. But in the turmoil of the Spanish defeat he shewed the courage and battle sense that were to win the respect of his admirals in the great sea fights of his brother's reign.

In the hard-fought action that left the town with no alternative but surrender it was generally agreed that the redcoats, and in particular Lockhart's regiment, won the honours of the day. Again the fleet's contribution, as so often with sea power, was preventative rather than positive. The great ships could not come close enough inshore to do much damage, a fact which Mountagu recalled in the next reign when the question of keeping the place or selling it was in agitation. In private conversation at his embassy in Madrid in 1667 he freely admitted, 'I was the first Man that ever moved the King to part with It . . . the Coast there was so tempestuous & the grounds so changeable & rouling upon every storme, as never to leave a certain steerage to that Port.' So cold a glance at the bottom line would not have been welcomed by the Protector, who understandably made the most of this triumph for English arms.

For Edward it marked his appearance, in his own right, on the European stage. He was presented to the young Louis XIV. He entertained Mazarin to a splendid dinner aboard the *Naseby* of which it was noticed that the Cardinal partook sparingly and drank only Rhenish wine. The visit was, however, a great success. Mazarin was shewn all over the ship and was delighted with her. He remarked of his host in a letter that he was 'un des gentilhommes du monde le plus franc et mieux intentionné et le plus attaché à la personne de M. le Protecteur'.

Dunkirk was captured at the end of June. Lockhart, who shared the Protector's enthusiasm for making it a rallying point for European Protestantism, was appointed Governor. But Oliver was not to be granted time to develop these schemes. By the time Edward returned to England early in August he was very ill. On September 3rd, his day of victories, he passed into history. He was succeeded immediately and without a ripple disturbing the surface by his son Richard.

Probably this is what Oliver had intended. The Petition and Advice had empowered him to nominate his successor but with well over a year to avail himself of this invitation he had failed to do so. On the other hand he had taken some steps to raise Richard's status. He had called him to his Upper House. He had resigned the Chancellorship of Oxford University in his favour. What mattered was that his Council of State issued orders for the proclamation of Richard and that Fleetwood, Richard's brother-in-law and Oliver's successor as Commander in Chief of the Army, accepted them. If there was any debate on that anxious afternoon we do not know. But we may be sure that, if there was, Edward would have been whole-hearted and outspoken for Richard. As it was he was quick to secure a loyal address from the navy. In so acting he was, as always, reflecting the general mood and preference. 'There is not a scrap of evidence' writes the most recent authority 'in either central or local archives that this response was anything but spontaneous.'[1] People who have lived through a civil war and have been kept awake by fear of anarchy are likely to support authority however dubious the title on which it rests.

For men such as Mountagu and Lockhart and Broghill there could be no thought of retirement into private life. Never had the support of the tried and capable servants of government been more necessary to the life of the country. The breach left in its defences against foreign enemies and domestic upheaval by the vanishing of so Titanic a figure as Oliver must be manned as best they could. Besides rallying the navy to instant obedience Mountagu was made on September 16th Colonel of a regiment of horse. The council of officers was the most serious potential threat. Stiffening the Protectorian interest there was essential. And abroad the pace of events was quickening. As Oliver lay on his deathbed Charles X of Sweden, once thought of as the lynchpin of the great Protestant alliance, had denounced the Treaty of Roskilde so patiently negotiated by the Protector's star diplomat, Philip Meadowe, and had attacked Denmark, who was sure to be supported by the Dutch. This meant that access to the Baltic was again in jeopardy. The Baltic was to the seventeenth-century maritime powers of Europe what the Persian Gulf is to the twentieth. Masts, spars, tar, plank and most other materials for the building and the motive power of ships came largely from there. The Dutch had long done their best to establish a supremacy or at least a preferential position over the Sound. And the Dutch were already giving trouble by providing facilities for the privateers that had previously based themselves in Dunkirk. Late in October, a month before the grandiose obsequies of the Protector, Mountagu took out a squadron of twenty nimble ships from Portsmouth to teach these pests a lesson.[2]

On November 23rd he and all the other leading figures of the regime attended the state funeral in Westminster Abbey. For the rest of the

1. Ronald Hutton, *The Restoration: A Political and Religious History of England and Wales 1658–1667* (1985) p. 22.
2. *C.S.P. Dom* 26th October 1958 Capt. Fras. Willoughby at Portsmouth.

winter he was active in issuing operational orders and obtaining supplies for the ships in the Straits squadron under Captain Stokes as well as for those being prepared for service in the fleet destined for the Baltic. The Dutch had lost no time in sending a powerful fleet which had got the better of the Swedes in an action inside the Sound and had succeeded in joining the Danish fleet in Copenhagen thus altering the balance of power on which Charles X's adventure depended. By then it was late in the season. Nonetheless the Council of State decided to send a force under Vice-Admiral Goodson. It was only twenty ships as against the Dutch fleet of forty-five. And the weather was what might be expected in the second half of November. Goodson managed to appear with the greater part of his ships off the Skaw on December 9th. But it was a tribute to English seamanship rather than a reinforcement of English diplomacy. On the 15th he wisely decided to return home. A fearful gale made survival a considerable achievement but by the end of the year they had all struggled home.

It is unlikely that Edward favoured this ineffective and potentially costly gesture. He was certainly an advocate of a strong line with the United Provinces but he was too experienced a seaman and too prudent a commander to risk his most powerful ships on so remote a possibility of any decisive result. He was himself to be sent out early in March with a much more formidable force, a fleet that would have given the Dutch pause for reflection had it been sent out the previous October. But by the spring the Dutch, anticipating the English reaction, had mobilized large reinforcements so that once again they disposed of superior force.

The Protectorate, in spite of the valiant efforts of its loyal and vigorous servants, was beginning to crumble. Early in December, while Goodson's force was being blown about the North Sea, there had been an equally tempestuous scene at the Council of State. Fleetwood and Desborough accused Mountagu and Fauconberg of conspiracy with Colonel Ingoldsby to kill or imprison them. Mountagu angrily denied this absurd allegation and challenged them to produce their evidence, which turned out to be an anonymous letter. The young Protector sided with Mountagu. Fleetwood, the Lord Lundy of the English Revolution, gave ground but Desborough stormed out of the meeting. Doubtless this defiance of authority was well known by the time Parliament met in

January. At all events the members very quickly got the bit between their teeth, and the Protector, after opening the proceedings with a speech that surprised everybody by its dignity and general good sense, made no attempt to curb them.

From the backwater of the new Upper House Edward could not be called on to stem the Parliamentary torrent. On March 11th he was granted leave from his duties there to take command of the fleet destined for the Sound, flying his flag once again in the *Naseby*. He sailed a few days later and anchored off Elsinore on April 6th.

For the second time as a General at Sea he found himself charged with the same sort of mission as the Grand Old Duke of York. His instructions were weak and ambiguous.[1] 'Deal very seriously with the King of Sweden touching his present war with Denmark.' Quite. Essentially they expressed the pious aspiration that the English and Dutch should mediate a settlement based as closely as was practicable on the Treaty of Roskilde. Certain limited contingencies in which force might be used were specified but the tone of the instructions was such as to warn any commander of the mortal political danger he would run by doing so. Even the careful restriction of the claim to make foreign vessels strike their colours 'in the British seas' was further qualified by a private note from the Protector 'to avoid all disputes of this nature, if it be possible, because war and peace depend on it'.[2]

Playing a weak hand uncertainly supported by an unselfconfident government calls for tact and restraint, two qualities for which Edward all his life was conspicuous. He was also fortunate in having Sir Philip Meadowe, the Protectorate's most experienced and trusted diplomat, on the spot to inform and advise him. But there his good luck ended. On April 22nd, barely a fortnight after he had arrived, Richard Cromwell capitulated to the Army chieftains and dissolved his Parliament. On May 7th the Rump was recalled and by the end of the month the Protectorate was at an end. Its two most formidable enemies, the military establishment and the Republicans, were struggling for power and neither of

1. Summarized in *Journal of the Earl of Sandwich* (N.R.S. 1929) ed. R.C. Anderson. Appendix I.
2. *Thurloe SP*, vii, 633.

them had any reason to believe that Mountagu was of their way of thinking. He had been walking on thin ice before but now the cracks were like pistol shots.

His difficulties were compounded by the slowness and uncertainty of communication. He had to deal on the spot with a military and diplomatic situation that was developing and ramifying rapidly from day to day, having at the pit of his stomach the certain knowledge that there was no longer a government behind him whose mind he knew and whose trust he enjoyed. In the first days of his arrival in the Sound, before the Dutch reinforcements under de Ruyter had entered the Kattegat and before Richard had been overthrown, he had acted with speed and decision. He had called on the Dutch admiral to join with him in bringing pressure on both combatants to settle and he had warned Charles X that he was not to expect any support from the English fleet that had now restored a balance of naval power unless he showed an immediate readiness to treat for peace. The Dutch reaction was cool and equivocal, the Swedish scornful. Charles X was a military gambler, not a peace-loving statesman. Why should he give up his game, the age-old game for which, in his view, kings should live, at the behest of some whey-faced Puritan? Edward consulted and kept the confidence of his captains at Councils of War; he kept in close touch with Meadowe; he seized the opportunities offered by the sudden weakening of the Swedish military position as the weight of Dutch sea power and Brandenburger troops began to tell; he went ashore and conducted a highly successful direct negotiation with the Swedish King and clinched his success by placing his fleet in a position to save a Swedish squadron from annihilation by the now united Dutch fleets of de Ruyter and Wassenaer.[1] The successes of English officers, notably Ayscue and Cox, who were serving as admirals in the Swedish service no doubt helped bring the King nearer to accepting the English position. A conference at The Hague between France, Holland and England had agreed an outline of settlement early in May, but it was another matter to secure the adherence of the warring countries and the other powers such as Brandenburg that scented advantage. With large bodies of troops and powerful fleets in constant motion, with only

1. This telescoped account is largely based on R.C. Anderson's introduction to the *Journal*. F.R. Harris and vol. v of Masson's *Life of Milton* supply some details.

the slender protection of short-term truces, the danger of a general war was very great.

If this had been Edward's only concern his part in the avoidance of disaster would have been a notable service. In the extraordinary circumstances of unknown and unforeseeable changes in the character of the government for whom he acted, changes of which he might or might not be adequately informed, at a delay subject to the chances of wind and weather, it was remarkable. Most obviously he could not, however conscientiously he discharged his duties, feel anything but anxiety and dismay on personal and political grounds. He had identified himself with the regime and with the family that was going down to defeat. At his last interview with the Protector just before joining his flagship he had advised him in the clearest terms to rely on his father's trusted servants and counsellors especially Broghill and Thurloe and not to allow himself to be manipulated by the army leaders. In retrospect he saw Richard's dissolution of his Parliament at the demand of Fleetwood and Desborough as the fatal step. That had taken place on April 22nd. By the time Edward heard of it the Rump had been recalled, the very men whom Oliver had expelled so dramatically six years earlier. By the time he heard of that, in the last week in May, Richard himself had been ousted and the Commonwealth once more proclaimed. Thurloe, the administrative hub of the military, diplomatic and intelligence system which kept both the country and its most powerful neighbours in awe, was dismissed two days later.

Who was running the country? Or, to put the question in more specific terms, with whom would one do business? The question recalls the axiom of the Greek philosopher Heraclitus that one could not step into the same river twice, refined by one of his followers to the point that one could not step into it once, since the flow of water would have altered its composition between putting one's foot in and touching the river bed. At first Richard's Council of State was stiffened by a strong admixture of the military. The restored Rump replaced the Oliverians by Republicans but perforce kept the soldiers. To conduct foreign affairs a subcommittee of six was appointed which, in those days of dizzying change, was so uncertain of its own identity that it continued to transact business in the name of 'the Most Serene and High the Lord Protector of the

66

Commonwealth of England, Scotland and Ireland', describing themselves as 'the Commissioners of His Highness the Protector'.[1]

Edward's position was difficult in the extreme. As a simple patriot and
as the only General at Sea in active command his first duty was, in the
phrase usually ascribed to Blake 'to stop the foreigner from fooling us'.
As a firm believer in monarchy and as a loyal and trusted friend of
the Cromwells he made no secret of his affiliations. He continued to
correspond with Thurloe until he was informed of his dismissal. He
then addressed himself, in a businesslike manner, to the new Council
but without any of the rapturous professions of love for the Good Old
Cause that were felt to be appropriate. Even as late as September, when
he had returned to England and had been summarily relieved of all his
appointments, he wrote to Richard Cromwell, now once again the squire
of a Hampshire village, as though he were still Lord Protector, styling
him 'Your Highness' and addressing him with the same deference as in
the days of his power. Contemporaries and later historians who dislike
what he stood for have sneered at him for a time-server and a turncoat.
Rather in that age of cant he may be admired for disdaining fashionable
hypocrisy.

At any rate the restored Rump regarded him with a clear hostility and
suspicion that only prudence prevented them from avowing. To declare
him a public enemy when he was out of reach and in effective control
of the fleet would have been the height of folly. Instead they resorted to
that familiar expedient of hard-pressed governments: they appointed a
Commission. The Commission was empowered to take over the peace
negotiations in the Sound and thus to control the use of the fleet in
those waters. It consisted of two harmless and obscure figures and one
thorough-going Republican, the aristocratic Colonel Algernon Sidney,
a distant relation of Edward's who was himself joined with the other
three in the Commission. On July 22nd they were welcomed aboard the
flagship at Elsinore.

They were not, however, the only new arrivals from England. One of
Oliver Cromwell's less inspired promotions had been that of his loutish
nephew Thomas Whetstone to a captain's place in the navy. He had

1. On a treaty made with the Dutch on 30th July 1659. This fascinating document
was unearthed in New Zealand by the late Philip Aubrey and quoted in his *Mr
Secretary Thurloe* (1990) p. 185.

been sent out with the Straights squadron under Stokes, one of Blake's captains who had succeeded to his responsibilities in the Mediterranean, and even before Oliver died had been in serious trouble for professional incompetence and actual disobedience. Most unwisely he attempted to defend himself by bringing charges against Stokes. What might have happened if the Protector had lived to influence the decision of the Admiralty Committee we cannot know: but with the death of the great man they had no difficulty in coming to a decision. Whetstone was recalled in disgrace and imprisoned before being discharged with the intimation that his services were no longer required. Edward himself had been party to this verdict and sentence, though Whetstone was probably ignorant of this fact.

An alert Royalist agent Samuel Morland saw in this disgruntled protégé of the Protectorate a promising contact with the all-important commander of the fleet. If Mountagu could be won over, if he could be induced to bring his ships back to support the great Royalist rising that was planned for the summer, the highest hopes might be fulfilled. Whetstone accepted with alacrity, crossed over to Bruges for instructions and letters from the exiled court and made his way to Copenhagen. There he was to get in touch with the Admiral's cousin who had shipped with him, yet another Edward Mountagu, conveniently abbreviated to Ned. Ned, the son of the Lord Mountagu of Boughton who had briefly served on the Navy Committee in 1647–8, was himself a Royalist agent. The meeting duly took place and the Admiral heard his cousin's account with every appearance of sympathy. Colonel Sidney's aggressive and uncompromising attitude had already given him grounds for thinking that the new government was preparing to supersede him at the earliest practicable moment. His suspicions were probably confirmed by Whetstone's information, obtained through Morland who was a highly placed official in the diplomatic and intelligence system inherited from Thurloe, that Algernon Sidney's secret instructions empowered him to do so.[1] Pepys, who had come over with letters for his master at the same time as the Commissioners, had no inkling of what was in the wind. And it is to him that we owe the story of Whetstone's crass ineptitude at a

1. I owe this conjecture to John Carswell *The Porcupine: The Life of Algernon Sidney* (1989) which gives an account of these matters decidedly hostile to Mountagu.

chance encounter ashore in Copenhagen told him by Edward (now styled 'my Lord') three years after the Restoration:

> . . . my Lord, being at dinner with Sydney, one of his fellow Pleni-potenciarys and his mortal ennemy, did see Whetstone and put off his hat three times to him, but the fellow would not be known; which my Lord imputed to his coxcombly humour (of which he was full) and bid Sydney take notice of him too; when at that very time he had letters in his pocket from the King – as it proved afterward. And Sydney afterward did find it out at Copenhagen, the Duch Commissioners telling him how my Lord Sandwich had hired one of their shipps to carry back Whetstone to Lubeck, he being come from Flanders from the King. But I cannot but remember my Lord's equanimity in all these affairs with admiration.[1]

Mountagu has left his own account, written within two or three weeks of the event, of the negotiations with the Swedes and the Dutch and, even more important, the fierce arguments between himself and Alger-non Sidney 'my mortal enimye' at the private discussions among the Commissioners.[2] Sidney's disdainful prickliness at a conference with the Dutch is vividly conveyed: 'Col. Sidney, while we discussed, leaned in the window by himself apart in a discontented manner, afterwards expressed himself against what we had asked and that he was fully satis-fied upon their obligation offered and walked about the room with Monsi-eur Slingelandt alone discoursing.' What was at issue was whether the fleet should remain in the Sound, should leave a token force of fifteen ships with the Dutch reducing their armament to a similar strength (a proposition that they steadily evaded), or should abandon what had become a pointless exercise and sail for home forthwith. Sidney was for the first or second, Mountagu for the third, arguing that the second would be an unacceptable task undertaken with no conceivable advantage and that the first, the only true alternative, was impracticable because provisions were already short, the ships had been at sea for four months and sickness had taken its usual heavy toll.

This view, unanimously supported by his captains and vigorously emphasized by his Vice-Admiral, Goodson, was accepted by the other commissioners. On August 24th the fleet set sail for England, leaving

1. *Diary* 8th March 1663.
2. Printed in Anderson *Journal*, 47–70.

behind a couple of frigates and a ketch to attend on the grimly furious Sidney and his two anxious colleagues. During the voyage Edward composed the narrative already alluded to and doubtless thought long and hard about what he was going to do and say, indeed about what situation he would find when the *Naseby* dropped anchor in Hosely Bay, as she did on September 6th. According to the secret conversations with Whetstone, a countrywide Royalist rising would have been synchronized with his return. Would he be required to bring over the King, to blockade the mouth of the Thames, to embark troops from Flanders or the Pas de Calais? By August 31st he knew that these possibilities need no longer concern him. The *Eaglet* ketch, bound for Copenhagen with letters for the Commissioners which he opened and read, must have brought the news of the comprehensive failure of the Royalist coup. What might the Council of State now have to say about his sudden decision to bring the fleet home?

Edward landed at Manningtree on September 7th. He did not hurry to London, spending that night at Colchester and the next at Chelmsford. Did he want time to pick up intelligence as to how things were going in Whitehall? The omens were not good. He had found three of the Admiralty Commissioners, among them his old Parliamentary rival Colonel Valentine Walton, waiting for him when he brought the fleet in. He was received by the Colonel on the morning of Saturday the 10th. They listened to the account he had prepared in frosty silence and ordered that it should be reported to Parliament and that a Committee should be appointed 'to examine the reasons of my sailing with the whole fleet from the Sound hither contrary to the directions of the Parliament'. The regiment of horse that Richard had given him was taken away and given to Colonel Alured, a heartwhole Republican, and the lodgings at Whitehall were to be vacated though Edward himself was not to leave London. Meanwhile Lawson, the popular left-wing admiral who had refused to go as Blake's second-in-command to the Mediterranean in 1656, had been appointed to command the fleet in the narrow seas, which in effect made him naval Commander in Chief for the time being.

Like many a political survivor Edward was saved by a combination of the speed at which events moved, the mistakes of his opponents and, last but not least, his rare ability to keep his mouth shut. A bare month after this virtual public disgrace, the government had fallen. The moving spirits of the Rump had tried to assert themselves by dismissing several of the army leaders, who had at once retaliated by turning them out and locking the Parliament house. The old fissures on which the more philosophic Royalists had counted from the beginning were opening up again. Edward took the opportunity of withdrawing to Hinchingbrooke where he took good care to keep himself well informed by Pepys and others watching out for him in London. The wheel was spinning fast, so fast that his sometime colleague, the temperamentally unadventurous, middle-of-the-road lawyer Bulstrode Whitelocke in the space of three weeks first advised the army leaders to attack Monck in Scotland in case he should bring in the King and then volunteered to go over himself to make terms with Charles.[1] Mountagu, by contrast, said nothing, signed nothing, risked no one else's neck. Like his hero, Oliver, his sincere desire was not to bring things into blood and confusion.

1. *The Diary of Bulstrode Whitelocke* ed. Ruth Spalding (1990), 547, 552.

VIII

Restoration

=====≈⊃⊂≈=====

THE COLOUR AND MOVEMENT of the scenes that accompanied
Charles II's restoration have caught the eye of the common reader of
history. The ball at The Hague on the last evening of the King's long
exile, the embarkation in the fleet, dressed overall with pendants streaming in the wind and the Royal Standard at the main, commanded by
General at Sea Mountagu about to exchange that rank for that of Admiral
and to rename his favourite flagship the *Royal Charles*, the landing at
Dover, the lining of the road to London, the sovereign's parade on
Blackheath, the delirium of cheering and drinking of healths as the
procession wound its way through the streets of London and Westminster, what pen but that of a glum statistician would not feel the ink
stirring in its veins? It is one of the great set-pieces of English history,
as much for those who shake their heads in disapprobation of the carnal
backslidings of God's Englishmen as for those who see it as the last
chapter of an adventure in which the characters settle down to live
happily ever after.

A great part of the enthusiasm with which the King was received was
a simple reaction of relief. The frightening instability of government, the
widespread alarm that anything might happen, that nothing could be
taken for granted, made the reappearance of traditional forms and institutions, whatever their well-known shortcomings, a boon to be seized.
The poet's advice to

> Always keep a hold of Nurse
> For fear of finding something worse

was never more apposite. The country, or more exactly London where its power and wealth were concentrated, had had the smell of anarchy in its nostrils and it did not like it. Troops had mutinied, for want of a firm and visibly established authority that might meet their exasperated demands for arrears of pay. The making and unmaking of governments by the army leaders had exhausted its limited potentialities. Once again, at the end of December, the Rump had been recalled: but recalled to what? No one, except those whose faith in the Good Old Cause was proof against evidence and perception, could believe that this political ghost had power to command the pikemen and musketeers that had raised it.

Logically the position of a Cromwellian who had become a Cromwellian because it offered the essential element of monarchy was perfectly clear. Either Richard must be restored or Charles must. Alternative military candidates, Lambert or Monck for instance, could not be established without a fresh *coup d'état* which would itself set a precedent for similar praetorian revolutions. For intimates of the Cromwell family such as Mountagu, Broghill or Lockhart there was no point in throwing good money after bad. Richard had had his chance and had fallen at the first fence. In Monck's expressive phrase he had deserted himself and his father's friends were thus released from any obligation of loyalty. Charles Stuart was therefore the only possible solution.

But the symmetry of a syllogism bears little relation to the unevenness of life. Mountagu was in a backwater, with no authority and no responsibilities. What about Lockhart, governor of Dunkirk? What about Broghill, once again away in Ireland? What about Whitelocke, who had served Oliver, albeit with reservations which he had reason to suspect were cordially returned? What about Milton, the régime's most brilliant controversialist who had exerted all his powers to defend what Mountagu and the rest had not defended, the execution of the King? What, above all, of Monck, secure in the command of the well-paid, well-found army that was now quartered just across the border in Scotland?

If we examine the thoughts and actions of these men, so far as they are known to us, we may perhaps glimpse the situation as it might have appeared to Edward as he celebrated Christmas with his young family at Hinchingbrooke. Lockhart had been approached by Royalist agents who had offered him a bribe to declare for the King and, probably no hard task, to bring his unpaid, underfed, unhappy troops over with him. He declined, more it may be suspected out of professional honour and personal pride than out of political conviction. He had good reason to believe that the restored Rump would relieve him of his command at the earliest practicable moment and then he would be at liberty to choose his allegiance. Broghill had certainly reached the same conclusions as Edward and, like him, had taken some preparatory steps without compromising himself. Whitelocke's readiness to jump on bandwagons had, as we have seen, led him for once into jumping the gun. The repudiation of his proposal to the army leaders to make terms with the King while they were still in a position to do so had left him dangerously exposed. While the Mountagus were celebrating the twelve days of Christmas by their own fireside Whitelocke was shivering in a field gate just outside London on a bitter snowy night, struggling in a high wind with a large periwig and 'unusuall clothes [which] did much disguise him; his man looked strangely att it, fearing lest his Master might have some design to robbe'. He was to remain in hiding for several weeks. Milton, characteristically, flew to the opposite extreme. As the odds on a Stuart Restoration shortened he staked everything on a fierce opposition to it, even by implication repudiating the monarchical constitution of the Protectorate that he had himself served. The bitter courage with which the blind poet defied the future Charles II, even invoking scriptural authority for his continued exile,[1] foreshadowed the awesome hero of *Paradise Lost*. That he survived to write the poem, or rather dictate it, may have owed something to the subject of this book. But that must be considered in its proper place.

Monck demands not a paragraph but a book to himself.[2] Almost every contemporary authority, from Pepys to the King himself who, uniquely, raised a commoner by non-stop lift through the gradations of the peerage to the supreme honour of a dukedom, acknowledges him as the chief instrument of the Restoration. On the question of what his intentions were when he crossed the Tweed with his army at Coldstream on 1st January 1660 there was, and is, no such unanimity. The French nickname

---

1. The allusion is made clear in Masson, *Life of Milton* v, 655.
2. He has more than once been accorded it. The best modern study is that by Maurice Ashley *General Monck* (1977).

for Hitler in the nineteen-thirties, Adolphe Légalité, is perhaps in point here. Monck was always at pains to profess, hand on heart, his loyalty and obedience to lawfully constituted authority. He had never had anything to do with, had indeed outspokenly deplored, the making and breaking of governments by his military colleagues. It was in fact to support the Rump, expelled in October and now recalled on Boxing Day, that he was crossing into England to confront Lambert who had been sent to bring him to heel. Lambert's troops, unpaid like their comrades in London and much less comfortably quartered, melted away, many of them only too glad to take service in Monck's well-found regiments. The General's southward march took on something of the aspect of a royal progress, crowds cheering, bonfires blazing, the gentry turning out on horseback to present addresses. Sometimes, as in the case of Fairfax at York, his hosts sought to secure, in confidence, a nod and a wink towards the King over the water. But the General held himself as straight as a ramrod, as inexpressive as a regimental button-stick. Afterwards of course the severe Republicans knew that he was just a bandit, out for all he could get, without the shadow of a scruple. Afterwards too his own family and friends knew that his heart was all the time bursting with loyal devotion to the House of Stuart. His latest biographer accepts neither view, presenting him rather as a patriot whose pragmatic temper disposed him to keep his options open until the limits of profitable action had sufficiently disclosed themselves. Although Edward later described him, irritably, to Pepys as a blockhead he may well have meant the same thing. It seems clear that he never thought of him as either a romantic or a crook.

If few would dispute that Monck was the instrument of the Restoration few would argue that he was its architect. There the claims of Sir Edward Hyde, later Earl of Clarendon, would seem the strongest. It was he who from the first had insisted that the monarchy could only be restored, indeed must sooner or later be restored, by the nation's recognition that the King's right was their right, their interest, the only warranty for their own security under the known laws. Clever deals with Scotch Presbyterians, the Pope, the French, the Spaniards, might embarrass or damage the usurping government but they could never displace it. That could only be achieved by winning back the loyalty of the disaffected and the misled. And the only way to do that was to sail under one's own colours, not play about with *ruses de guerre*. Now, at last, Hyde's policy was vindicated. The City, the only source of ready money for satisfying the justly resentful soldiery, was almost raucous in its royalism. All over the country the cry was for a free parliament and fresh elections which the Republicans well knew would be swept by a royalist backlash. Now, with success simply a question of how and by whose initiative, what did Hyde think? Letters of intelligence poured in on him from his own agents, many extremely well informed. Two highly placed servants of government, George Downing and Samuel Morland, had already committed themselves to passing on everything they knew and had been promised lavish rewards for their treachery. Hyde was thus as well placed as anyone to form a judgment, certainly better placed than Edward lying doggo at Hinchingbrooke. It is interesting that up to the final stages Hyde remained consistently distrustful of Monck, on whom many of the exiled court were pinning their faith. Hyde's old colleague in Charles I's government, Colepeper, had shewn astonishing prescience in forecasting as long ago as September 1658, on the morrow of Cromwell's death, that Monck 'who commandeth absolutely at his devotion a better army (as I am informed) than that in England is, and in the King's quarrel can bring with him the strength of Scotland, and so protect the northern counties that he cannot fail of them in his march' was the man who would serve their turn. 'I need not give you his character, you know he is a sullen man . . . and much believes that his knowledge and reputation in arms fits him for the title of Highness and the office of Protector, better than Mr Richard Cromwell's skill in horse-races and husbandry doth . . . the way to deal with him is . . . to shew him plainly, and to give him all imaginable security for it, that he shall better find all his ends (those of honour, power, profit and safety) with the King, than in any other way he can take.'[1] Yet as late as 17th March 1660, when the tide of Royalism had for weeks past been running so high that the King's health was drunk openly in London, Hyde was still preparing countermeasures in case Monck should prove 'peevish and obstinate', a possibility much enhanced, he thought, by 'the giving away of Hampton Court to Monck and his heirs'.[2] In fact Monck had declined this gift,

1. *Clar S P* iii, 413.
2. *ibid.*, 701.

voted by the Commons after the re-admission of the Secluded Members, in favour of a substantial cash payment.

It was on Mountagu that Hyde pinned his faith. When earlier that month one of his most trusted agents reported rumours that Mountagu was conspiring with Thurloe (now restored to his secretaryship) and others to bring back Richard Cromwell[1] Hyde would have none of it: '. . . so ridiculous that I cannot believe it'. His opinion can only have been confirmed by the report of another informant a few days later that Mountagu had severed all connexion with this group 'and doth now wholly cleave to his Father-in-law, and his Party is as true. And he said within these three days to a great intimate of his and mine thus, "Sir, the true reason why I have left the one and adhere to the other is, because I plainly see there is an utter impossibility of settlement without bringing in the King; and I profess I had rather the nation were settled, though I and my whole family suffer by it, as I know I shall." '[2] In view of the King's welcoming invitation, no doubt drafted by Hyde, which had been secretly extended to him at Copenhagen, we may feel that he protests too much. But that is not to deny the sincerity of his motives, even if he flatters himself in their (reported) expression.

The rapid development of events after Monck marched into London on February 3rd is evoked with incomparable freshness in the pages of Pepys's *Diary*. The arrival of the post at Hinchingbrooke must have been a moment of mounting excitement. Although Edward corresponded with his young cousin in cipher it is clear that his communications gave nothing away, for when Pepys decided to go down to Hinchingbrooke towards the end of the month to give his master a full account of events he found that Edward had left for London the day before he himself had set out in the opposite direction. The re-admission of the Secluded Members had at once restored Edward to place and power. On February 23rd Parliament elected him a member of the Council of State. On March 2nd it appointed him, together with Monck, General at Sea. Since Monck was Commander in Chief of the Army this gave Edward in practice sole command of the fleet. He was also made a Commissioner of the

1. *ibid.*, 693.
2. *ibid.*, 703.

Admiralty and both his regiment of horse and his lodgings at Whitehall were restored to him. In fact Pepys had been given the key of these apartments by Sir Anthony Ashley Cooper, to whom the Army leaders had allotted them, as early as January 19th. Ashley Cooper, who had considered his talents and services insufficiently appreciated by Royalists, Parliamentarians and the Protector in turn, was going to make sure that he was not left out when the King came in.

The chief hazard that confronted Mountagu in establishing himself as the effective Commander in Chief of the fleet was the presence of John Lawson in that very capacity. Lawson, it will be remembered, had refused to go as Blake's Vice-Admiral to the Mediterranean on grounds that were manifestly political and had resigned his commission. A year later he had been briefly taken into custody on suspicion of being involved in a Fifth Monarchy conspiracy against the Protectorate and had not been subsequently employed by either Oliver or Richard. On Richard's fall he had at once been recalled by the Rump to command the fleet in the Channel, obviously as a counter-weight to Mountagu then commanding the fleet that had been sent to the Sound. On Mountagu's return and dismissal he had been confirmed as sole Commander in Chief and had demonstrated his loyalty to his Republican employers by bringing the fleet into the Thames and threatening a complete blockade of London when the Army leaders turned the Rump out. On the face of it he had acted in naval terms exactly as Monck had in bringing his troops to the defence of the government against a military coup. But everyone knew that Lawson was a strong partisan of left-wing opinions in politics and religion and no one knew whether Monck had any opinions at all.

In a way perhaps Lawson had provided Mountagu with his card of re-entry. On February 21st, before the Secluded Members had returned to elect a new Council of State but after Monck had declared himself for a free Parliament, Edward's father-in-law invited Pepys to dinner and told him that '. . . upon Monkes desire, for the service that Lawson had lately done in putting down the Committee of Safety, he had the command of the Sea for the time being. He advised me to send for my Lord forthwith, and told me that there is no Question but, if he will, he may now be imployed again.' Monck had no reason to promote Mountagu's interest. They scarcely knew each other. But he wanted a safe pair of hands, not a known zealot, in charge of the navy. Edward was the obvious man, as his father-in-law at once saw.

By the time Mountagu had left Hinchingbrooke for London he had already been elected a member of the new Council of State from which Lawson had been dropped. When Pepys, hurrying back from his trip to Cambridge, at last met him on February 28th in the house of his brother-in-law Sir Harry Wright, Edward must have known that he was to be given the command, since Pepys was told so next day by another of his servants. The vote made it public on March 2nd. Was Lawson, who still held his Vice-Admiral's commission, going to accept the preferment of an officer whose politics were so clearly and so diametrically opposed to his own? On March 10th he signified his acceptance. So far, so good. But how much reliance could be placed on anyone's professions of loyalty? Consider the oaths that Monck had sworn within the last few weeks. Lawson was a popular officer, a bred seaman not a government nominee. He had shewn that he was ready to risk his position for his beliefs.

Mountagu, at any rate, was taking nothing for granted. On the day after his appointment he confided in Pepys his fears that Monck might be aiming at dictatorship. Clearly there was no time to be lost in getting aboard his flagship. But once he was there he would, in the fluid, uncertain state of affairs, need a secretary in whom he could confide, whose political antennae would be sensitive, and with whom, above all, he could relax. On March 6th he offered the post to his cousin, with consequences memorable in the history and the historiography of Restoration England. Pepys's record of the event shows why Edward was so much liked: '. . . he called me by myself to go along with him into the garden, where he asked me how things were with me . . . He likewise bade me look out now, at this turn, some good place; and he would use all his own and all the interest of his friends that he hath in England to do me good. And asked me whether I could without too much inconvenience go to sea as his Secretary, and bade me think of it. He also began to talk of things of state, and told me that he should now want one in that capacity at sea that he might trust in. And therefore he would have me to go.' The considerate courtesy of this glittering invitation from one in the front rank of public life to a young relation of some promise but no achievement would be notable in any age.

Pepys, as we know, accepted. On March 23rd he and his employer embarked in the *Swiftsure* at Greenhithe. As soon as Mountagu's flag was broken at the main, Lawson came on board 'and seemed very respectful to my Lord and so did the rest of the Commanders of the frigates that were thereabouts' whose guns had gone off bravely in salute. This was a great point gained for though Lawson had not concealed his strong Republican sympathies no one thought him devious. He might not like the way things were going but that was no reason why he should not, like so many others, accept what he saw he could not alter. In fact he was to prove a loyal and successful flag officer in the navy of the Restoration. He accepted a knighthood in September 1660. He was entrusted with an important independent command in the Mediterranean on two successive occasions in the early years of the reign and died of wounds received in the first battle of the war against the Dutch in June 1665.

But not all the senior officers of the Commonwealth Navy were as philosophic or as straightforward. Many of them, probably most of them, were not personally known to their General at Sea. There were constant reports of murmurings and possible refusals of duty. And the central authority of government was still, when Mountagu was appointed, in a state of flux. As we have seen he himself thought that Monck might attempt to take power. It was not until March 17th that Monck, in the strictest privacy, plumped irrevocably for the King, and not till the 23rd, the very day that Edward hoisted his flag aboard the *Swiftsure*, that Sir John Grenville arrived at Brussels with Monck's letter. After that politics, at least, became plain sailing. It was bonfires and beanfeasts all the way to the King's landing at Dover two months later. But the navy was an altogether different matter. It was, as it long remained, a world of its own, insulated from the ordinary life of the nation, less affected by prudential considerations than men whose occupation did not daily expose them to risks of life and limb, dominated to an extraordinary degree by the personality and quirks of captains whose narrow authority was all but absolute. Tact, caution and firmness were called for in the handling of this formidable and uncertain force.

The first essential was to find out as discreetly as possible which captains were likely to give trouble. What a groping in the dark this was can be felt from Mountagu's confiding in Pepys his doubts of his own flag captain, Roger Cuttance.[1] By that time they had shifted from the

1. *Diary* 11th April 1660.

Swiftsure into the *Naseby*, Mountagu's familiar flagship which had been in dockyard hands at the time of his appointment, and things were settling down. A complete list of all the Captains with their supposed political or religious inclinations had been drawn up,[1] evidently with the loyal if perhaps reluctant co-operation of Lawson, and the potential firebrands had either been relieved of their commands or else detached to escort convoys to the Straits. The first and most difficult steps in the re-modelling of the corps of sea officers had been successfully taken.[2]

Mountagu can justly claim credit for achieving this delicate transition but it would hardly have been so swift and painless without Lawson's support. Clearly the two men got on. 'Hither came the Vice-admirall to us and sat and talked and seemed a very good-natured man.' 'While I was at dinner with my Lord, the Coxon of the Vice-Admirall came for me to the Vice-Admirall to dinner; so I told my Lord and he gave me leave to go. I rise therefore from table and went, where there was very many commanders and very pleasant we were, on board the *London*, which hath a stateroom much bigger than the *Nazeby* – but not so rich.'[3] Naval officers and ratings have much to teach the rest of us in the difficult art of living together at close quarters. Mountagu certainly benefited from this admirable quality and equally certainly exemplified it.

On March 16th, a week before Mountagu had assumed his command, the Long Parliament had dissolved itself and issued writs for the sum-moning of a new one on April 25th. The last scene had been worthy of its passionate character. Mountagu's father-in-law had moved that the house should not dissolve without first expressing its abhorrence of Charles I's execution, a sentiment that was by that stage of events almost conventional. Up sprang the fierce old regicide and Republican Thomas Scott to declare his wholehearted adherence to the revolution then in-augurated and to claim that he could wish no higher honour than that the inscription on his tombstone should read 'Here lieth one who had a hand and a heart in the execution of Charles Stuart.'

Victrix causa deis placuit sed victa Catoni

---

1. Carte MSS 73 f. 402, 74 f. 490.
2. For an excellent account see Bernard Capp *Cromwell's Navy* (1989), 357–361.
3. *Diary* 11th and 24th April 1660.

So bold a defiance of an encroaching tide dignifies human nature.

The Parliament that met on April 25th, known as the Convention Parliament because it lacked the usual constitutional antecedent of a royal summons, would have had no place for Scott. It had, however, ample accommodation for Edward Mountagu, who had been returned in his absence at sea for Weymouth and had even been invited to sit for Cambridge. His fellow Cromwellian Broghill was returned for Arundel, but like Edward was absent from Westminster on other duties concerned with the promotion of the royal cause. In December he had joined with Sir Charles Coote to secure Ireland from Republican control and in March he and his officers had declared for a free Parliament before the Rump had dissolved itself. Indeed a letter from his confrère Coote inviting the King to land in Ireland had been received at Brussels a few days before Monck's message conveyed by Sir John Grenville. The last of the three Cromwellian Royalists, Lockhart, was not so situated, as the others were, as to act for himself. He had been continued in his combined posts of ambassador to France and Governor of Dunkirk and in these capacities had been offered enormous bribes by Mazarin and promises in the name of Charles II to betray Dunkirk to France or to the exiled King of England. His sympathies inclined him to the latter but, unlike George Downing at The Hague, he did not consider it honourable to accept one allegiance while representing another. He was relieved of his posts immediately after the Restoration and neither proceeded against nor employed by the administration of Clarendon.

Clarendon's favourite of all the Cromwellians, indeed of all those who had fought for the Parliament and now wanted to bring back the King, was always Edward Mountagu. He did not have any direct contact with Lockhart until he himself was once again at the very end of his life a banished man and Lockhart, by the turn of fortune's wheel, was once again England's ambassador in Paris. On that occasion, touched by the personal generosity of a man he had never met, he wrote to thank him:

'I doe therefore choose, though in a hand at best illegible and now shaking through much weakenesse, to assure you that I have a very just sense of your kindnesse to a man, soe totally forgotten in the world, and that I shall never forgett it.'[1] Broghill he came to know well: two of his

1. Lister *Life of Clarendon* iii, 484–5.

own children married the children of Broghill's elder brother the Earl of Burlington: but he seems never altogether to have liked or trusted him. Certainly at this point his reception was distinctly frosty.[1] Mountagu on the other hand was trusted absolutely, indeed was from the moment of Monck's declaration of allegiance to the King seen as a counterweight of true moderate Royalism against the possible machinations of a military adventurer.

Edward's first encounter with the King and his great minister was now close at hand. On May 2nd the Convention Parliament had thrown itself at the King's feet and begged him to return with all convenient speed. On May 3rd Pepys read the Declaration of Breda and the King's letter to the fleet before all the commanding officers assembled in a council of war aboard the *Naseby* and drew up a loyal vote in reply which was passed without apparent dissent 'though I am confident many in their hearts were against it'. However after a convivial dinner to which they were all entertained by the Rear-Admiral Sir Richard Stayner, with whom Mountagu had served on Blake's last voyage, Pepys went round the whole fleet and found the enthusiasm of the ships' companies unmistakable. The vigour and economy with which he described the scene to a colleague in London is not to be surpassed.

> He that can fancy a fleet (like ours) in her pride, with pendants loose, guns roaring, caps flying, and the loud *Vive le Roy*'s echoed from one ships company to another he and he only can apprehend the joy this enclosed vote was received with, or the blessing he thought himself possessed of that bore it.

There was, it seemed, little more to do but spread the canvas before a favourable wind and sail across to Holland where the King was waiting. In practice it was not quite so simple. Victualling, storing and fitting out a fleet for a mission that would attract the eyes of all Europe could not be done in the usual scrambling, hand-to-mouth fashion. Besides the fleet itself still wore the emblems and the heraldry of the Protectorate. The figure on the *Naseby*'s prow showed Oliver trampling underfoot the enemies of his régime, which included by implication if not direct portrayal the monarch she was now to bear home. This, and the replacing

---

1. e.g. Hyde to Rumbold, 26th March 1660, *Clar S.P.* iii 707.

of the State's arms by those of the King, would have to be attended to.[1] And a world of silk for the pendants and scarlet taffeta for the waist-cloths to dress the ships overall would somehow have to be obtained. Neither the material nor the money to pay for it was easily found. A weather eye had still to be kept on the apparently docile corps of sea officers and a sharp ear cocked for the premonitory rumblings of any desperate explosion of the Good Old Cause. On April 23rd Sir Anthony Ashley Cooper wrote to inform him that Lambert, who had escaped from the Tower and tried to raise the country against a restoration of the monarchy, had been taken in Daventry fields together with Colonels Okey, Axtell, Creed, Sir Arthur Haslerig's son and others. 'God has blasted the wicked in their reputations and bloody designes' he remarked sententiously.[2] Finally the Commander in Chief had to provide ships for an endless succession of royalist agents, confidential messengers and anxious bigwigs streaming across to secure the favour of their future master. That Mountagu had the temperament for great place is shewn by Pepys's record of his ability to relax, to unburden his mind in conversation or in making music with his young cousin. Above all he had the ability to delegate.

In the press of affairs he did not forget his family. On May 10th his eldest son, Ned, came aboard. At twelve years old he would enjoy the excitement and colour of a historical occasion that was to exhaust the vocabulary of panegyric and Pepys could look after him when his father was too busy. On the same day he received a short message from Monck urging him to bring the King over as soon as wind and tide would serve. Edward at once sent Monck's emissary over to Charles warning him to be ready and set sail out of the Downs the following day. Since he had been earlier charged to carry over the Commissioners from Parliament he paused impatiently off Dover, sending his Rear-Admiral ashore to find out whether they had arrived. Since they had not, he sailed without them, an act which Clarendon asserts was never forgiven him by his intended passengers.[3]

The fleet dropped anchor off The Hague on the 14th and sailed back

1. Oddly Oliver's effigy continued to adorn the ship for another three years. It was finally taken down and burnt in December 1663 by which time Pepys thought the replacing it a waste of money: 'God knows it is even the flinging away of 100*l.* out of the King's purse.'
2. Mapperton MSS Letters to Ministers i, f. 23.
3. *History* XVI, 237.

to England with the King and the two Royal Dukes on the 23rd. During these days of ceaseless entertaining, of landing people and taking them off, the General never set foot on shore, although once he prepared to do so, in a suit of clothes as splendid as gold and silver could make them, in order to wait upon the King. Charles sent a civil message saying that he would himself come to meet him on the shore but he was detained. The two men therefore did not meet until the morning of the day of embarkation when the King 'did with a great deal of affection kiss my Lord' before coming aboard for a grand dinner at which all the royal party were present. Later in the afternoon the Queen of Bohemia, the Princess Royal and her son the Prince of Orange, the future William III, went ashore, the Duke of York went aboard Lawson's flagship and the Duke of Gloucester Stayner's 'and with a fresh gale and most happy weather we set sail for England'.

Among Mountagu's guests had been the famous Dutch admiral Obdam whom he was to meet in battle five years later and the Duke of York under whom he was to serve on that occasion. This first meeting called for all Edward's tact since the Duke had from boyhood enjoyed the title of Lord High Admiral and had every intention of asserting the powers of that office. He must too have met for the first time the Chancellor whose trust in him had first turned the King's eyes towards him and whose steadfast support was to sustain him when his own conduct came under fire. Pepys gives a charming account of taking young Ned to see the great man, bedridden with gout, at The Hague but there is no record of any conversation between Clarendon and Sandwich, as we must learn to call them, on the voyage. Probably Clarendon did not wish to see anyone he did not have to. He was certainly exhausted, probably still suffering from gout and was always sick as a dog the moment he found himself aboard ship. And Sandwich himself had his hands full attending to the comfort of his royal guests, the movements of the fleet and the directions and inquiries of his new Lord High Admiral. Once the King was safely ashore, clasping the Bible presented to him by the burgesses of Dover and embracing General Monck, there was time for relief:

> My Lord almost transported with joy that he hath done all this
> without any the least blur and obstruccion in the world that would

give an offence to any, and with the great Honour that he thought it would be to him.

He had reason. Pepys had noted, as did one of the Petty Officers aboard, Edward Barlow, that when the long-awaited moment came for the King to re-enter his kingdom, he had refused the splendid craft specially adorned for the occasion, preferring to go ashore in Mountagu's own barge. Barlow's description shows that the personal compliment was at once recognized and sets it in the context of national rejoicing:

'The Parliament had fitted a "brigitine" [brigantine], rowing like a galley with twelve oars, with galley sails and three small guns of brass over the prow, galley fashion, and gilt most bravely with silk colours ... yet His Majesty would not go ashore in her, for he went ashore in the General's barge, the same boat he came aboard in. And all the earls and lords accompanied him ashore in other boats, whilst all the ships rang him a peal with their ordnance, which made the very hills and Dover cliffs to sound the echo with like harmony, as though they were all glad to bear him up and have the happiness to welcome home the true sovereign, King Charles II, for whom the land had so long grieved.'[1]

1. *Barlow's Journal* ed. Lubbock (1934) i, 44–5.

IX

Rewards and Opportunities

THE PLEASING SENSATIONS of a child waking up on Christmas morning and feeling the weight of a well-filled stocking lying on the bedclothes rarely recur in adult life. Yet Edward Mountagu must have enjoyed them in this year of Restoration. Twenty-four hours after the royal party had landed Clarendon wrote from Canterbury in his own hand to tell him that the King had conferred on him both a barony and an earldom. The day after that the King made him a Knight of the Garter. Pepys gives a rapturous account of the ceremony held in the great cabin of the *Naseby* (now re-named the *Charles*) in the presence of all the commanders, the King's letter lying on a crimson cushion presented, with three genuflections, by Sir Edward Walker, Garter King of Arms. Clarendon wrote again next day, another friendly personal letter, asking him to arrange convoy for his mother-in-law and his children, his books and papers and 'the little goods' left behind in Zealand.[1] Everything was being done to make him feel as much at home in the intimate circle of the new government as he had been in that of the Protectorate.

In the character of Sandwich which Clarendon drew ten years later in his autobiography he emphasizes his lack of pushfulness: 'nor did he ever contribute to any advancement to which he arrived, by the least intimation or insinuation that he wished it, or that it would be acceptable to him'. This restraint must have been especially congenial to Charles II who, one of his ministers observed, had a lively aversion to 'an asking

1. Carte MS 73 f. 462.

face'. His rewards were not the less substantial. To support the honour of his earldom he was granted lands worth £4000 a year: he was made a Privy Counsellor and a Commissioner of the Treasury and, richest of all prizes had he bestirred himself to exploit it, Master of the Great Wardrobe. Few departments of the Royal Household can have offered greater opportunities for the generally recognized douceurs on expenditure or the perquisites from the disposal of alleged superfluities. Imagination boggles at what Pepys would have extracted from such a goldmine. But Sandwich, though an acute and informed student of economic affairs when in government, was lazy and careless about money. Not that he was indifferent to its charms or blind to its necessity. In the same kindly character that Clarendon gives of his friend he concedes that '. . . avarice . . . was the sole blemish (though it never appeared in any gross instance) that seemed to cloud many noble virtues in that earl'. Other less conspicuously lucrative but still useful offices continued to accrue to him during the next year, Master of the King's Swans, Bailiff of Whittlesea Mere. As he remarked to Pepys on October 3rd he could ask anything he wished. It was his wisdom not to press this advantage.

Where he did ask it was generally for his friends and relations. Protection and advancement were expected of a grandee who would be thought to diminish himself as well as his followers if he did nothing for them. While they were still at Dover he assured Pepys of his future. 'We must have a little patience and we will rise together. In the meantime I will do you all the good Jobbs I can.'[1] What would not brook delay was protecting people from the vindictiveness of embittered Royalists. Edward's brother-in-law, Sir Gilbert Pickering, had been a member of all the Councils of State during the Interregnum, even serving on the Committee of Safety in the autumn of 1659, and had steadily opposed the Restoration. Without a doubt it was the new Earl of Sandwich who prevailed on his colleagues in the House of Lords to pardon him.

He may well have had a hand in a far more important, and far more difficult, act of public mercy. Why, if a mere buffoon such as Hugh Peters should suffer the hideous penalties of high treason for having exulted over the captive Charles I (for whose execution he was in no way responsible), should Milton escape? Milton, who had justified the

1. *Diary* 2nd June 1660.

killing of the King in the most powerful, most famous, piece of propaganda produced by the English Republic *The Tenure of Kings and Magistrates*, had reiterated his arguments in subsequent works, had poured scorn on the sacred text of the cult of the Royal Martyr the *Eikon Basilike* (The Image of the King) in a work resoundingly entitled *Eikonoklastes* (The Image Breaker), and had compounded his offences a bare two months earlier in a pamphlet invoking scriptural authority for keeping Charles II in permanent exile. Surely vengeful Royalism must have licked its chops as it contemplated the fate in store for him.

Yet in spite of the fact that the Commons moved on June 16th for his arrest and for the public burning by the common hangman of his *Defensio Prima* and his *Eikonoklastes* Milton got off with only a short period in custody. No one mentioned *The Tenure of Kings and Magistrates* or the virulence of his recent pamphlet. With so many merciless men in full cry there must, as David Masson brilliantly demonstrated in one of the most readable of giant Victorian biographies, have been very powerful forces working in the opposite direction and the Lord Chancellor must have given them tacit support. Clarendon, who was Milton's almost exact contemporary, of course knew all about him and had good reason to dislike what he knew. Pressure, not personal preference, must supply the explanation. But whose? Traditionally Milton had obtained mercy for Sir William Davenant under the Commonwealth and the Royalist poet was now reciprocating his deliverance. But Davenant was not a figure of sufficient weight to have had more than marginal influence on so sensitive a political issue. The same was true of a better poet and a closer friend, the back bencher Andrew Marvell. Two of Monck's political protégés to whom both the King and Clarendon would have wished to seem gracious, Sir William Morrice and Sir Thomas Clarges, are said to have been active on Milton's behalf and so, certainly, was Arthur Annesley, an important leader of the Presbyterian party whose adherence to the King was rewarded by an earldom in the Coronation honours. But none of these men were at all intimate with Clarendon. Two people who were, and to whose solicitations he might well have listened, were Lady Ranelagh, Broghill's sister, and Edward Mountagu. Lady Ranelagh, whose husband and son both turned out badly, had received sympathetic advice from Clarendon about the difficulties of her position. His connexions with the Boyle family were close. Apart from his friendship, later cemented by intermarriage of the two families, with her brother the Earl of Burlington he is also said to have urged her favourite brother, Robert, the great scientist (for whom she later kept house) to take holy order with a view to enriching the intellectual resources of the bench of bishops. And Lady Ranelagh was a great favourite with Milton, who had at one point tutored her son. Edward's connexion with Milton was nothing like hers. But the high compliment paid him (by a writer whose good opinion was not easily earned) in the *Defensio Secunda* is evidence that it was not negligible. And Edward's good nature and gentleness of temper would prompt him to intercede for a friend.

Where he was powerless was to protect the memories of the great men who had given him his opportunity, had taught him by example the arts of war and of high command, had fitted him for the business of government and diplomacy, and had trusted him with great responsibilities. Cromwell and Blake commanded his fullest admiration and loyalty, and there is no evidence that he ever by deed or word went back on his opinion or his attachment. On the contrary what Pepys reports of his private talk shows no diminution of their strength. Best of all evidence is the final assessment of the two men in Clarendon's *History of the Rebellion.* Clarendon scarcely knew Cromwell though he must have come across him in the two parliaments of 1640: Blake he had never met. Yet both portraits breathe a grandeur that is notably absent from that of a figure of comparable importance such as Hampden whom Clarendon himself knew. Clarendon's obvious source – the only man he knew well who had known both these men well – was Sandwich. Both Monck and Broghill could have supplied personal recollections of the greatest interest – Monck like Edward had served with both men – but neither was sympathetic to Clarendon.

Yet though Sandwich may be credited with having helped justice to be done to these heroes of the English Republic in the pantheon of English Royalism, he was never to see, he almost certainly never knew, what service he had rendered to their memory. That part of Clarendon's *History* was written during his final exile in France, when it would have been out of the question for the two men to be in touch, and the work itself was not published until thirty years after Sandwich's death. By good fortune he was spared the shame of witnessing the insults and indignities inflicted on the remains of the two great captains when they were disinterred from Westminster Abbey since his duties as Admiral of the Narrow Seas[1] required him to convey members of the Royal Family to and from the continent. Henrietta Maria and her daughter Henriette, Charles II's much loved sister, had elected to return to France at this particular moment.

But this is to anticipate events. Sandwich was back in London on June 9th. On the 19th he received the thanks of the House of Commons for his services to the country in bringing back its King. On the 21st he was sworn a Privy Counsellor. On the 26th he chose Portsmouth for the suitably maritime seat of his earldom (Huntingdon, the obvious territorial choice, already belonged to the Hastings family), altering it a fortnight later to Sandwich, as one of the Cinque Ports, the cradle of the Royal Navy. On the 27th he was dined by the officers of his regiment.

It was clear that the new régime, with the touchy and jealous exception of the Duke of York, was anxious to give Sandwich the fullest scope it could afford to maintain and develop the navy that, in less than ten years, had raised England to the front rank of European powers. Monck was needed to control the army, above all to supervise its demobilization. Penn, the only other surviving General at Sea and with much longer and more diverse experience of the sea service than either, was from the first firmly relegated to a subordinate position. He remained, none the less, a potential threat to Sandwich's position, particularly should the Duke of York wish to override it. Penn could supply the necessary background of specifically naval expertise. It was, perhaps, the uneasy consciousness of this that made Pepys so unrelenting and so extravagant in his hostility towards him. For the Duke, justly proud of his own military record and of the golden opinions he had earned from Turenne, was determined not to be a fainéant Lord High Admiral but the fighting leader of a fighting service.

Perhaps this unconcealed ambition counted in Sandwich's favour with the King and with Clarendon. Both had only too recent and too vivid recollections of how headstrong and injudicious James could be. Tact and temper, sympathy and judgment were essential to the handling of a service whose experienced officer corps was overwhelmingly Crom-

1. A post conferred on him two months after the Restoration. It is interesting that the King's letter giving him the Garter describes him as 'one of our Generalls at Sea'.

wellian. The handful of Cavaliers who had served under Rupert from 1648 to 1653 might add a seasoning of Royalism but they could not of themselves form a line of battle or, till they had had some experience of fighting in one, be entrusted with a flag command.

Sandwich saw his opportunity. Even before he had received his official commission as Lieutenant-Admiral to the Duke of York and Vice-Admiral of the Narrow Seas for which the warrant was issued on July 28th he must have discussed the composition of the Navy Board with Clarendon and the King since he insisted, against the open opposition of Monck, on having his own nominee, Samuel Pepys, appointed Clerk of the Acts, in effect its Secretary. Although the Board was in name an old pre-Civil War institution dating from Henry VIII in fact it was an administrative innovation, higher powered and more highly paid than any before it. Like the various Committees of the Admiralty and the Navy or of the Admiralty and the Cinque Ports which had run the war at sea for the Parliament and had subsequently controlled the large permanent navy of the Commonwealth and Protectorate, it was not simply an office that looked after the King's ships, supplying them with masts, spars, sails, cordage and the rest of it and providing facilities for docking and construction. It did all this of course. But far more importantly it kept an eye on the sea officers – whose selection and appointment belonged to the Lord High Admiral – and was from the start ready to extend its activities into fields which were still the province of separate administrative authorities such as those which dealt with Ordnance or Victualling.

The seasoned timber of the old Parliamentary navy that, next to Cromwell's Ironsides, had done most to defeat the King was represented by Sir William Batten and Sir William Penn. The Royalists, veterans of the Civil War or even the pre-Civil War navy of Charles I, were the able Sir Robert Slingsby who died before making his mark, his lightweight successor Sir John Mennes, and the formidable Sir George Carteret who as Treasurer was the most highly paid and most influential member of the Board. The strength of Carteret's position was more broadly based than that of any of his colleagues. Like Batten, he had served both as a sea officer and as a junior member of the Board in the time of Charles I. Unlike Batten he had an impeccable, indeed a distinguished, record as a Royalist sea officer during the Civil War, recapturing his native

Jersey for the King and holding it as a base for Royalist privateers for several years after Charles I had surrendered. It was during this period that he had given sanctuary to Clarendon and the young Prince of Wales who was now established on his father's throne. Carteret's hospitality and the warmth of his courage in that dark hour had won him the rare reward, which Edward was now to share, a place in the affections and loyalties of both the King and his great minister. They had many of the same qualities: a great capacity for hard work and a determination to master their job; easy, unassuming, attractive manners; steadiness of character without priggishness; a fondness for conviviality without the sottishness so common in that age; a happy and affectionate family life shared by a wife whom everyone admired and liked. It is not surprising that the two couples took to each other and that a marriage was arranged between their children as soon as they were old enough – indeed from Pepys's account rather before that point was reached.

Our perceptions of the Navy Board of the Restoration are of course mediated through the sharp eye and sharper mind of Samuel Pepys. However much one allows for his prejudices, his self-importance, his partisanship, '*tamen usque recurret*' – it will keep coming back, that vitality, that directness. And although Pepys came to the Navy Board, and knew that he came, as the client and follower of Sandwich, his independence of mind, his insatiable curiosity, were bound to lead him to conclusions and opinions of his own. His passion for orderliness, so constantly provoked by his wife's untidiness, for lucidity, so often thwarted by the devious transactions of Sir William Batten or the muddling incompetence of Sir John Mennes, drove him into a close alliance with the one member of the Board whose brilliance and articulacy surpassed his own, Sir William Coventry. Coventry was anything but a natural ally of Sandwich. He had been put on the Board because he was the Secretary of the Lord High Admiral. He was a friend and admirer of Sir William Penn and he was a bitter and long-standing enemy of Clarendon. As time went by he became more and more the model on which Pepys, in his serious moments, wished to form himself: that of the upright, capable public servant bent on replacing nepotism, muddle and corruption by efficiency, accountability and the career open to the talents. This had the effect of distancing him from his original patron, not because Sandwich stood for

93

the bad old ways but because Coventry, in the world of politics and the court, was the champion and ultimately the martyr of the good.

Sandwich, anyhow, unlike Pepys and Coventry, was not primarily interested in naval administration. He was a sea officer, interested above all in the practicalities of sea power, that is to say in the purposes to which it could and should be applied and in the means by which it could be made most effective. His membership of the Privy Council Committee for the Navy must have given him considerable influence behind the scenes. Until Rupert was added to it late in 1663, Sandwich and Monck were the only two members with naval experience. And Monck, though a formidable fighting leader, had not, as Sandwich had, an analytical turn of mind.

To take first Sandwich's ideas as to the nature and future development of English sea-power. These had been formed, as had his own naval career, under the direct inspiration of Cromwell and Blake. Both were blue water men, believing that the function of the navy was to protect and expand the ocean trades, not to bicker with the Dutch over the herring fishery in home waters. Both were keen to wrest from Spain the wealth of the Indies. Sandwich subscribed in particular to Cromwell's primary objective, the securing of a permanent base at the entry to the Mediterranean, preferably Gibraltar. This would mean that a strong squadron would always be in a position to hinder Spain and France from uniting their Mediterranean and Atlantic fleets, to harry and pillage the treasure convoys returning from Spanish America and, inside the Mediterranean, to teach the pirates of Tripoli and Algiers and their no less rapacious Christian rivals the Knights of St John at Malta and those of St Stephen at Pisa a much-needed lesson. As we have seen Edward had already surveyed and made drawings of Gibraltar on his first Mediterranean cruise. His journal shows that he revisited it at the first opportunity after the Restoration.

But by that time the treaty of marriage between Charles II and Catherine of Braganza had presented England with Tangier, a well-fortified position on the African Atlantic coast just outside the Straits. The harbour, or rather the roadstead, was not one in which ships would ride in all weathers, but it was generally agreed that the construction of a mole could remedy this deficiency. Here, with the gift of Bombay thrown in, was all that the blue water school could desire. Sandwich at once and enthusiastically identified himself with the proposal. The alliance with Portugal offered two inestimable advantages in the wider field of imperial policy: an open backdoor into the closely guarded Spanish empire of which Portugal was, in Spanish eyes, herself no more than a rebellious province; and secondly a means of preventing the Dutch from picking off the ripe fruit of Portugal's colonies in Africa, the Far East and South America which Portugal lacked the strength to defend. Besides Sandwich would not have forgotten Blake's insistence on the supreme value of access to the great naval base of Lisbon which Tangier, even with its projected mole, or the rock of Gibraltar, an unsupplied anchorage on a potentially hostile coast, could never hope to rival. His cousin the Earl of Manchester was a strong partisan of the policy, as indeed was Monck, who had approved the signing of a treaty with Portugal only a month before the King's return. This was naturally superseded by the change of régime and the initiation of fresh negotiations.

Portugal's revolt against Spain in 1640 could never have been sustained without the diversion of Spanish military effort into the long, exhausting war with France. The Peace of the Pyrenees in 1659 obliged the French to abandon their support for Portugal so that an English alliance with Lisbon might seem to risk antagonizing both the major powers. But for France the peace was a mere tactical move in a struggle she was confident of winning and ready at her chosen moment to resume. One of her best generals, Schomberg, was in effect seconded to Portugal to direct the war against Spain, and an important part of the forces he was to command was to consist of ex-Cromwellian troops paid by the Portuguese. To avoid an open violation of the peace treaty Schomberg was sent by way of England where he had long and friendly conversations with Charles II during the course of which he urged the advantages of the Portuguese alliance. Schomberg's mother was Anne Dudley, daughter of Earl Dudley and a relation of the Mountagus, as Edward noted in his journal when the two men saw a good deal of each other in Lisbon some eight years later. Strangely it does not appear that they met on this occasion, perhaps because Sandwich was absent for most of the month of September fetching the Princess Mary from Holland and had been down at Hinchingbrooke for the second half of August. Schomberg sailed for Portugal early in October so that the two men must both have been in London simultaneously for at least a few days. Both their relationship and their strong common interest in the business of Portugal would have provided good reason for a meeting. On one issue however their views were diametrically opposed: Schomberg urged Charles II on no account to relinquish the possession of Dunkirk. With England's naval superiority to both France and Spain it would be a permanent and instantly effective check to hostile action on the part of either power. Sandwich on the other hand was on his own confession the leader of those who held that its vast expense was out of all proportion to its usefulness and the sooner it was sold the better. Perhaps the difference of view was essentially that between a soldier and a sailor. Schomberg was dazzled by the potentialities of an unassailable base at the exact point where French and Spanish possessions were most vulnerable. Sandwich had found by experience that the Dunkirk roadstead offered no good holding ground for ships anchored there and that the approach to the harbour was fouled by constantly shifting sandbanks.

Dunkirk was an issue on which the government's naval experts were unanimous. Both Monck and the Duke of York agreed that it should be got rid of. But the Duke of York's other ideas as to how England's sea power could best be employed did not coincide with Sandwich's. The protection and expansion of overseas trade had little interest for him. It was not the ultimate purposes but the immediate excitement of warfare that attracted his attention. To lead the nation in battle was still seen as the true function of monarchy by contemporaries such as Charles X of Sweden, Louis XIV of France and his own future son-in-law and sup-planter, William III. Should there be no promising war in the offing the navy could be used for adventure. On 3rd October 1660 Pepys noted

> This day I heard the Duke speak of a great design that he and my Lord of Pembroke have, and a great many others, of sending a venture to some parts of affrica to dig for gold-ore there. They entend to admit as many as will venture their money, and so make themselfs a company. 250L. is the lowest share for every man. But I do not find that my Lord doth much like it.

This was the germination of the Royal African Company, incorporated two months later, and at once drawing the Royal Navy into its affairs. A squadron under Robert Holmes sent out down the West African coast early in 1661, followed up by a second expedition under the same warlike commander three years later laid a powder train to the explosion of the Second Dutch War. Sandwich, it will be observed, was unenthusiastic though he later thought it tactful to become a shareholder.

On the same tide that Holmes sailed for the warmer southern latitudes Sandwich took the fleet across to France, landing the Queen Mother and the King's sister Henriette at Le Havre at the end of January. The voyage was uneventful except for an incident that once again showed Sandwich's self-control to advantage. While ashore at Le Havre he and the Duke of Buckingham and the Queen Mother's favourite the Earl of St Albans sat down to a game of cards. Buckingham lost money to Sandwich but instead of paying up pocketed his stake, making insulting reflections on his honour. 'Which my Lord resenting, said nothing then; but that he doubted not but there was ways enough to get his money from him. So they parted that night, and my Lord sent for Sir R. Stayner and sent him the next morning to the Duke to know whether he did remember what he said last night and whether he would owne them with his sword and a second; which he said he would, and so both sides agreed. But my Lord St Albans and the Queene and Abbot Mountagu [Sandwich's cousin, brother to the Earl of Manchester, who had been converted to Roman Catholicism while in France in Charles I's time] did waylay them at their lodgings till the difference was made up, much to my Lord's honour, who hath got great reputation thereby.' Pepys had the story from two of his colleagues in Sandwich's entourage but the affair got into the newspapers and did indeed raise Sandwich's standing.

He took, as Pepys noted with a touch of apprehension, easily to court life. The king distinguished him by unusual marks of affection: 'with what kindness the King did hugg my Lord at his parting'.[1] He enjoyed spending money, declared that he would have a Master of Horse and that his wife and daughters should wear patches. Unlike most contemporary men of fashion he does not appear to have exceeded in drink but he certainly shared the passion for building and for laying out pleasure grounds that was one of the most attractive features of the age. On March 4th, a month after his return from France, he went down to Hinchingbrooke taking his building contractor with him. The remodelling of the house was extensive: two storeys were added to one

1. 3rd September 1660.

wing, a new kitchen was built; and various other changes made which cannot be exactly identified since no architect's drawings survive and the house was altered again after Edward's time. That he himself had a hand in the designs is highly probable as he certainly did in the ornament and laying out of the garden and grounds. The journals he kept while ambassador in Madrid are full of scale drawings of fountains, statuary, walls, gates, railings and suchlike, even down to the details of door knockers and latches. The eagerness and pride with which he showed Pepys his improvements in September 1663 are those of an artist as much as a proprietor. Pepys on this and other occasions admired the taste of his patron but deplored the imprudence of the expense.

The visit to Hinchingbrooke was the briefest of retreats into private life. Sandwich was one of the few entrusted with the secret of the King's decision to marry the Infanta of Portugal which even Pepys did not hear of until a few weeks before the King announced it to Parliament early in May. Sandwich was assigned a role part naval, part military, part diplomatic. He was to take the fleet to Lisbon to secure the very considerable cash payment which was part of the deal, go on to secure the occupation of Tangier which was another part which might well be frustrated by the direct action of either the Dutch or the Spaniards, and finally to return to Lisbon in order to bring the new Queen of England home with him. In the interstices of this complicated mission he was to show the flag and impose, if he could, new treaties on the Barbary corsair bases of Algiers, Tripoli, Tetuan and Sallee.

The drafting of instructions and the preparations for mounting so extended and diverse an operation, the disposition of personal affairs and responsibilities consequent on so long an absence, took up time. Since he was required to set out early in June there was none to spare. Yet much of April was taken up with ceremonial occasions. On the 15th he was installed as a Knight of the Garter and a week later on St George's Day he was prominent among the lay officiants at the Coronation. In the Abbey he carried the staff of St Edward, a strange echo of carrying the Sword of State before Oliver, handed the golden pall to his cousin the Lord Chamberlain and was one of the four Knights of the Garter who held the canopy over the King during the anointing.

Sandwich took barge at the garden stairs of Whitehall on June 13th, immediately after taking leave of the King. He had been charged with

Fashion drawing: 'The habite taken up by ye king and Court of England
November 1666 which they call a vest'

the most important military and diplomatic mission of the new reign but he never wanted self-confidence and his previous experience, both with Blake and on his own at the Sound, no doubt fortified him. 'My Lord and we very merry' noted Pepys as they dined on their way down river. The treacherous channels of the post-Oliverian period were far astern and he was heading for the open sea.

X

A Mediterranean Man

THE MEDITERRANEAN in the middle of the seventeenth century was
still a sea of high risk. The Eastern basin was entirely controlled by the
Ottoman Empire which had by no means abandoned its aggressive
designs. Since 1645 it had been attempting to wrest the island of Crete
from the Venetians, who by 1661 were closely confined to their strongly
fortified base at Candia. Obviously Venice was not strong enough to beat
off the immense forces at the disposal of the Sultan, particularly as he
could also call on the North African ports in the Western basin such as
Tripoli and Algiers over which he claimed suzerainty. These cities had
for centuries lived by piracy so that sea-fighting was their speciality.
Should Crete fall, as it certainly would unless other maritime powers
came to its support, Malta, Sicily, southern Italy might expect the attentions of the Ottomans. Only twenty years later they were to come close
to capturing Vienna. The great victory at Lepanto in 1570 had been an
evanescent triumph. The Mediterranean might easily become, if not a
Turkish lake, a sea in which the nations of Western Europe would find
their trade exposed to such violence and extortion as to make it no longer
worth their while.

France and Spain as Mediterranean powers themselves might well
wish to assist Venice as the English and the Dutch, the main trading
nations, also would. But no one would care directly to antagonize the
Ottoman Empire and thus put at risk their trading posts at Smyrna
and Constantinople: and all the powers had long-standing rivalries and
resentments between themselves, the French against the Spanish, the
English against the Dutch, that might at any time flare into war. Direct,

co-ordinated action in support of Venice was therefore all but impossible. But what was perfectly practicable and easily justified was retaliatory action against the piratical bases in the Western basin which constituted the most serious immediate threat to the beleaguered Venetian forces. And there was no reason why such action should not be unofficially co-ordinated by the naval forces that would undertake it.

In fact there is no evidence of such collusion though as R.C. Anderson has pointed out the French had actually sent troops to reinforce the Venetian garrison in 1660 and were preparing to attack the Barbary ports in 1661, as were the Dutch 'so that it seemed likely that no less than three different countries would shortly be sending fleets through the Straits of Gibraltar on the same errand'.[1] The French squadron did not get to sea till the following year but a powerful Dutch fleet under de Ruyter had already left port by the time Sandwich sailed in the *Royal James*. Whereas the English made straight for the Mediterranean the Dutch had first to meet and convoy their inward bound East Indiamen coming northabout round Scotland. On June 27th Sandwich detached a ship to go into Lisbon with a letter from Charles II to prepare for the later stages of his mission and on July 4th he anchored off Malaga. It was about this time that de Ruyter set off from the Texel in his wake.

Sandwich lost no time in sailing for Algiers but he was suddenly struck down by a high fever. Off Alicante the fleet hove to and the Admiral was sent ashore. After a week he was sufficiently recovered to return aboard and four days later, on July 23rd, to resume his voyage. The first news of his illness reached Pepys on August 12th whose immediate reaction was concern for Lady Sandwich and the children 'if he should miscarry, God knows in what a condition would his family be'. Next day his own career comes uppermost: 'my mind is yet very much troubled about my Lord of Sandwich's health, which I am afeared of'. On the day after, a letter dated July 15th tells him that Sandwich is recovering 'which doth give me mighty great comfort'. On the following afternoon he paid a visit to 'my Lady', now in advanced pregnancy, 'and there told her of my Lord's sicknesse (of which, though it hath been the towne talk this fortnight, she had heard nothing) and recovery, of which she was glad – though hardly persuaded of the latter'.

1. *Journal*, xxxii.

By this time Sandwich had been and gone from Algiers. Arriving on July 29th he called the commanders on board for a Council of War and sent off his demands which were as promptly and as categorically refused. The death of Cromwell, said the Algerines, had abrogated Blake's treaty and they were not going to sign another. Sandwich had already prepared his plan of attack, of which there is a sketch in his journal reproduced in R.C. Anderson's edition, and the Algerines moved the boom into position at the mouth of the harbour to stop him. The weather favoured the defence. An adverse wind was followed by thick fog: thick fog by great seas that prevented the intended manoeuvres and the sending in of fire-ships. In the exchanges of artillery fire the land forts, as usual, got the best of it. The fleet stood off to wait for better weather. After a week a second Council of War decided to call it a day. Sandwich took five ships with him to Lisbon leaving Lawson with ten ships of the line to ply off Algiers and make as much of a nuisance of himself as he could.

On the way Sandwich was forced by contrary winds to shelter in a bay near Malaga where he found de Ruyter and part of his fleet. De Ruyter gave him news of English reinforcements met at sea which would certainly have already arrived in Lisbon. At the Barbary port of Tetuan just within the Straits Sandwich obtained satisfactory assurances from the Governor. It was a much less important place than Algiers and so weak that there had been thoughts of seizing it in Cromwell's time, a strategic initiative now rendered superfluous by the prospective acquisition of Tangier.

Sandwich dropped anchor in the Tagus on September 6th. He spent most of the next four weeks ashore where he was soon joined by the regular ambassador fresh out from England, Sir Richard Fanshawe. Fanshawe was a placid, cultivated, Royalist gentleman of the old school whose talent for languages (he had a distinguished reputation as a translator of literary texts) was perhaps his chief qualification as a diplomat. The memoirs written by his wife Anne reveal a passionate and protective devotion to her mild and ineffective husband, whom she had married in the parish church at Wolvercote when the Court was at Oxford during the Civil War. Clarendon had been one of the two witnesses at this romantic wedding and had befriended them as they trailed round Europe, loyal but penniless followers of the Court in exile, each stage marked by the grave of a much loved child. Such griefs would have unhinged a steadier temper than hers. She was by now a bitter partisan of a husband whom she saw as wronged, particularly bitter against Clarendon because Fanshawe had not been made Secretary of State. The wildness of her resentment is sufficiently evidenced by her accusation that Clarendon had appointed Sir William Morrice Secretary of State as a creature of his own whereas Morrice, a dim figure whom Clarendon had never met, was the nominee of Monck who had consulted him as an old family friend on the delicate negotiation that preceded the Restoration. No doubt she looked on Sandwich's position as ambassador extraordinary with the deepest suspicion but there is no evidence of any outburst on her part at this stage.

Besides the harmless ambassador and his jealous wife Sandwich would have had the assistance of one of the most remarkable representatives ever sent to Portugal. Consul Maynard, originally appointed by Thurloe in the middle 1650s, was still in office, despite some acrimonious passages with English merchants in Lisbon, in the last decade of the century. Maynard was not an easy man but he was extremely well-informed and astute.[1] And Sandwich needed all the help he could get if he were to achieve a smooth transfer of sovereignty at Tangier and the payment, either in cash or in marketable colonial produce such as sugar, of the huge dowry promised by a Crown that was already hopelessly embarrassed for money.

Soon after his arrival in Lisbon news reached him of a substantial success gained by Lawson against the Algerines. Two merchant ships and two men of war had been captured and another driven on shore. Considering that part of his mission sufficiently discharged Sandwich sent orders to Lawson to join him in Tangier Bay. With a Dutch fleet as powerful as his own in the offing it would not be prudent to divide his forces at the delicate moment – (if it were to be a moment: Maynard had doubtless had something to say about Portuguese dilatoriness) – of transfer.

A few days before sailing for Tangier on October 3rd Sandwich attended a bull-fight. Although the whole city was *en fête* for the King's wedding Sandwich makes no mention of these junketings among the

1. On Maynard see Professor C.R. Boxer's too brief sketch in his introduction to *Descriptive List of the State Papers Portugal 1661–1780 in the Public Record Office London* (Lisbon 1979).

staccato entries of ship movements and letters sent or received. It is the more noticeable that he spreads himself on a minutely accurate description, revealing more of the talent of a fashion correspondent than of a sports reporter:

'After 3 or 4 bulls were tired and killed by the footmen then was another let out and the Conde de Sarzedas came in upon a fine well ranged horse very richly equipped, having 74 lackeys came in before his horse, half in red liveries with silver lace and half in green with silver lace.'

He was certainly a mathematick admiral. How many observers would have counted the 74 lackeys? And he had an eye for colours and textures.

If his journal tells us nothing about the quality of life in Lisbon it tells us less about his own anxieties during the most exacting part of his mission that was to follow. He anchored in Tangier Bay on October 10th and sent in the four Portuguese caravels which he had convoyed from Lisbon. The town was illuminated for the King's marriage and Sandwich's ships fired celebratory salutes each night but these civilities appear to have elicited no response from the Governor. The fourteenth of his line to have held that office he declined absolutely to betray the heroic traditions of his ancestors by handing over this stronghold to foreigners and heretics. In the end he had to be recalled and superseded by a more compliant grandee, bribed by the promise of a six year term as Governor of Brazil.[1] Sandwich of course only knew of this indirectly, either from the Portuguese emissary he had brought down from Lisbon or from the letters he received from Fanshawe and Maynard. The Governor, frigidly disregarding his presence, communicated only by sealed packets directed to the Governor of the Algarves at Lagos. Meanwhile Sandwich was faced with the problems of maintaining a large fleet with its requirements of food and marine supplies for an indefinite period in an anchorage exposed to violent winds and seas on a coast where the Moors outside the town or the Portuguese inside could at best be counted unreliable and might well be openly hostile. Seventeenth-century ships were neither comfortable nor healthy and the climate at Tangier as described by Pepys twenty years later sounds foul.

On the 15th Sandwich was joined by Lawson and some of the ships

1. E. M. G. Routh *Tangier* (1912) p. 10.

under his command. Next day 'we had a Council of War and resolved
how to dispose the fleet for the best service'. It was a difficult question.
They had to keep an eye on de Ruyter since the Dutch were still at war
with Portugal and the seizure of Tangier by sudden *coup de main* might
well be expected of so bold and accomplished a commander. They had
to watch the Spaniards who were known to be encouraging the Moors
to grab Tangier and massacre the Portuguese. They had to be on the
spot to cover the landing of the English garrison and Governor when
they should appear, but this much desired fixture seemed to come no
closer. And so large and expensive a naval armament would be expected
to provide convoy for English trade coming in and out of the Straits
and to take every opportunity of attacking the corsairs.

The journal for the last three months of the year is full of these last
two duties. The movements of the Dutch gave less and less cause for
alarm. De Ruyter seemed to be attending to the business of dealing with
the Barbary pirates. Lawson had anchored alongside him at Malaga on
his way to join Sandwich at Tangier and they had exchanged signal
books so that they could recognize each other by day or night when
pursuing their common enemy. There was thus no need to concentrate
the whole of the English fleet in Tangier Bay. Just how widespread were
its units and commitments may be seen from the entry for December
10th:

> With me in Tangier Bay – Royal James, Mary, Montagu, Portland,
>   Princess, Yarmouth, Hampshire, Augustine.
> In Gibraltar Bay – Swiftsure, Fairfax, Anne, Constant Warwick 2
>   ketches.
> At Cadiz – The Colchester and Martin.
> At Faro – The Greyhound.
> At Lagos – The Newcastle.
> At Lisbon – The Gift.
> At Leghorn – The Assurance.
> At Zante – The Crown and Nonsuch.
> Plying in the mouth of the Gut – The Assistance.

But there was still no news of the troopships sailing from England and
precious little sign of a thaw in the icy relations with the Portuguese
authorities ashore. On November 1st a Portuguese cavalry colonel and
his son, a judge and two other gentlemen had come to dinner aboard

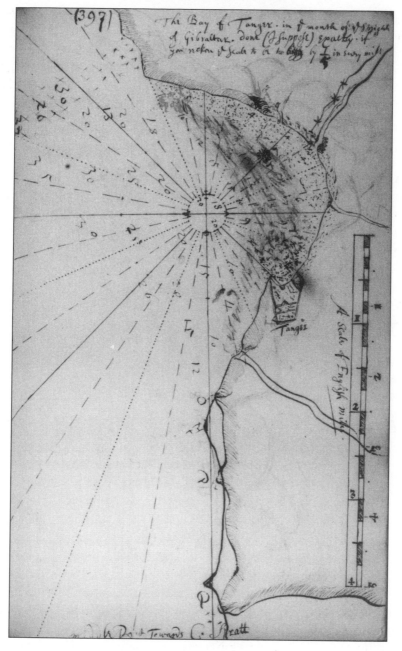

Tangier, done in November 1661

the flagship. On the 18th the Town Major took passage aboard a frigate for Lagos, ostensibly to make arrangements for handing over to the English. But it was nearly Christmas before there was any apparent result from these endeavours. On December 17th 'the Aidill of Tangier' (presumably the Chief Magistrate) dined aboard. Next day there was news that the English expedition was at last ready to sail as soon as the wind came fair. The last vestige of alarm about the Dutch was removed by de Ruyter taking the whole fleet to Minorca to clean.

But there was still no real sign that the Portuguese were ready to budge. Even Sandwich's patience showed signs of wear. On January 4th and again on the 6th he sent Fanshawe's representative with the Governor an offer of four hundred men from the fleet to reinforce the Castle against a possible Moorish assault. There was no answer. But on the 12th the Governor overplayed his hand. A party of 140 horse, probably the main effective cavalry of the garrison, made a sally into the country for booty. They caught the Moors unprepared and were returning in triumph with 400 cattle, 30 camels, some horses and 35 women and girls when a well-armed and doubtless enraged force of 100 Moors fell on them a few miles outside the walls and routed them, killing over fifty of the cavalry and capturing their horses. This was a serious loss. Horses were at a premium in Tangier. Without them reconnaissance and local supply were impossible. The Governor was obliged to ask Sandwich for reinforcement. On the 16th 80 sailors from the *Royal James* and the *Princess* manned the defences of the lower castle and frigates were busily shuttling to and from Cadiz bringing in provisions. By the 23rd Sandwich had 'between 3 and 400 men in the Town and Castles, and the command of all the strengths and magazines.' He had secured his objective without the use of force. A week later the Earl of Peterborough, Governor Designate, arrived with twenty-seven sail and marched into the town at the head of his own regiment. The Governor handed over the keys together with 'a horse, rich saddle and bridle, scimitar, silver spurs and a lance'. England's first Crown Colony in Africa had been planted.

The rest of Sandwich's time at Tangier was taken up in transporting across to the Algarve such of the Portuguese as wished to leave and in surveying the harbour for the building of the mole. The foul weather for which the place was notorious made this and other boatwork hazardous: 'in my boat to sound again and advise about the mole; which as we were doing came up a great storm, with spouts with a levant wind, and so I rowed aboard.' The suddenness with which the seas got up was disconcerting. Sailing at last for Lisbon on a gentle gale and a calm sea Sandwich accepted an invitation from Sir John Mennes who had commanded the fleet that brought the Governor from England. During dinner it came on to blow so hard that it took three hours in his boat to get aboard his own ship again.

At the end of January the *Royal Charles*, Sandwich's old flagship, sailed from the Downs for Lisbon. Once again he was to hoist his flag in her and with the Royal Standard at the main bring home the new Queen. Her presence, together with Mennes's squadron, gave him so large a superiority over the Dutch that he could afford to detach a powerful squadron under Lawson to re-enter the Mediterranean and resume oper-ations against the Algerines. In this Lawson was once again successful, even extorting a treaty from them later in the year.

Extorting the promised dowry from the Crown of Portugal, had it been possible at all, would have required the same strong-arm methods or at least the combination of bullying and threats that came so naturally to Sir George Downing, our ambassador at The Hague. Neither Sand-wich nor Fanshawe could act in that character. In the end Sandwich disobeyed his instructions and accepted Bills of Exchange for a great part of the money. He had already spent a month and a half in Lisbon. Further delay in bringing home the Queen would not do. Portugal any-how was *in extremis*. The expense of the war with Spain was beyond her resources and an immediate peace with the Dutch was essential even if it meant conceding them the same trading privileges in the Empire as those accorded to England by the marriage treaty. Sandwich sailed on April 15th and anchored at Spithead on May 14th. The unfortunate Queen had been seasick from the moment they cleared the Tagus. The passage had been long and rough. She was still in bed when her husband first set eyes on her but he too, as he explained to Clarendon, was in no position to claim his conjugal rights. Sandwich was present at the official ratification of the contract and formal blessing of the union by the Bishop of London in the King's House at Portsmouth on the 21st. On the 23rd he was reunited with his family at the Wardrobe.

Edward's journal, which ends a week later with the State Reception of the King and Queen at Hampton Court, records his frequent letters to his wife. That she was no less affectionate a correspondent is clear from many surviving letters. Anxiety for his health, the progress of the work at Hinchingbrooke, the urgent need for ready money and a recurrent fear that they are spending far too much of it, the ruinous effects of debt, the illnesses of the children, the kindness of other people, above all the quiet longing to see him home again provide the matter for the unstudied, unselfconscious, generosity of spirit expressed in them.

The two main events of family life during his absence had been the birth of a daughter and the departure of the two eldest sons on the Grand Tour. Both had taken place in August 1661. The parents had meant to call the little girl Sarah but Lady Sandwich decided instead to christen her Katherine 'you having the honour to bring our so much desired queen I thought we might allsoe have the honour to have her name'.[1] She was a delicate child but was to live to a great age. Her mother's care of her appears in a letter written when Sandwich was once again abroad as ambassador in Madrid:

> I have sent little Kat to London to Mr Pers the Serg that belongs to the Duke [Pepys's friend, James Pearse, who was surgeon to the Duke of York] ther being they say the famostes Docr. in Iingland for sore eies; he did a mirackeulus cure on the Dutches daughter, the Lady Ann [the future Queen], and now cam up to the Dutches of Richmon [la belle Stuart] who by the smale pox had one of her eies much hurt.[2]

Sending the two boys abroad to acquire the *ton* and the polite accomplishments of the best Parisian society was a further stage in the transition from the world of Cromwell to that of Charles II. Pepys saw them off at the end of August and they were met on their arrival in Paris by Sandwich's cousin, the abbé Mountagu. No better introduction to the most exclusive circles of an exclusive society could have been obtained. The charming infinitely experienced old man took great trouble over his young cousins. A governor was engaged: so were the best masters for Latin, for dancing, for horsemanship. As soon as they were both old enough they were sent to the most fashionable of all academies, that of

1. Carte MS 74 f. 351.
2. Harris, ii 182.

M. du Plessis. Accounts were opened at the best bookshops and at the best tailor. One way and another it cost a pretty penny.

Lord Hinchingbrooke's application to his studies does not seem to have been proportionate to the expense. Like his father he was fond of music, perhaps, thought his tutor, too fond 'for those yeares att which we are to learn usefull things rather than to meditate delightsome ones'. After a year of intensive tuition he had apparently not heard of either Xenophon or Moses. But his riding master spoke well of him. Sydney, the younger brother, who was to be closest to his father, showed on the other hand neither aptitude nor taste for horsemanship but was lively company and quick to learn any subject.

They were to be in Paris for nearly three years. Sydney came home in May 1664 while his elder brother went on the full Grand Tour, down to the Loire, to Lyon and so to Italy, returning in August 1665. In spite of their absence it was a large and loving family that Edward found at his house at the Wardrobe. 'Wee all longe much for your safe returne which wee have beene in great expectation of but now I hope it will be very sudingly' his eldest child Lady Jemimah had written as long ago as early December.[1] Altogether the Sandwiches were to have eleven children, seven sons and four daughters. The careful preservation of childish effusions among the graver papers of state shows how much their father valued and enjoyed them. Brought up by so enchanting a mother it was hardly surprising that their family life should set a pattern of happiness and affection.

1. Carte MS 223 f. 149.

XI

Slack Water

━━❦━━

AT FIRST SIGHT Sandwich's public situation in the summer of
1662 appeared as enviable as his domestic. He had brought back the
Queen: he had secured Tangier: and news had just arrived of the
Algerines having at last been forced to sign a treaty. The gratitude of his
master was signalized by an immediate and substantial cash grant and
the Portuguese authorities also made him a handsome present of gold
cruzados.

But success won by honest service and the rewards that went with it
were dangerous attractions in the greedy, spiteful, jealous court of
Charles II. Men were not wanting to point out that the great proportion
of the Queen's dowry remained unpaid and that the operations which
had ultimately brought the Algerines to heel had been carried out by
Lawson. The rapid dissatisfaction of the King with his new Queen, the
growing credibility of the widely disseminated report that she was
incapable of bearing children not only wiped out the gains of having
been prominently associated with the Portuguese marriage but converted
them to loss. Clarendon stood fair and square in the eye of the wind, a
wind which rose to hurricane force with the sale of Dunkirk in the
autumn. His standing with the King, for so long towering over all com-
petitors for royal favour, was beginning to crumble. Not only was he
answerable for the Queen being Queen, he had taken her part when her
caddish husband bullied her into accepting Lady Castlemaine as one of
the ladies of her bedchamber. Sandwich with his easy manners took
trouble to remain on good terms with the King's mistress. She had
lodgings near his in Whitehall and gossip, reported by Pepys with the

languor of disbelief, suggested an affair. It seems unlikely. But Lady Castlemaine was Clarendon's bitterest enemy and by the next year everyone, including Pepys, agreed that the Chancellor was flat on his back, past rising again. This had grave implications for Sandwich, by now a close personal and political friend.

Not that Sandwich's own ambitions were, or ever had been, political. But his passionate concern for the navy, his vision of his country's future on the pathways of the seas, required a political base. And here, where he might least have expected it, he came up against opposition in the bosom of his political family, Clarendon's son-in-law and the King's brother, James, Duke of York. James did all he could to play down Sandwich's success in his recent mission because he wished to replace him as the active naval Commander in Chief in any future war. In his endeavours he was ably seconded by his Secretary, Sir William Coventry. As we shall see they came close to success. Like all men who rise by merit of service Sandwich had no broad base on which to maintain his position.

He had returned in cheerful mood. Pepys noted how well he looked and remarked on his gaiety, reflected in his preference for fiddler's tunes, simple airs, over the fantasias that they had been used to playing together. As soon as he could he went down to Hinchingbrooke and was delighted with the improvements and extensions. There was no stinting when the Master of the House was at home, however much the careful and unselfish Lady Sandwich might economize when he was away. Pepys's exquisite epicurean friend Mr Povey went to stay there the following year and has left a description whose laboured opulence makes it clear that no expense was spared in the comforts and elegances of life. This is amply confirmed by such accounts as have survived.[1]

Sandwich was determined to live as a nobleman of his time ought to live. He was not content to keep up a grand establishment. He wished to increase it and to fill it with books, furniture, pictures and tapestries, to adorn his table with silver and glass, to commemorate his services to the state by possessions such as the barge that the King had used at his restoration. He had brought from Tangier a fine Barbary horse – the era of the thoroughbred was just dawning – on which he rode about the

1. Harris i, 253–5.

estate or went hunting or hawking. And the estate too was steadily enlarged by grant or purchase. All this was expected of a man in his position. Was he not Lord Lieutenant of the County? And were not Kimbolton and Boughton, the seats of his cousins, twin spurs to magnificence? As in international relations so in maintaining the fabric of social order, reputation was the *sine qua non*. How it was all to be paid for was a secondary question.

Nonetheless it could not be altogether disregarded. The Wardrobe, in theory, should have supported the lifestyle of a grandee. On June 22nd Sandwich was back in London partly to press for the money due to him in respect of his embassy and partly to make arrangements for going over to France to fetch the Queen Mother. Pepys called on him early on the 27th and Sandwich rose from bed for a long and confidential *tour d'horizon* in his dressing gown. His first concern was to straighten out, if possible, his tangled finances and then to decide what course to take about his future employment at sea. He made no bones about the Duke's desire to have him out and identified Coventry as his enemy. He made one remark which mystified Pepys, as well it might: 'Hitherto I have been supported by the King and Chancellor against the Duke; but what if it should come about that it should be the Duke and Chancellor against the King?' Clarendon never found his son-in-law a sympathetic personality and never concealed his detestation of his clever secretary, William Coventry, under whose spell Pepys himself was beginning to fall. From Pepys's point of view a rift between the Lord High Admiral, supported by Coventry, and Sandwich, to whom his own first loyalty lay, spelled disaster: for his own career, for Sandwich's, and for the sea service. But ten days later the clouds began to lift. At another tête-à-tête at the Wardrobe Sandwich told him that Coventry had been singing his praises 'wherein I am much pleased.' Before the interview was over Coventry himself was announced 'and so my Lord and he and I walked together in the great chamber a good while, and I find him a most ingenuous man and good company.'

To work for this rapprochement became one of Pepys's chief concerns. Sandwich however though never haughty or huffish had his pride. His service was long and distinguished: his professional skill as a seaman and a navigator recognized by those who had sailed with him. He gave fresh evidence of it that July. As Admiral of the Narrow Seas he chose to sail in the King's yacht to bring over the Queen Mother while the Duke of York and William Coventry took passage in the warship escort. A fierce storm in the Channel scattered the flotilla, dismasting the Duke's ship and endangering the rest. Coventry wrote to Pepys warning him that Sandwich's fate was unknown. It had been, as Sandwich later told him, a close call. From other sources Pepys heard of his calmness while the courtiers aboard gave themselves up for lost.

This was his only sea service for many months to come. During the early autumn he was fully employed in the small secret committee that negotiated the sale of Dunkirk. Otherwise he was left to his own devices as the thunder of another war with the Dutch rumbled closer. The exploits of Sir Robert Holmes's first expedition down the West African coast, commissioned by the Duke of York's Royal African Company, had angered their High Mightinesses. His second, for which the Duke signed the instructions, drafted by Coventry, on 10th November 1663, led to the actual occupation of Dutch colonial possessions. There could not be much doubt what the consequences of that would be. Why, Sandwich must have asked himself, was the Government's principal naval adviser and most senior flag officer not consulted? But he wasn't. The squadron that he had left under Lawson in the Mediterranean had come home at the end of the year. In the spring of 1663 Lawson had been sent out again with a few ships to show the flag in Lisbon, at Tangier and off Algiers, returning again in the autumn. He was sent on the same errand yet a third time in January 1664 and in June of that year exchanged courtesies off Alicante with a Dutch squadron under de Ruyter who was at that moment under secret orders to sail down the Guinea coast and attack the English forts in reprisal for Holmes's activities. It was at this eleventh hour, in the midsummer of 1664 when hostilities might open at any minute, that the Duke of York decided to offer employment to the Earl of Sandwich.

For all the imperturbability of his manner Sandwich was highly strung. The months of neglect had preyed on his mind. 'My Lord Sandwich is still in good esteem, and now keeping his Christmas in the country' Pepys had written at the end of 1662. It was perhaps the warm glow of satisfaction with which he contemplated his own prosperous situation that coloured the judgment. Sandwich rather appeared restless and dissatisfied. Besides his house at the Wardrobe[1] and his lodgings at White-hall he took rooms in Chelsea. To visit him there, as Pepys did at the end of April 1663, was to make a country excursion. Ought a public figure with ambitions to serve his country to put himself so far out of the world? Sandwich had been very ill early in the year and needed a fresher air. But gossip, to which Pepys never failed to listen and perhaps too readily believed, ascribed his withdrawal to an amour with the daughter of the house in which he was living. Pepys was appalled. It was not that he was a rigorist in the matter of sexual morals, though like many loose livers he was surprisingly censorious. It was much more a matter of snobbery. So provincial and undistinguished a liaison exposed a man of Sandwich's importance to ridicule. In any case such an attachment must necessarily keep him away from court where the King had already remarked on the infrequency of his appearance. Pepys's decision to put these considerations to his employer in 'my great letter of reproof' took several months to reach. Sandwich was not at Chelsea during the whole of this period. For a great deal of the summer and autumn he was at Hinchingbrooke, his health restored, his manners as agreeable as ever. Patron and protégé met there in that atmosphere of relaxed informality that the Sandwiches so evidently and so unaffectedly preferred. Sandwich took pains to distinguish Pepys among his house party and asked his opinion about the walls and walks that he was laying out or remodelling. Pepys's itch to tell other people what they ought to do was for the moment stilled. But when he got back to London the effects of gossip, self-importance and a strong, if submerged, Puritanism were too much for him. He wrote the letter; and things were never the same again between them.

At least Pepys seems to have thought so. His description of Sandwich's reception of that extraordinary document is the more convincing because he does not seem to have understood it. Sandwich's coolness, firmness and, ultimately, kindness caught him off balance. But then Pepys, for all his wonderful powers of observation and shrewdness of judgment, does not altogether seem to have been tuned in to his cousin's wavelength. We have seen how completely he had misread him after the fall of

1. The site is still commemorated in the name of the church in Queen Victoria St., St-Andrew-by-the-Wardrobe.

Richard Cromwell. It is permissible to wonder how much weight should be given to his opinion that Sandwich was 'a man amorous enough' or, specifically, that he had made overtures to Pepys's wife through the agency of Captain Ferrer, his master of the horse. To say that Pepys had sex on the brain is perhaps to underrate the susceptibility of his other members. One thinks of the lather he worked himself into over his growing certainty, for which he later admits he had no evidence at all, that his wife was having an affair with her dancing-master. Similarly, though less candidly, he owns to his surprise at finding the lady in this question, when he at last met her, a very different person from the seductress he had imagined. She did not set the hormones racing. She was rather plain. She was extremely agreeable company.

It was when Sandwich had returned to London in November that the letter was delivered. His affairs were still in the doldrums. The Chancellor, his great ally, was still under heavy attack. The King had again, according to Pepys's friend the eminent surgeon James Pearse, remarked on Sandwich's prolonged absence from Court. The Wardrobe accounts, now that the bills for the Coronation had all come in, looked bleaker and bleaker. It may have been with some intention of selling that office, as he ultimately did, that Sandwich took the lease on 20th January 1664 of a house in Lincoln's Inn Fields, a neighbourhood familiar to him as the home of his father-in-law Lord Crew. At any rate it was a good way from Chelsea. He began to come to court again, sometimes playing cards with the King. But he was still kept at arm's length by the Duke amid the growing preparations for a war with the foremost naval power in Europe.

Rumours of Holmes's activities on the West African coast filtered through in March. By early May they were well known both in London and in Amsterdam. Without humiliating concessions by one side or the other war was now inevitable, perhaps only a matter of days. Yet still no summons came. The Duke of York's great objective, the command of the fleet in a major war, was almost within his grasp. And the Cavaliers were resentful of the continuous employment of old Commonwealthmen like Lawson or Cromwellians like Sandwich in the most important flag appointments. Why should not the Royalists have their turn? Old Sir John Mennes had been sent out to join Sandwich at Tangier as Flag Officer commanding the escort of Lord Peterborough's expeditionary force but no one seriously thought of putting him up against Kortenaer or de Ruyter. A start had been made by giving Thomas Allin, who had served under Rupert in the fleet that revolted to the Royalists in 1648, the command in the Downs in the summer of 1663. Allin was that rare bird among Royalists, a professional seaman: he was continuously employed from the Restoration onwards. But if Allin had claims, what about Rupert? If he were to be invited to serve it could hardly be under anyone less exalted than the Lord High Admiral himself. And where would that leave Sandwich? At best Rear-Admiral of a fleet he had so recently commanded.

These considerations seemed to offer the Duke a way out of offering him anything at all. Monck after all had the finest fighting record against the Dutch of any surviving General at Sea yet the King had insisted that he was too essential to the safety of the state to be put at risk. Could not the same compliment excuse the offering of a subordinate command to so great a man as his co-architect of the Restoration? William Coventry was deputed to sound out Pepys as to how his master would react.

It was diplomatically done. On Whitsunday May 29th, the King's birthday as well as the day of his Restoration, Pepys was invited over to Coventry's lodging at St James's. They talked shop about the navy and the approaching war with the Dutch. Coventry expressed his scepticism as to the necessity for any such conflict and enlarged on the natural advantages enjoyed by England, winds, harbours and manpower. 'But it is our pride and the laziness of the merchant.' Many contemporaries thought that Coventry himself had been a prime mover of the aggressive policies from which he was now distancing himself.

'The main thing he desired to speak with me about was to know whether I do understand my Lord Sandwich's intentions as to going to sea with this fleet; saying that the Duke, if he desires it, is most willing to it; but thinking that twelve ships is not a fleet fit for my Lord to be troubled to go out with, he is not willing to offer it him till he hath some intimations of his mind to go or not. He spoke this with very great respect as to my Lord, though methinks, it is strange they should not understand one another better at this time then to need another's mediacion.'

Sandwich shared these misgivings when, two days later, Pepys communicated this message. He had been seeing the Duke every day and been treated with every appearance of friendship, but no word had ever been said about a flag appointment nor had his advice ever been asked about any of the Captains so far named. He was hurt and insulted by such treatment. Nonetheless both Pepys and he agreed that it would be 'wholly inconsistent with his Honour not to go with this fleet'.

Pepys therefore signified his acceptance and was surprised – Sandwich would not have been – that Coventry seemed displeased and irritably asked whether he had made it plain to Sandwich that the Duke did not expect him to go. 'I told him I had.' The prospect of a breach between Pepys's patron and Coventry and his patron was almost too terrible to contemplate. But even against his will, realism would not be denied.

Sandwich for his part was far too perceptive not to have observed the growing influence of Coventry over his cousin and protégé and not to understand how valuable such a connexion must appear to a young man with his way to make. But to understand is not necessarily to approve. In a conflict of loyalties was Pepys to be reckoned his liege man? The matter was, like so many others, bedevilled by his own overspending. He had borrowed money from Pepys and had induced him to back a bill for a thousand pounds. This altered the relationship. Absurd though it might be, Sandwich was to that extent Pepys's client instead of the other way about. And Pepys had shown signs of growing restive about this commitment. Doubtless this nettled his patron. Pepys noticed, and was offended by, what he considered off-hand treatment when he waited on him on June 20th.

By this time the news that Sandwich was to be given a command was widely known. On the 30th the fleet of twelve sail was ready in the River. On July 4th the King and Queen were received aboard by Sandwich. Pepys was not in attendance. Indeed although he still saw a great deal of Lady Sandwich and the children his relations with his cousin seemed more distant than ever. Then, on the 14th, everything changed. 'Depend upon it, if a man knows he is to be hanged in a fortnight it concentrates his mind wonderfully.' Sandwich's courage was anything but blind: he knew, none better, that fighting the Dutch at sea could not be undertaken lightly or wantonly but soberly and in the fear of God. If he were to be killed, did he want to leave Pepys as the engaged, whole-hearted defender of his family and all that was dear to him, or as a regretful but uninvolved former connexion? The question answered itself. On the evening of the 13th Pepys was summoned to attend him next morning.

The Diary entry for the 14th opens with an evocation of unfocused anxiety that a poet might envy:

'My mind being doubtful what the business should be, I rose little after 4 a-clock, and abroad; walked to my Lord's and nobody up, but the porter ris out of bed to me. So I back again to Fleet-street and there bought a little book of law; and thence, hearing a psalm sung, I went into St Dunstans and there heard prayers read, which it seems is done there every morning at 6 a-clock, a thing I never did do at a chapel, but the College chapel, in all my life.

'Thence to my Lord's again; and my Lord being up, was sent for up, and he and I alone: he did begin with a most solemn profession of the same confidence in and love for me that he ever had, and then told me what a misfortune was fallen upon me and him: in me, by a displeasure which my Lord Chancellor did show to him last night against me in the highest and most passionate manner that ever any man did speak, even to the not hearing of anything to be said to him.'

The cause of offence, for which Pepys had no difficulty in showing that he was in no way responsible, was the marking of standing timber in Clarendon Park for felling by the navy purveyors acting under a warrant from the Treasury. Clarendon's temper at the best of times was at a short fuse. Inflamed by gout and irritated by the pettishness of unrestrained power a waft of thistledown was enough to detonate its explosion. He clearly liked Pepys and esteemed Sandwich. Within two days he was pacified, indeed pleased that both men now made it their business to exempt his property from its statutory liabilities. During the course of these conversations Clarendon gratified Pepys by telling him of the high character Sandwich had given of him.

Was the whole affair an innocent stratagem on Sandwich's part to restore their old intimacy and mutual dependence? It certainly produced that effect. He talked to Pepys without reserve of his own political position, of the difficulties occasioned by his good relations, which he wished to maintain, with the rising star Harry Bennet, the future Lord Arlington, who was the bête noire of the Chancellor to whom his deepest loyalties must ever lie. He talked of the Duke of York who, after the prolonged snubbing of his professional opinion, had drawn his commission in the most generous terms so that any future fleet or flag that might be added should be subordinate to his own. 'He tells me, in these cases ... and all others, he finds that bearing of them patiently is his best way, without noise or trouble; and things wear out of themselfs and come fair again. "But", says he, "take it from me never to trust too much to any man in the world, for you put yourself into his power; and the best-seeming friend and real friend as to the present may have or take occasion to fall out with you; and then out comes all." '

This, if ever, is Sandwich distilling his deepest convictions into axioms of conduct. The calmness that he showed in action, in the aftermath of a coup d'état, in the face of the Duke of Buckingham's insults, in the absence of proper instructions or promised support, in imminent danger of wreck in the Channel, was all of a piece. Was there a specific as well as a general warning in his final admonition? Did he think his young cousin too flattered, too bewitched, by the wit, the intelligence and the friendship of William Coventry? No doubt he would have thought it flat-footed to ask so direct a question.

The occasion was a solemn one, pleasurably heightened by Sandwich's mother-in-law breaking in to tell him that his wife was safely delivered of yet another son. Sandwich was seriously worried at the deplorable state of his finances. 'Then as to the voyage, he thinks it will be of charge to him, but that he must not now look after nor think to encrease ... "This," says he, "is the whole condition of my estate and interest; which I tell you because I know not whether I shall see you again or no." ' Three days later he had set out for the Downs.

XII

Command at Sea

WHEN SANDWICH BOARDED his flagship the *London* in the Downs
the fleet of twelve ships that had been thought too paltry for his acceptance had grown to eighteen. Allin, the ex-Royalist, was his Vice-Admiral
and Teddiman, a Commonwealth veteran, his Rear-Admiral. Allin was
soon to be detached to relieve Lawson in the Mediterranean but Sandwich, who always took trouble to cultivate good relations with his brother
officers, dined aboard him a week after assuming command. Although
war had not yet been declared he rightly regarded himself as responsible
for putting the affairs of the fleet on a war footing. He went ashore to
visit the harbours and docks that he would have to rely on. He visited
lighthouses and, when at sea, recorded pilotage details and noted the
flow of tides. He called on the mayors of the coastal towns who might
in an emergency be of more use than officials operating from London.
Above all he took his ships to sea and noted their sailing qualities. He
had not been a colonel in the New Model Army for nothing: it was not
numbers so much as discipline and efficiency that counted.

In tactical terms discipline and efficiency spelled formalism; that is,
fighting in a prescribed line of battle according to instructions previously
circulated to the fleet. Only so could the refinements of the sail plan
developed over the last century and the enormous hitting power of the
great guns carried on the broadside be employed to their full effect. The
old chance medley of each ship seeking to grapple the nearest enemy
belonged to the days of hand-to-hand fighting, when indeed the real
fighting was the business of soldiers carried aboard for the purpose.
Once the ship herself had become a weapon to be aimed at an enemy

on her beam the offensive power of a fleet could only be maximized by making sure that one ship did not mask another, and that meant fighting in line ahead. In Sandwich's day this was still a novel doctrine. As was emphasized at the beginning of this book he was its most important champion: indeed he was ahead of his time in perceiving the implication, unquestioningly accepted within a decade or two of his death, that a true line of battle could only be formed of warships, built with the sole purpose of carrying guns on the broadside. Logically there was no place for the armed merchantmen temporarily pressed into service, with which Drake and Frobisher had sailed to meet the Armada.

Sandwich had called a Council of War aboard the flagship on the second day of his command and, to quote his journal, 'Agreed our Sailing and Fighting Instructions.' Is it fanciful to see in that wording the spirit of Nelson's Band of Brothers? It is certainly not how the Duke of York would have put it, though he like Sandwich was a strong formalist and lost no time in issuing his own – substantially the same – when he hoisted his flag as Lord High Admiral. But for the summer of 1664 Sandwich enjoyed his own command, plying up and down between the Isle of Wight and the approaches of the Thames, providing passage for envoys and other persons connected with the court to and from France and Holland, taking stellar observations and on one occasion recording a waterspout, of which he made drawings, off the mouth of the Thames:

> The appearance of it was upon the surface of the water as if in a round of some 50 yards diameter the water did rise out of the sea with a white breach and tumbling itself furiously like black smoke out of the mouth of a furnace, and from this breach up to a black cloud that was over it was a pillar of water of some 5 or 10 yards diameter continued. At the last about the middle it separated and the one half shrinked itself upwards; the other half in the shape of a cone with the sharp end downward, fell to the water.
>
> Presently after the end of it we had a great thunder clap and from the N.W. very much rain for one hour and ½.[1]

In the middle of October Sandwich was ordered to report to Whitehall together with Sir John Lawson, whom Allin had relieved at the Straits. The day after he left Portsmouth Rupert anchored there with the squad-

1. Journal 4th August 1664.

ron that had been fitting out in the Thames to sail in support of Holmes's exploits in West Africa. De Ruyter's comprehensive obliteration of them – as Pepys put it 'our being beaten to dirt at Guiny' – was to frustrate this mission. Rupert, whose pride and aggressiveness is so often described by both Clarendon and Pepys, wrote Sandwich the civilest of letters, expressing his readiness 'to serve with you or in any other place'.[1] When Sandwich returned at the end of the month the Prince was still there and they paid each other regular visits. This was the prelude to the arrival on November 9th of the Lord High Admiral himself to take the whole fleet out on a Channel cruise. In spite of all that Sandwich had done, sending his own men to help rig the vessels in harbour, pressing seamen wherever he could find them, the ships were not ready and the weather was not propitious. On the 24th his old flagship, the *Royal Charles*, came in with 15 sail and the Duke removed into her. On the 27th the whole fleet now numbering 41 men of war, divided into three squadrons with Rupert as Admiral of the White and Sandwich of the Blue, set sail with a hard gale at north-east. They cruised for three or four days off the Channel Islands and the Cherbourg peninsula but were soon back in harbour. On December 4th the Duke and the Prince returned to London, leaving Sandwich once more in command.

He remained aboard all December and January, ready to snap up any Dutch vessels that might risk the Channel passage. Watching the transit of the Blazing Star across the cold clear heavens was the principal relief of a thankless monotony. During the middle watch on December 17th he obtained his best view: 'The body of the star was dusky, not plain to see his figure or dimensions, but seemed 4 or 5 times bigger than the Great Dog, of a more red colour than Mars. The tail of him streamed in the fashion of a birchen besom towards the Little Dog the one half of the distance between them.' On January 22nd he sailed from St Helens with fifteen ships in company to sweep the Channel up as far as the Downs. The weather was filthy and the only ships they sighted were a fleet of French fishermen and a solitary English merchantmen homeward bound from Malaga. On the 28th they anchored in the Downs.

Here intelligence indicated an imminent Dutch attack on the anchorage. Sandwich exchanged out of the *London*, assigned to Lawson as his

1. Mapperton MSS. Letters from Ministers i, 37.

flagship for the fleet to be set out for the spring, into the *Revenge*. In spite of the horrible weather, snow showers, extreme cold, a hard gale and a chopping sea, they kept out most of the time so as not to be caught with insufficient sea room. At last it became clear that the Dutch were not coming, or not just yet. On February 21st Sandwich hauled down his flag and went ashore. On his way to London he hoisted his flag aboard the *Prince*, then lying at Chatham, in which he was to sail as Admiral of the Blue at the end of March.

The month he spent in London was much taken up with business. Pepys glimpsed him several times at meetings of the Tangier Committee. Their relations were still excellent. Sandwich took care to tell him how highly the Duke of York spoke of him. Indeed it was the Duke's initiative, encouraged by Sandwich, that replaced the incompetent but well-connected Povey by Pepys in the lucrative post of Treasurer of Tangier. The warm glow of approaching wealth fortified Pepys against his consciousness of the fearful deficiencies in the fleet that would soon have to do battle with the best-led, best-found and most experienced navy of the age. Sandwich, who knew about these matters from months of direct observation, had good reason to be preoccupied. He had been ten days in London before he had leisure to dine at home as Pepys, who was there, recorded: 'And a pretty odd demand it was of my Lord to my Lady before me: "How do you, sweetheart; how have you done all this week?" – himself taking notice of it to me, that he had hardly seen her the week before.'[1]

Sandwich went aboard his new flagship at Gravesend on March 23rd and joined the Duke's flag in the Gunfleet on the 27th. Just before sailing he had been horrified by the loss of his old ship the *London* in an explosion from which only a handful of her company survived. The discipline and safety procedures of the Restoration navy left much to be desired. Drink was much too easily available and drunkenness ran right through society. Sandwich's journal gives repeated evidence of accidents or court-martial offences arising from this cause. A more interesting court-martial on which he sat with the Duke and Prince Rupert within ten days of joining the fleet was that of an insubordinate Lieutenant who had compounded his offence by taunting his Captain and another officer

1. *Diary* 5th March 1665.

'with their having been rebels and served under Cromwell's commission'. He was promptly cashiered.

For all its deficiencies the fleet that the Duke of York commanded at the Gunfleet was the most powerful that England had ever fitted out, totalling well over a hundred sail of which eighty-four were men of war. The fighting and sailing instructions followed closely those issued by Sandwich earlier in the year and in one particular exactly reproduce a provision of his for signalling a change of formation.[1] The Duke as Lord High Admiral commanded the centre, assisted by Sir William Penn serving in the unique appointment of Great Captain Commander. As on the brief cruise in December Rupert had the Van or White squadron and Sandwich the Rear or Blue. Every ship had her station in the line and each of the three divisions replicated that of the fleet with a Vice-Admiral in the van and a Rear-Admiral astern. One further refinement was added during the second and third Dutch Wars. In case the fleet might have to fight in reverse order the Vice-Admiral of the Blue squadron took station in the rear, not the van, so that whatever happened the line would be led by a senior flag officer. Formalism could no further.

Sandwich's Vice-Admiral was Sir George Ayscue, whom he had served with at the Sound when Ayscue was seconded to the Swedes, and his Rear-Admiral Teddiman, who had held the same appointment in the small Downs squadron. Though he had had no say in choosing his flag officers they were exactly the kind of professionals with whom he preferred to serve. But the navy was not yet wholly professional: courtiers and favourites easily obtained the consent of the King or the Duke to serve as volunteers or reformadoes, that is an officer without specific duty or the pay that went with it. Some of them were very grand and conscious of their grandeur. The Duke of Monmouth, the King's favourite among his growing tribe of illegitimate children, was apparently entitled to attend at Councils of War though still in his teens. The Duke of Buckingham claimed the same privilege by virtue of his membership of the Privy Council. When the Duke of York refused him admittance he rushed back to Whitehall in a fury, demanding an order from the King himself. This absurd request was not granted but he was nonetheless allowed to return to the fleet and was wished on the unhappy Sand-

1. See R.C. Anderson's introduction to the *Journal*, especially xlvii ff.

wich, who would hardly have chosen as a shipmate the arrogant brute who had insulted him at the card table. He was more fortunate in his other passengers, the good-natured, amusing Harry Savile whose intemperance and indiscretions prevented him from fulfilling the promise of his abilities, and another young courtier, the brother of la belle Stuart,[1] whom Sandwich liked well enough to take with him in his retinue to the Madrid embassy.

But this enormous and expensive fleet had work to do. Apart from meeting the threat from the formidable armament known to be already mobilized in harbours within a few hours' sail on a favourable wind there was a rich Dutch convoy expected home northabout round Scotland and down the North Sea. Charles II seems never to have lost the hope that foreign policy and its extension into war could be made to pay. The first Dutch War fought in the Interregnum had certainly had that effect. The prizes taken had doubled the size of the English merchant fleet.[2] Geography had put England astride the two routes by which Dutch ships must sail to reach the oceans. As the Dutch Pensionary succinctly remarked on the failure of negotiations for a peace: 'The English are about to attack a mountain of gold, we a mountain of iron.'

To achieve both purposes a cruising ground in the North Sea suggested itself. But whereabouts? On April 21st the fleet weighed from the Gunfleet and stood over to the Dutch coast, hoping to intercept the Zeeland squadron before it could join the main body of the Dutch fleet then in the more northerly anchorage of the Texel. Nothing was sighted. The Duke then proposed going in close to the entrance to the Texel in the hope either of discouraging the Dutch by this confident show of force or of provoking them to come out and fight. Sandwich opposed this, arguing that a position well out to sea to the north-west would give a much better chance of intercepting the returning merchantmen and would still enable the fleet to fall on Kortenaer if he did decide to bring his ships out. He was outvoted at the Council of War and they spent two days close enough for Sandwich to make out with his telescope two Admirals and two Vice-Admirals among the abundance of ships' masts.

1. The court beauty whom the King ardently desired to make his mistress and even, some thought, his Queen. Her unexpected marriage to the Duke of Richmond certainly enraged him.
2. Ralph Davis *The Rise of the English Shipping Industry* (1962) p. 12.

His main reasons for opposing this disposition of forces was first the danger of exposing the fleet to the risk of violent weather so close to the banks and shoals of the enemy coast and second the obvious discouragement of a sortie by the Dutch fleet, whereas the sooner the battle was fought the better: 'since we are superior to them in force and stronger now than we are like to be hereafter, and shall shortly be necessitated to go off their coast to recruit water and beer'. This was professionalism, not over caution. Both Rupert and he supported the idea of forcing the Texel and attacking the Dutch at their moorings but 'both the enterprise and the circumstance of the Duke's person commanding the fleet make it of very great weight to determine, and therefore was left with us to ruminate further upon.'

In fact they sailed next day, May 1st, to the position Sandwich had originally suggested and three days later snapped up all eight merchantmen of a convoy whose escort got away through the fault of a commander keener to get his hands on a prize than to chase enemy warships. Intelligence suggested that the great body of returning ships of which this convoy formed part had already slipped into port and that nothing more of any value was to be expected until the Smyrna convoy, which was still sheltering in Cadiz, or the East India convoy due in June or July. The project of forcing the Texel was considered in detail and finally abandoned because the great ships all drew too much water for the entrance channels and only the fourth-rates could be reasonably certain of getting in. This difference between Dutch and English ship construction – 'Their ships being so much floatier than ours' as Pepys put it – dominated the tactics of fighting the Dutch on their own coast. It was therefore decided to send the main fleet into Harwich to store and revictual in readiness for a long campaign when the Dutch came out, leaving a squadron of fourth and fifth rates to watch their movements and report.

Hardly had the decision been taken when a storm blew up from the south-south-west, the very direction in which the course of the fleet would lie. When a day or two later the wind abated a further Council of War was called at which the decision was re-affirmed, against Sandwich's advice. A large fleet caught in a gale was always in danger of running aboard each other, especially at night, with consequent damage and loss of effectiveness. He also thought that, 'riding still at an anchor until we had a leading gale of wind homewards' they might surprise the Dutch who might well take advantage of the same wind to come out after the storm 'to pick up our straggling ships or small squadrons'. And there would be the battle that everyone wanted.

His guess was right. The Dutch did come out and found, not the English fleet ready and waiting, but a valuable English convoy from Hamburg freighted with much needed naval stores. The Dutch took the lot, escort and all.

News of the reverse and of the Dutch fleet being out and ready to seek battle reached England in the last week of May. The Duke took the fleet to sea and on the 31st called a Council of War at which Sandwich advanced his proposal for taking the merchantmen out of the line of battle to form a division of their own in the rear 'by which means our ships of force of the King's would have had their strength contracted into a lesser room (by near a league) than when they are intermixed with the merchant ships. They would have been much stronger to make an impression on the enemy in any part, or to resist any combined force of the enemy attempting us. They would have had no impediment by bad sailers. And the commanders of the King's ships more entire and resolved to aid one another than it is to be feared the others are.'

A Mathematick Admiral indeed. It would be hard to find as lucid and succinct a statement of the difficulties inherent in the new and promising method of fighting in line. The fact that abstracting twenty-four merchant ships would reduce the length of the line 'by near a league', that is, by nearly three miles, brings home how a fleet of a hundred ships would stretch over the horizon ahead and astern of its commander, assuming that such a number of vessels of, as Sandwich points out, unequal sailing qualities could ever be deployed in such a formation. To keep any control of the battle once action was joined was out of the question. Signalling was in its infancy and even if it had reached the stage to which Kempenfelt brought it more than a century later the smoke from the guns and from the attacks of the fireships would have rendered it at best uncertain and at worst useless. Hence the importance of Fighting and Sailing Instructions. And hence Sandwich's efforts to improve them. He notes that Lawson 'was for this the day before and others seemed to like it, but now nobody was forward to speak, and so agreed to continue our former order of battle'.

Next day Rupert reported the sighting of the Dutch by two ships scouting ahead, lowering and hoisting his ensign 'to make us take notice'. The Dutch were to windward 'had the weather gage of us' as the seamen put it which meant that they could choose when or whether to attack. For two days Obdam kept his distance, the English ships cleared for action. Why he did not use his advantage is an unsolved mystery. But early on June 3rd the wind changed 'a fine chasing gale. We had the weather gage of the enemy.' The Dutch, who never wanted fighting spirit, tacked to meet the English line led by Rupert's van division and the battle began about four o'clock in the morning. It lasted till eight at night and ended as Sandwich records in a glorious victory. The blowing up of Obdam's flagship and the mortal wounding of Kortenaer on whom the command devolved led to confusion disintegrating into rout. Sandwich, leading the pursuit, had his main topsail shot away and was overtaken by the Duke as darkness came on. By an act of incredible folly on the part of one of the courtiers aboard the *Charles* pretending to have the Duke's authority, sail was shortened and the Dutch escaped annihilation. Such an opportunity was never to recur.

Both Rupert and Sandwich had distinguished themselves in the hottest of the fight. Sandwich had engaged Obdam's flagship supported by a Dutch Indiaman of 75 guns and was having a rough time of it until the Duke's flagship and another vessel came to his aid. He says little of his own exploits but repeatedly and emphatically praises Rupert's courage. The humanity after victory for which Nelson so memorably prayed is shewn by his anger with a fireship commander who burnt two badly damaged ships that had already struck their colours. 'This cruel fact was much detested by us as not beseeming Christians.'

The English casualties, in the Battle off Lowestoft, though only about a twentieth of the Dutch, had not been light. Among the killed was Robert Sansum, the Rear-Admiral of Rupert's squadron. Rupert requested that the vacant flag be given to Robert Holmes, his companion in arms from the days of cavalry actions in the Civil War and their subsequent adventures with the Revolted Fleet. The Duke demurred and in the end gave it to his own flag captain, Harman, having first offered it to Sandwich's flag captain, Roger Cuttance, 'but he chose out of friendship to me to stay in this ship and obtained the Duke's leave to do so'. It is a telling instance of Sandwich's power of engaging the trust and affection of those who served with him, the more striking since Cuttance was one of the captains whose loyalty Sandwich had doubted on the eve of the Restoration.[1] Lawson though not killed in action died shortly after from a serious wound that had turned gangrenous. The veteran Royalist Earl of Marlborough, who was granted the status of a flag officer though not holding a flag appointment, was killed as a private captain in the Duke's squadron. Even the Duke himself had had a close call. Three courtiers standing beside him had been killed instantly by chain-shot. The brains of one had been dashed in the Duke's face, offering material for gallows humour about supplying his intellectual deficiencies. It also gave the King unanswerable grounds for forbidding his brother to take such risks with a still precarious succession.

Who then was to command the fleet in his place? Sandwich's claims had been reinforced by the skill and courage he had displayed in the battle, recognized in the warmest terms by the King himself in a letter written in his own hand. But Rupert too had done well and had served in the senior post. There was always the sensitive issue, unmentionable though it might be, of Cavalier and Roundhead. In the eyes of the House of Commons Clarendon and the Clarendonians such as Sandwich were unsound on this. Rupert was the cavalier *sans peur et sans reproche*. Neither the King nor the Duke liked him or, in their private circle, took him seriously. But to pass him over might disturb the none too steady equilib-rium of the régime. In the end they decided to offer both men the joint command.

Sandwich, accommodating as always, accepted. But Rupert refused, demanding instead that the fleet should be divided into two separate commands, one to be held by himself, the other by Sandwich. It is not clear why. He had accepted a similar proposal, which had not actually come into effect, the previous autumn. And his letter to Sandwich of October 19th already referred to expresses a readiness to serve with or under him. Was he annoyed with the Duke for passing over Holmes for Sansum's flag? Rupert was a proud man and the Duke was neither tactful nor discreet. Had Rupert heard of the mimicries and mockeries that William Coventry had witnessed and had subsequently reported to Pepys? His refusal is the more surprising when it is remembered that

1. *Diary* 11th April 1660.

he accepted the joint command with Monck, hardly so easy and agreeable a colleague, on exactly the same terms in the following year.

The result was that Sandwich was appointed Commander in Chief and Admiral of the Red at the beginning of July. Penn was to have the White and Allin the Blue. The temporary command of the sea obtained by the defeat of the main Dutch fleet opened two mouth-watering possibilities: the overpowering of de Ruyter's small squadron returning in a no doubt weakened state from its long absence in the Mediterranean and the unhealthy climate of West Africa and, even more desirable, the capture of the immensely rich Indiamen whose return could no longer be covered by their own fleet. It was a golden opportunity and no time was to be lost. Sandwich had only come ashore on June 18th and his flagship had not just to be victualled and stored but refitted after the battering she had taken. There were family matters to be attended to. The negotiation of a marriage between the Sandwiches' eldest daughter Jemima and Sir George Carteret's son Philip had reached the stage of signing the settlements. Lady Sandwich was unwell and had gone to Groombridge to take the waters at nearby Tunbridge. On July 2nd, the day after the King had given him the supreme command, he was called to her bedside, which suggests a serious alarm for someone so unself-regarding. The urgency of his orders permitted no more than the briefest visit. Penn had already taken his squadron to sea to cruise off the east end of the Dogger Bank and Sandwich, sailing on the 4th, joined him there on the 6th. Even then the fleet still lacked Allin's squadron, so intense had been the pressure on dockyards and resources, but it numbered a formidable sixty-nine vessels. Neither the Indiamen nor de Ruyter's squadron had yet got home. The prospects of success looked excellent.

A cloud no bigger than a man's hand might however be discerned in the last sentence of the fleet's instructions. There the eventuality of Dutch vessels taking refuge in Norwegian harbours (then part of the Kingdom of Denmark) was specified and the order given: 'if you find you are able to take or destroy them, or any considerable part of them within those harbours, you are not to neglect the opportunity of doing it'. The obvious tactic of rich, unprotected merchantmen making for Holland from northabout was to creep down the Norwegian coast and bolt into the nearest harbour for sanctuary if danger threatened. But our ambassador in Denmark had indicated the Danish King's readiness to break his agreements with Holland and allow his neutrality to be violated in exchange for a half share in the proceeds. It was this proposed collusion that no doubt inspired these instructions.

When Sandwich put to sea the plague whose ominous appearance Pepys had noticed in early June had begun to reach alarming proportions. The autumn session of Parliament was to open in Oxford and meanwhile the Court removed to Salisbury. On his way there Clarendon wrote from his house at Twickenham on July 26th a letter of the warmest friendship and encouragement:

> I will not begynne my journey towards Salisbury without first kissinge your handes and assureing you of my most faythfull service whilst I lyve. I pray to god with all my hearte for your good successe and that wee may meete agayne and both outlyve this devouringe warr and once more see our country settled in peace with all the world.
>
> '... I must congratulate you for my owne sake for the good Allyance you are now makinge with my frende the Vice-Chamberlain [Carteret, whose son Philip was to marry Sandwich's daughter Jemimah]. I have not two frends I am more concerned in and therefore I cannot but wish all imaginable happinesse to the young couple, who must be mutuall comfortes to you both; I shall add no more then to desyre you to lay any commands upon me you thinke me worthy of, and to assure yourselfe, that if I outlyve you, I will serve all who relate to you with the utmost care and diligence I can, and with all the affection I have professed to you, and in this I am sure I cannot fayle, beinge with my whole heart, my deare Lord, your Lp's most affect. faythfull servant.
>
> Clarendon C.[1]

Clarendon's horror of war, so rare in a statesman of the seventeenth century, and his deep sense of its danger, both to the régime he was trying to consolidate and to his friend who was going out to fight, breathe through every line.

Within a week of going to sea Sandwich had heard that some Dutch merchantmen had taken refuge in a south Norwegian port. But he was at first content to leave them there and wait for Allin's squadron to join

1. Carte MS 223 f. 279.

him in sweeping the North Sea for signs of de Ruyter or the Indiamen. Allin came up with him forty miles to the north-east of Flamborough Head on the 17th but as the wind continued southerly a fleet of Indiamen coming from the north would have offered an easily discovered prey as they hove to or tacked across the likely course of their pursuers. At a Council of War held a few days later it was agreed that they were far more likely to steal down the coast of Norway. This appreciation proved correct. Indeed had it been acted on a few days earlier it would have caught de Ruyter, whose twelve men of war and a few prizes would have stood no chance. But by a stroke of luck which the Dutch chose to interpret as direct divine intervention the two fleets missed each other by a couple of hundred miles and de Ruyter slipped into port early in August. The fleet of Indiamen following more or less the same route six days behind him were more cautious. Probably they had picked up some intelligence of the movements of the English. Anyway on July 29th ten of them took refuge in Bergen where a large number of Dutch merchantmen were already sheltering. These, as it happened, Sandwich had already decided to attack in accordance with his instructions and on the 30th he detached a powerful force of some twenty-two ships and two fire-ships under Teddiman.

The English had some difficulty in bringing so large a number of ships into the approach channels but Teddiman and part of his force entered the harbour in the early evening of August 1st when there was still plenty of light left to do the job. He found the Danish governor unexpectedly uncooperative. He had had, he claimed, no such orders as Teddiman had been led to believe. He insisted on delay till instructions should reach him from Copenhagen. The argument went on all night, enabling the Dutch, even with many of their men ashore dead drunk, to land cannon from their ships, to manoeuvre the vessels up to the narrows where a few ships moored in a close line could form a boom behind which the rest could shelter, and to reinforce with their own gunners the forts which protected the whole anchorage. By morning an already difficult situation had deteriorated so disastrously that Teddiman could delay no longer. He must either turn tail or fight under the most unpromising circumstances.

He chose the second and, after suffering severe punishment with no corresponding damage inflicted on the enemy, broke off action and

134

retired while his ships had still spars and cordage to enable them to do so. As so often brave men had paid in blood for the blunders of the clever. Sir Thomas Clifford,[1] the future architect of the Secret Treaty of Dover, was present as a volunteer and had taken the lead in the fruitless negotiations with the Danish governor. As the client of Arlington he had doubtless had a hand in devising the policy that had backfired and it is characteristic of his courage that he should have exposed himself to its risks. Among other volunteers were the court poet and wit, Lord Rochester and Sandwich's son Sydney, both of whom survived. Edward Mountagu, the son of Sandwich's cousin Lord Mountagu of Boughton, was killed. 'Were poore Ned Mountagu to be lost' wrote Clarendon in another affectionate letter written from Salisbury on August 28th 'I am gladd the circumstances of it were much to his advantage. I do not meane his dyinge a Romanist if that be soe, that is reported.'[2]

The Bergen fiasco seems clearly attributable to the instructions Sandwich was given and to the shoddy execution of the shoddy diplomacy that lay behind them. But Commanders in Chief have to await the passage of time before the stains left by political interference or mismanagement

1. Much the best account of the backing and filling on the part of the Danish governor and of the difficulties thus presented to the English admiral is to be found in Cyril Hughes Hartmann *Clifford of the Cabal* (1937), which is based on the very full report Clifford himself wrote aboard Teddiman's flagship on the voyage home. Clifford's relations with Teddiman and Sandwich were excellent. He testifies to Sandwich's thoroughness in making preparations for the attack (pp. 79–80):
'The service tis true was looked upon as very difficult by my Lord Sandwich and the whole Council of flag officers, but the probability of the Danish assistance counterpoised the danger and ill accesse to the place. I did never in my life see greater care and industry taken in any affaire than his excellency tooke in informing himselfe of the difficulties of the place. There was scarce a pilott in the fleet that his Lordship could heare had ever bin att Bergen but that he sent for him and discussed the matter over with him, and for a whole weekes time the Map of this place and the discourse and questioning upon it was his whole entertainement, which could not but produce good councells and resolves, and the execution of them hath bin performed with as much good conduct as could have bin expected . . .'
It seems clear that from the start the idea of honour among thieves played no part in Danish calculations. Still less had they any motive for pulling England's chestnuts out of the fire.
The account given in my text is telescoped almost to the point of economy with truth. The affair is completely elucidated by Hartmann, supported by a reading of R.C. Anderson's introduction to Sandwich's journal for naval detail.
2. *ibid.*, f. 287 On Edward Mountagu's secret Romanism see below p. 203.

fade from their reputation. Sandwich had not only to contend with the malice of those at home who were jealous of his previous successes but with the practical responsibility of protecting his badly mauled squadron without letting any more Dutch ships evade his search. The weather did not help. After detaching Teddiman's squadron the fleet had been carried steadily northward by the violent southerly gales. Provisions, especially beer and water, were running short. It would be easy to find oneself too far to the north to work back into any effective position. Sailing ships, especially the great men-of-war, were labour-intensive: they were also very unhealthy: crowding, poor diet, the want of dry quarters or clean clothes always led to serious outbreaks of disease. To sail a ship and fight an enemy depended on human energy: and human energy required proper food and drink. Sandwich therefore took the fleet into the anchorage of Bressay Sound in the Shetlands before it was driven any further. Shetland was, he found, 'a very barren country. Not one tree of any sort in all the island nor any sort of game, landfowl or beasts, except a few conies. The fruits of the island not ½ enough to feed the people of the island the year round.' But at least there was water – of a sort: 'for condition very badd, being such as draines from the topps of hills, through turffs, which collours the watters redd and is very unwholesome for our men to drinke, though it serves turnes to boyle withall'.[1]

It was as he was coming out of Bressay on August 13th that he heard of Teddiman's defeat and of the Dutch being out once again under the inspiring leadership of de Ruyter. This time luck was on the English side. De Ruyter missed Teddiman's battered ships by a few miles. On the 18th Sandwich met them at the rendezvous off Flamborough Head. On the 21st the whole fleet was safe in Southwold Bay, landing the sick and wounded and pressing for men and provisions. A week later they sailed again for their old cruising ground between the Dogger Bank and the Texel.

The northerly gale that kept them from their intended station proved a stroke of good fortune. On September 3rd just south of the Dogger they sighted half-a-dozen Dutch ships to leeward and after a chase of

1. Rawl. MS 468 printed in Colenbrander *Bescheiden* . . . (The Hague) (1919) i, 259.

several hours took them in the evening, two very rich Indiamen escorted by four warships. De Ruyter's fleet was once again not far away and the two admirals missed each other by a narrow margin. Sandwich kept his prizes with him for greater security. He knew that though the great part of the returning merchantmen were now safe in their home ports there were still a good number who had been separated by weather and might still be picked up. He therefore chose a cruising station as close to the Dutch coast as he dared, not fearing the irruption of the enemy so much as a westerly gale driving his deep-riding ships into the dangerous shallows. His judgment proved right. On the 9th 'At break of day we saw 15 sail of Hollanders ahead to leeward and chased them, and about 9 oclock in the morning took of them 4 men of war, one of 70 guns, the other 3 of 40 guns and upwards; in them 931 prisoners, two West Indiamen and 5 or 6 other flyboats and vessels . . .'

As the English stood off with their prizes on a westerly course they encountered some thirty men-of-war under de Ruyter's Vice-Admiral. Some fire was exchanged but it was late in the day. 'We did not think reasonable to tack after these and engage them, because the night was all misty and thick weather, and besides chasing them would have drawn us too near a lee shore, and if we had tacked in the night endangered a huge separation of our fleet.'

It was a rich haul. To stay out longer would risk the fleet and its prizes for at the best trivial gains. As it was the weather turned very violent. Sandwich sent his frigates to the anchorage of Hosely Bay on the Suffolk coast, taking the prizes and the great ships, the first and second rates, into the mouth of the Thames. He dropped anchor at the Nore about sunset on September 13th concluding his journal with the words 'And I do not hear of any ship of the fleet or prizes missing. Deo Gratias.' He had much to give thanks for. But storms of which he had no inkling were brewing far inland from the familiar waters of the Channel and the North Sea.

XIII

Recriminations

ALTHOUGH SANDWICH CLOSED HIS JOURNAL once he had dropped anchor at the Nore he did not, as one might expect after all those months at sea, step thankfully ashore to enjoy the fresh delicious smells of early autumn after the stink of a ship in which several hundred men had been cooped up in insanitary conditions. He was still Commander in Chief and regular intelligence from Holland – the packet boats ran throughout the first summer of the war and our ambassador remained in residence – told him that the Dutch fleet had not paid off and come in for the winter. Not that he was able to go out against them with any expectation of success. The fleet that he had brought in was badly knocked about by having been so long at sea in bad weather. They had had no beer for three weeks and had been on reduced rations of dry provisions for longer than that. The fleet had not been properly stored and manned when it was hurried out in July. It was to this that he attributed the miscarriages of the summer campaign, when he came to write his report a few weeks later. The ships had been

> . . . very badly furnished with victualls, liquor, yet worse wanting
> 2500 men of what these ships had in the last engagement; some
> shipps, boats and men left ashore for hast of getting out, most of
> which defects would have been in some considerable measure
> cured, if the fleete had stayed but one entire day or twoe in Sould
> Bay, supplys of provisions being but at Harwich, and the instruc-
> tions though they did direct losse of noe time, yett it was tempred
> with takeing along such shipps as were in condicion of sayling . . .
> which God knows very many shipps then in the fleete were not,

and a short stay in Sould Bay would allsoe have had the good effect of makeing an entire fleete (Sir Thomas Allen coming in thither the very next day, as I take it), and the shipps refitted at Harwich might easily have beene gotten thither also, which indigent and disunited condicion of the fleete is necessary to bee noted, being the root whereunto in all probability may bee assigned the missing de Ruyter in his returne, and surpriseing the Dutch East India shipps in the open sea before they had put themselves into any port of Norway.[1]

The instructions, drafted by William Coventry, had left too little to the discretion of the Commander in Chief. The golden rule 'Tell the man on the spot what you want him to do and leave him to work out the best means of doing it' has too often been disregarded by over zealous ministers and bureaucrats. Sandwich had learned about logistics from one of the great masters of maritime strategy and tactics. The Duke of York, chafing at the denial of active command, and his secretary Coventry, jealous of Sandwich's high standing with the King and the Chancellor, were the last men to give him a free hand and the first to criticize and to play down such success as he might achieve. His own imprudence and carelessness in financial affairs gave them everything they needed.

When at the end of that long summer of disappointments and frustrations Sandwich had taken his rich prizes, Pepys and his colleagues on the Navy Board had gone wild with joy. A few days earlier they had been in the deepest dejection. Pepys had lain awake a whole night 'full of melancholy thoughts':

> The fleet came home with shame to require great deal of money, which is not to be had – to discharge many men, that must get the plague then or continue at greater charge on shipboard. Nothing done by them to encourage the Parliament to give money – nor the Kingdom able to spare any money if they would, at this time of the plague. So that as things look at present, the whole state must come to Ruine.

Now at last the war was paying a dividend. Not the huge wealth that Bergen might have yielded if only the Danes had kept their nerve and not tried to double-cross their partners in crime: their half-share, it was

1. Colenbrander, i, 251–2. Rawl. MS A 468.

agreed, would have extinguished the Danish national debt and left plenty over: but the prizes still afforded a comfortable sum which would at least permit the ships required for sea service to be victualled and, perhaps, some of the seamen to be paid.

The procedure to be followed when a prize was taken was well established. The seamen who took her were entitled to grab whatever they found lying between decks, that is the personal property of those they had captured. But on no account were they to break open the holds and rummage the cargo, 'breaking bulk' as it was termed. As soon as the prize crew brought the ship into port she was to be handed over to the Prize Commissioners who, after she had been condemned as lawful prize, would be responsible for selling, and accounting for the whole value of, both ship and cargo. The proceeds would then be divided, after suitable deductions, between the admirals, captains, officers and men who could lay claim to a share.

Most unwisely Sandwich had sanctioned an immediate partial share-out among the flag officers including himself. It was characteristic of his too easy-going ways as his long-suffering wife could have testified. That it was not mere avarice is clear from his assigning part of his share to Pepys and Brouncker on very generous terms when on September 18th they sailed down to the Nore in the Navy Board yacht to congratulate him. By then neither he nor they had any notion of what was in store. Indeed only two days earlier the King had written a letter, in his own hand, a rare and uncongenial exertion, from Ashley's house at Wimborne St Giles congratulating Sandwich on his handling of the fleet in general and, in particular, approving his conduct in breaking off the pursuit of the Dutch squadron when night and the proximity of the enemy coast might have exposed his ships to unacceptable risks.[1]

The marked approval of the King, the jubilation of the Navy Board, the lip-smacking of the flag officers as they contemplated the enjoyment of the fruits of their labours no doubt combined to relax the vigilance required of high responsibilities. On September 21st Sandwich signed an order for a preliminary distribution of prize goods amongst himself and his colleagues, apparently at the solicitation of Penn, his Vice-Admiral, who, according to Sandwich, assured him 'that the King and

1. Mapperton MSS. Letters to Ministers i, ff 42–5.

Duke of York intended him a perticular favour'.[1] Feeling uneasily that he might have exceeded his authority he wrote to Carteret, who was with the court at Oxford preparing for the assembly of Parliament, asking him to inform the King and Duke of what he had done. On the 28th Carteret replied in the most reassuring terms. His action was entirely understood and would be underwritten. Unfortunately to gain the Duke's approval he had had to show the letter to William Coventry who had remarked, ominously: 'Heere my Lord Sandwich has done what I durst not have done.' Although everything was going to be all right Carteret indicated that it would be prudent to restrain his admirals from actually selling the goods until he had the King's authorization in writing.[2]

This eminently sensible advice was disregarded. Before long rumours were flying round the city of fabulously profitable bargains to be obtained in silks, spices, china and all the most expensive luxury goods of the East India trade. Albemarle, always jealous and resentful of Sandwich's apparently effortless rise in a few years to positions that it had taken him a lifetime to win, heard, enquired and acted. The customs authorities were empowered to seize the goods and legal proceedings, it was clear, would follow against all those involved. Pepys, more alert than his master, instantly sensed danger. He wrote at once to warn him and began to make his own plans for getting out of the business as quick as he could.

As a nobleman, as a prominent public figure, Sandwich was too stately in style, too proud of his position as active head of a great fighting service to imitate the ignominious agility of his clever young cousin. He determined to bluff it out:

> The King hath confirmed it, and given me order to distribute these very proportions to the flag-officers, so that you are to own the possession of them with confidence; and if anybody have taken security from them upon seizure, remand the security in my name, and return their answer. Carry it high; and own nothing of baseness or dishonour, but rather intimate that I know who have done me indignities. Thank my Lord Brouncker and Sir John Minnes for civilities and tell them I expect no less in reality, for I have befriended them; and that I shall very ungratefully hear of news of base examinations, upon any action of mine.[3]

1. Colenbrander, i. 266.
2. Mapperton MSS. Letters to Ministers i, 51.
3. Penn *Memorials of Sir William Penn* ii, 365.

The King was indeed as good as his word and issued a written authorization of Sandwich's action. But unfortunately it was post-dated: and
what might have slipped by as a minor anticipation of official sanction
had been blown up into a cause célèbre to which all the failures and
missed opportunities of the war at sea were to be attributed. The gradual
development of the Prize Goods Scandal helped Sandwich's enemies to
identify two entirely separate issues at his expense. It was not until the
first week in October that he realized that he must mend his fences at
court and appear in person at Oxford. Before leaving he called a Council
of War to examine the state of readiness for sea of the ships under his
command and to decide in the light of these reports what further action
was possible. The conclusion was easily foreseen though the extent of
the still unremedied deficiencies was hardly imaginable. Only four ships
of the line were fit for sea. To risk an encounter with the Dutch in
such puny numbers was suicidal. The Council with Sandwich's entire
concurrence recommended the laying up of the great ships to fit them
for the following year.

Whoever was responsible for this appalling state of affairs it could
hardly be the Commander in Chief. Rather the finger might be pointed
at the Lord High Admiral, the Navy Board, or, above all, the government
which had blithely taken on the foremost maritime power in Europe
without a single ally of its own and the strong probability, now amounting
to a virtual certainty, that France would also be ranged against us. Political misjudgment on such a scale was bound to lead to humiliation. The
brilliant success of the fleet in the Battle off Lowestoft, in which Sandwich had played so notable a part, might if it had been properly exploited
have turned the unequal tables. But the mismanagement of that victory
compounded by the mismanagement of the situation it had created had
dissipated the advantage. Now the reality of the country's danger was
brought home by the presence in mid-October of a Dutch fleet off the
mouth of the Thames. And where was the English Commander-in-
Chief? In Oxford, defending his own conduct against a chorus of skilfully
orchestrated criticism. The embarrassing fact that he had no fleet to
take to sea could be easily concealed behind the personal invective for
which the age deployed such talents.

Coventry and the Duke of York behaved throughout as though they
disposed of perfectly adequate forces. On September 27th, a fortnight

Undated drawing, bearing the legend 'L.ᵈ Sandwitch Sʳ Peter Lilly fecit'.
The ascription is rejected by Sir Oliver Millar who is also sceptical
of the identification of the sitter

Above: The earliest Lely portrait; dated on stylistic grounds about 1649-1650

Opposite, above: Lady Sandwich, probably painted at about the same time, artist unknown
below: Sandwich as one of Cromwell's Generals-at-Sea *c.*1657, certainly painted by Lely

Edward J. E. of Sandwich.

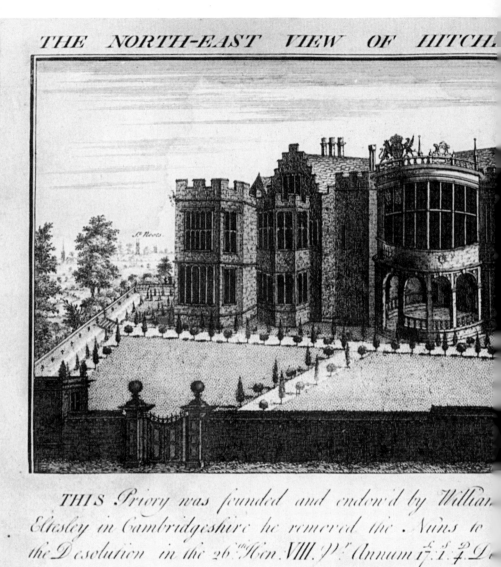

THIS Priory was founded and endow'd by William Eltisley in Cambridgeshire he removed the Nuns to the Desolution in the 26th Hen. VIII. Pr Annum 17.1.4 D

Hinchingbrooke: the Buck engraving, made half a century after Sandwich's death, gives a good idea of the house and gardens after his improvements.

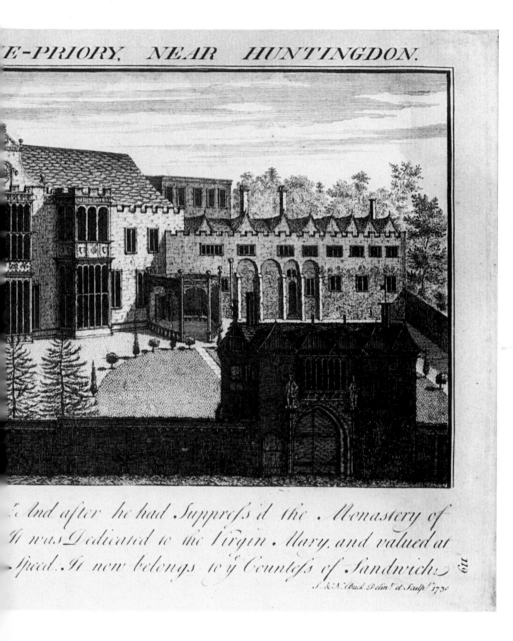

And after he had Suppress'd the Monastery of
It was Dedicated to the Virgin Mary, and valued at
Speed. It now belongs to y Countess of Sandwich.

S. & N. Buck Delin.t et Sculp.t 1730

Edward 5 E. of Sandwich.

Above: The portrait painted by Feliciano in Lisbon in 1668 to celebrate the signing of the peace between Portugal and Spain. The sitter describes it in his journal and judges it 'an extraordinary like Picture'.

Opposite: Sandwich in his Garter robes, by Lely, *c.*1670

Solebay. The tapestries now in the Royal Collection executed from drawings by
Van de Velde. The first shows the two fleets just before action was joined,
the Dutch coming on in line abreast and the English trying to scramble into
line ahead, with many of their ships masking each other. The second shows the
battle in the afternoon. The blazing wreck to the left is the *Royal James*.

after Sandwich had brought his storm-beaten, half-starved fleet into the Nore, Coventry wrote him a long letter from Oxford proposing the mounting of two expeditions both of which demanded substantial – and in fact non-existent – resources: the first the sending of a squadron under Sir Christopher Myngs to Guinea to reverse de Ruyter's conquests and the second the despatch of a strong force of frigates to the Straits. But all this, he conceded, must be left to Sandwich's discretion as the Dutch were reported to be still out.[1] When the Dutch were off the approaches to the Thames the Duke wrote to Penn, who as Vice-Admiral was in command during Sandwich's absence in Oxford, urging that a strong force of frigates should be sent out to draw them off. The real state of the country's defences was better stated on October 21st by the Governor of Deal Castle in a letter to Sandwich reporting the withdrawal of the Dutch who had been cruising off the Goodwins and had even entered Margate Roads 'Terrified by fower old Hony-combd gunns, which everytime they were shott of more endangered the gunners than them'.[2] It was in fact a succession of violent storms that scattered them and left them, weakened by sickness, thankful to be able to limp into their harbours for the winter. When Sandwich who had hurried back to the Nore in the last week of October managed to get together a squadron to send out under Harman[3] on November 4th there was no sign of them.

Their departure left the field free for the development of the offensive against Sandwich. Coventry unmasked his guns by moving in the Commons that the breaking of bulk aboard a prize should be made a felony. Soon there was talk of an impeachment. Sandwich was roused to anger, even to an uncharacteristic bitterness. He considered the Duke ungrateful for the loyalty and service rendered: he was understandably furious with Coventry not only for the overt malice of his present activities but for his past misrepresentation of the great part Sandwich had played in gaining the victory off Lowestoft. He even thought that Clarendon, on whose friendship he had entirely relied, had not done him justice in his speech at the opening of Parliament in which, naturally, he had defended the Government's record in the conduct of the war which was certain

1. Mapperton MSS. Letters to Ministers i, 49–50.
2. Carte MS 223 f. 293.
3. Its composition is listed in Carte MS 223 f. 295.

to be attacked. Pepys ventured to differ: 'I told him that I and the world do take my Lord Chancellor, in his speech the other day, to have said as much as could be wished.' This judgment was to be vindicated, though neither was to live to read it, by the account given in Clarendon's auto-biography, which enlarges with convincing circumstantiality on the passionate resentment felt by the Duke of York at Sandwich's having presumed to usurp his own privileges as Lord High Admiral and having compounded the offence by applying through Carteret to the King, and not to him, for pardon.

Carteret's long suit was loyalty to colleagues when the hiss of the world was against them. His staunchness to the King and to Clarendon when all had seemed lost long ago in Jersey could never be forgotten. Sandwich was glad to have bound the two families together by marriage, not the less perhaps because, as he told Pepys, it intensified the antagon-ism of William Coventry who disliked Carteret. Both families, like the Clarendons, founded their manners and morals on deep domestic affec-tion. In August while Sandwich was still at sea his wife had written to tell him that their eldest son Ned had caught the small-pox at the Carter-ets but could not be in better hands. 'She is a discreet woman and a most true and faithfull friend to us. She is a very good woman. I have more and more opinyon of her the longer I know her ... She liveth very handsomely and all things caried on with so much quietnes to wonder. I wish I could in some degree fallow her.'[1]

Two decidedly unClarendonian figures who proved unexpectedly friendly were Prince Rupert and Arlington. Rupert perhaps had a fellow feeling for a professional fighting leader whose achievements had been denied their proper recognition. Why, one wonders again, had he refused the joint command he was now on the point of accepting with Albemarle? At any rate Sandwich left Pepys in no doubt. 'That Prince Rupert and he are all possible friends in the world.' About Arlington he was equally emphatic. 'That my Lord Arlington is his fast friend.' Indeed it was from this that he deduced Clarendon's coldness towards him, a false deduction as Pepys rightly thought, confirmed a month later by Carteret's reporting Clarendon's own words to him. 'By [God], I will not forsake my Lord of Sandwich.'[2] But by far the most important ally was the King.

1. Carte MS 74 f. 354.
2. *Diary* 25th October and 27th November 1665.

Sandwich was probably right in guessing that the staunchness of this far from rocklike figure proceeded at least in part from irritation with his brother who, we know from Clarendon, was vehement against Sandwich. The Duke of York's hyperactive stupidity was a constant hazard in the difficult business of stabilizing an unsure régime. He had also, according to Sandwich, chosen this moment to compete with the King for the favours of the leading court beauty, la belle Stuart, whose brother Walter was to be a member of Sandwich's ambassadorial retinue. Doubtless there were other considerations. Though loyalty was not a principle with the King (witness his subsequent treatment of Clarendon) he was too shrewd not to appreciate its value in the market of politics. 'I shall not forsake my friends, as my father did.' Probably, too, he saw what a capable and trustworthy servant Sandwich was. Probably, too, he liked him. Certainly we know from Clarendon's autobiography that Charles had been annoyed by Sandwich's carelessness in not obtaining permission before instead of after breaking the rules, which makes his support a clear act of policy whatever its foundations.

Sandwich hauled down his flag on November 21st. He had already made up his mind, in consultation with Pepys, not to solicit further appointment in the sea service. He was still not clear of the consequences of the Prize Goods affair although the bill for making it felony to break bulk was not proceeded with in the Commons and the disapproval of the King, Clarendon and Arlington made an impeachment less likely. But the political outlook was deeply unsettled. The plague, the mismanagement of the war and the threatening attitude of France put the country at risks that an angry House of Commons was not going to accept. The leadership required to secure Parliamentary co-operation was conspicuous by its absence. 'That nothing at Court is minded but faction and pleasure, and nothing intended of general good to the Kingdom by anybody heartily, so that he believes, with me, in a little time confusion will certainly come over all the nation.' Thus Pepys and Sandwich on October 25th. It was, surely, a natural and rational assessment. It was only five years since constitutions had been changing in England with a volatility that astonished our neighbours. With more than three centuries of hindsight we observe that the outward forms were there to stay: but the premonition that there were to be radical changes both in the distribution of power and in the tone and character of the principal institutions was to be justified in the near if not the immediate future.

In this uncertainty prudence required Sandwich's presence at the centre of things, which in November 1665 was still Oxford. The Parliamentary session had ended on October 31st but the plague was still raging in London and Clarendon, suffering agonies from the gout, was confined to his bed at Cornbury, his Oxfordshire estate. With France about to come into the war on the Dutch side it was imperative to effect a *rapprochement* with Spain. Cromwell's unprovoked attack on Hispaniola which had resulted in the less valuable acquisition of Jamaica was still fiercely resented in Madrid. Even worse was the alliance, cemented by marriage, between England and Portugal, with whom Spain had been at war for a quarter of a century. Nothing but the common threat presented by the growing and aggressive power of France could have reconciled such profound and recent antagonisms. But Spain had so much else at stake and had so little hope of withstanding the French that she had no choice. Secret talks had led to a draft treaty and then in September, just when the Government was preparing to meet Parliament at Oxford, Philip IV chose that moment to die, leaving a gravely handicapped infant son and an empty-headed widow as Regent. The possibilities of mischief were increased by the too evident inadequacy of our ambassador, Clarendon's old friend the amiable Sir Richard Fanshawe, whom we last saw as ambassador in Lisbon. His recall had already been decided on before this latest turn of events. Whoever relieved him must combine high standing, a thorough knowledge of military and naval realities and, preferably, a sympathetic understanding of the policy that underlay the acquisition of, and investment in, Tangier. Above all, though he must possess sufficient initiative to seize an opportunity he must not be an adventurer or an amateur who would take it on himself to solve difficulties by exceeding his instructions as Fanshawe had done. In Sandwich all these qualities were united, together with a well-informed interest, unusual in a nobleman, in overseas trade and economic affairs generally. That he was personally congenial to the King, Clarendon his chief minister and Arlington the Secretary of State was an added recommendation. And his prolonged absence abroad would both spike the guns of those who wanted to pillory him over the Prize Goods and postpone indefinitely the threatened parliamentary inquiry into the conduct of the war at sea which could hardly take place without him. A fortunate, if trivial, coincidence was his sudden passion for the guitar 'which he now commends above all Musique in the world, because it is bass enough for a single voice, and is so portable, and manageable without much trouble'.

Pepys heard of the appointment from Albemarle early in December and was overjoyed. But there was still much to be settled before Sandwich eventually took ship at the beginning of March. His instructions were not drafted till late in February when the full extent of Fanshawe's folly had been revealed to his incredulous government. Early in December he had signed a treaty with Spain which not only conceded a number of points to which no English government could agree but – horror of horrors – was drawn up in Spanish and not Latin, the accepted language of the documents of European diplomacy. Such abject deference to another power was unthinkable. The Council refused to ratify the treaty. The new ambassador, charged to renounce what his predecessor had just signed, was not going to be met with smiling faces and a warm welcome.

That, at any rate, would be a challenge. What was deeply dispiriting was that the Prize Goods affair, which might have been assumed to have lapsed in the blaze of so signal a display of favour, still rumbled on. Albemarle, the Duke and William Coventry took care to keep it stirring. Pepys urged his patron to obtain a comprehensive pardon under the Great Seal. In January a pardon was offered under the Privy Seal but in such inadequate terms that Sandwich indignantly refused to accept. They were duly amended but it was humiliating to have had to ask. The sense that his services had not been properly recognized, that his friends in high places were not as friendly as they professed themselves, weighed him down. The Madrid appointment which had seemed so splendid began to lose a little of its lustre. Perhaps as he kept his Christmas at Hinchingbrooke he felt as Pepys did in his summary of the year:

> The great evil of this year, and the only one endeed, is the fall of my Lord of Sandwich, whose mistake about the Prizes hath undone him, I believe, as to interest at Court; though sent (for a little palliateing it) Imbassador into Spayne, which he is now fitting himself for. But the Duke of Albemarle goes with the Prince to sea this next year, and my Lord very meanly spoken of; and endeed, his miscarriage about the prize-goods is not to be excused, to suffer

a company of rogues to go away with ten times as much as himself, and the blame of all to be deservedly laid upon him.

One severe penalty of the new post was that once again it meant separation from wife and family and absence from a home in which he took such pleasure. No one seems to have thought of Lady Sandwich accompanying him. There were so many young children to be looked after and Lady Sandwich was a careful and unselfish mother. Foreign travel, especially in Spain, was apt to be a hit or miss business, even for the grandest. Clarendon's account in his letters to his wife of going ambassador to Madrid in 1650 sounds like a qualifying round for some endurance award.

The elder children needed a parent to supervise the all-important arrangement of a suitable marriage. The Carteret alliance was only the first move in the game. Ned, the eldest son, Viscount Hinchingbrooke, had returned from his very grand Grand Tour (he had been received by Louis XIV) in August and had, as we have seen, caught the small-pox while staying with the Carterets. Carteret himself had revived negotiations which Sandwich had initiated two years earlier for the hand of Miss Mallett, the richest heiress of her day. Her trustees had then rejected Sandwich's bid, but this time it seems to have been the lady herself who thought Ned too insipid. She certainly obtained all the colour she could require in a bridegroom by bestowing herself on the poet Rochester, who confessed to Bishop Burnet on his deathbed that for great tracts of his life he had never been entirely sober. It was Carteret who in the end found an excellent partner for this agreeable if unexciting young nobleman in Lady Anne Boyle, daughter of the Earl of Burlington. This reinforced the Clarendonian connection. The Chancellor's second son Laurence had married her sister and the Earl's brother, Roger, now Earl of Orrery, had been the Lord Broghill with whom Sandwich had been associated in Cromwell's intimate circle. Indeed Sandwich had told Pepys how much he missed Orrery's friendly influence at Court (he was once more back in Ireland) when the Prize Goods business erupted.[1]

Sydney, the second son, was once again to accompany his father. He was much the more intellectual and lively of the two and if he could survive a long campaign at sea he had nothing to fear from the rigours

1. *Diary* 17th November 1665.

of travel in Spain. Some of his shipmates were to accompany him in his father's household, notably John Werden and Walter Stewart. Werden (often spelled Worden) had served as a volunteer aboard Sandwich's flagship. Sandwich had evidently formed a high opinion of his aptitude for diplomacy as he sent him to Copenhagen in July 1665 to confirm Sir Gilbert Talbot's supposed agreement with the King of Denmark.[1]

Of the affairs to be settled before departure the Wardrobe would have to be left, as it largely had been, to be run by the Deputy Master, whose efforts to extract money due from the Treasury rarely yielded more than 'a peece of paper stuft with nasty Language, nothing to the purpose'.[2] One of Sandwich's early letters from Madrid to his son Ned urged him to interest himself in these accounts '. . . wherein you doubt anything you may safely advise with Mr Vice-Chamberlain [Carteret] . . . To see ye account speedily past in ye Exchequer follow it hard and have no patience till it be done . . . Account this affaire of great importance to your and my safety as well as Profitt and therefore you cannot take paines in a thing or more moment and besides give you a handsome introduction sometymes to be known to the King.'[3]

The other great matter was to prepare his defence against any future inquiry into his conduct of the campaign of that summer and autumn. This he did in close cooperation with Pepys, in whose hand the report is written.[4] Since it is based on his journal most of the points made require little comment. Two concerning the Bergen affair are fresh: first the specific statement that the King and Duke had told him that he might expect the help of the King of Denmark and second that the stakes justified the gamble:

'But that the adventure may not appeare foolish neither: wee were ledd thereunto by the vast consequences of our successe therein, in all probability to have given an unsupportable blow to the Hollanders, all theire East and some West India shipps being lodged therein, together with theire rich shipps from Smyrna, Spaine, Portugall, the Bay of Biscay.

1. *Journal* 248. Some of the drawings in the Spanish volumes of the Journal are by him. For his subsequent career see D.N.B.
2. Harris, i, 257.
3. Carte MS 223 f. 133.
4. Rawl. MS A468.

I am apt to believe scarce at any time in one place soe great a mass of wealth was ever heaped together.'

Perhaps the most illuminating general reflection is on the technique of command:

> The method of useing councells of warr in all weighty millitary affaires I have ever seene in my time, and taken it to be the constant practice of generalls, and the best and wisest proceedings, many persons of experience and fidelity being likelier to conclude the best then one; and I have found it in most if not all instructions to commanders in cheife (when the oppertunity admitts the assembling the councell of warr) a command to use theire advice upon emergencies which happen in all humaine affaires; and perticuler instructions can bee but lame, and prescribe the scope of a designe only, but noe man can serve well that does not vary the particuler steps as circumstances arise; but I acknowlidge the authority and shelter of a councell of warr hath never swayed mee to one action wherein theire reason had not prevayled upon my understanding first . . .

There is a boldness and largeness of mind about this that Nelson would have approved. No wonder that Sandwich wrote sharply to Clarendon and his own cousin Manchester to protest at the continued pettifogging delays and arrests of his goods to which the Prize Commissioners and local customs officers at Lynn were still subjecting him.[1] The beautifying and enriching of Hinchingbrooke was never far from his thoughts, little time though he was given to enjoy the place. 'The garden here,' Lady Sandwich had written to him that August '[is] very hansom, much beyond what I could expect. My Lady Pickering [Sandwich's sister] saies she doth extraordinary like it, the walkhouses and garden houses are very fine and to the walls very hansom. The lower part doth exceeding well. There is every day company in the Bowling Aley of the better sort of our Nebours . . .'[2]

Hardly a post was to pass between England and Madrid without their writing to each other.

1. Carte MS 75 f. 422 29th December 1665.
2. Carte MS 74 f. 354.

XIV

The Spanish Experience

WHEN SANDWICH SET OUT for Madrid with secretaries, gentlemen, a chaplain, cooks, footmen, a master of the horse, pages and whatnot he was not dependent on this imposing entourage for the weight that he carried as the representative of his country. Reputation, the word itself, and the concept it expressed, was by common consent of the great powers, the cornerstone of effective diplomacy. Few of his contemporaries could rival him in the elements of experience, achievement and social standing out of which this quality was compounded. He had commanded a regiment in the New Model Army, that famous body whose veterans were among the best soldiers at the disposal of Portugal in her long frontier war with Spain. He had for several years been a member of Cromwell's Council and subsequently that of Charles II. He was well versed in public finance and foreign trade. He had commanded the fleet in the greatest naval war in which his country had ever been engaged and had given proof of his outstanding skill and courage in the fiercely fought battle off Lowestoft. He was a nobleman who added to the expected acquirements of his rank an unusual taste and curiosity, indeed an intellectual distinction that made his Fellowship of the Royal Society no mere honorific title. He sounds like some senatorial figure whose long and distinguished record has raised him above the clamour and the ignominies of conflict. Yet he was only forty, the father of a young family, constantly embarrassed for money (largely, it must be admitted, through his own carelessness), open to fresh impressions, responsive not marmoreal.

From the beginning it is evident that he embraced his appointment as a means of widening his knowledge and perceptions of the human condition and recognized, rightly, the negotiations with which he had been charged as a long and difficult campaign in which the tactics of attrition by boredom must not be allowed to wear him down. Just as he had, when chosen to assist Blake, spared no pains to make himself into an expert seaman and navigator, he observed and analysed the manoeuvres and purposes of the personalities in the Spanish government with whom he had to deal and was never too proud to learn from his fellow diplomats, even from the representatives of such tiny states as Lucca or Mantua, both of whom supported a permanent mission to Madrid. He mastered his instructions, no easy task when the feebleness and faction of Charles II's government led to frequent inconsistencies and occasional outright contradictions, and laboured, not always successfully, to establish swift and secure communications with the Secretary of State.

The years of Sandwich's embassy are the period at which we can see him clearest because he kept, largely in his own elegant hand, a journal on a scale that dwarfs all his other productions of the kind. It is not, like his cousin's immortal diary, intentionally self-revelatory. He was not, so far as one can see, interested in his own psychology. He appears to have thought himself a rational man acting from rational motives which therefore require no examination or elucidation. What he was interested in, passionately interested in, was other people and their way of doing things. Sometimes this led him to speculate as to what they thought, but not often and not far. His curiosity was admirably defined

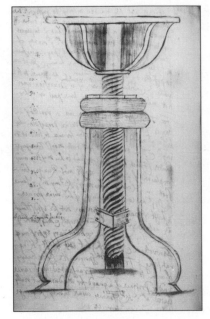

A lampstand for ladies (see p. 153)

by the motto of the Royal Society: *nullius in verba*. Accurate description and mensuration is the keynote of the journal. In the long treatment of

The *canfonilla*, the instrument played by Gallegan street-musicians

the preparation and consumption of chocolate every aspect of the subject, social, sexual, digestive, is carefully considered and the kitchen utensils employed are drawn and measured. So is furniture such as the simple leather armchair common in Madrid. A lampstand for the use of ladies is sketched and its height – about eighteen inches – given, with the note that its shortness is explained by the female custom of sitting on cushions on the floor. The theatre at Madrid seats a total of 2132 persons but the men and the women sit in separate parts of the auditorium, except in the boxes where they are allowed to mix: but even here it is expected that they should belong to the same family. The Spaniards are very fond of dancing and move most elegantly, making frequent use of castanets to emphasize the rhythms. Sometimes it is an all male performance, sometimes men and women together, but in either case they avoid bodily contact. An extreme example of this inhibition was cited by the Duke of Medina de las Torres from the treaty negotiations at Fuentarabia in 1659:

He said when ye K. Philip 4° came first into sight of ye Reyna Madre of France his sister, she accordinge to ye accustomed freedome used in France made Hast towards her Brother (whom of many yeares she had not seen) with her armes spread to embrace him, but when she came neere, He putt his hand to her Breast and shoved her off whereat she was in greate Coller and swore oaths to her selfe, but at last, asked ye K's pardon for that of many yeares she had been used to customes of other Countrys and overjoyed to see him, had made her exceede ye fashions of Spayn in expressinge her gladnesse.[1]

All this and much, much more is described in the spirit of an anthropologist, a scientific observer, rather than that of a man chiefly concerned with politics and war. Even when he records a practice of repulsive cruelty, such as the putting out the eyes of beggar children so that they can earn their living as blind street musicians, he may flinch at the inhumanity but he rarely passes any kind of moral judgment. Similarly in describing religious observances or beliefs which clearly seemed to him superstitious, or allegedly miraculous phenomena which he perceived to be fraudulent, he does not colour his account with the vivid denunciatory language so characteristic of his age. There is a coolness of temper, a courtesy of mind, that transcends his mental environment. The same liberation from the barriers of the past is expressed in the very orthography of the journal. He punctuates, as few other seventeenth-century writers do, in a manner that would present few difficulties to a modern compositor. He uses colons and semi-colons: he even uses decimals.

Thus it is that in the two and a half years' absence in Spain and latterly in Portugal and Tangier we are brought closer to him than at any other period of his life. We see, in detail, how his mind worked and what his tastes were: even, to a lesser degree, what he thought and felt. What is most obvious about him is what a good messmate he was. Living at close quarters with people one might not have chosen for congruity of taste or charm of personality is an art for which, in England at any rate, the services are still the best school. Sandwich, unlike the general run of noblemen in great place, is never haughty, contemptuous or dismissive. He could not write, as even so warm-blooded and unaristocratic a figure as Clarendon did, of 'dirty people with no name'. He was not a snob, though, like Cromwell, he accepted without question the stratification of the society he knew, and amused, or perhaps shocked, Pepys

1. Mapperton MSS. J. iii f 84 22nd October 1666.

by saying that he would rather his daughters were to die than to marry into the City. He was clearly on the easiest and friendliest terms with his staff and took an interest in his servants, recording their mishaps and their qualities. He observes the Spaniards with whom he dealt, from the Grandees in high office to the more shadowy and shifty persons from whom intelligence might be obtained, with the same interested curiosity, the same readiness to listen.

'But I, as I am in all things, curious . . .' His cousin's phrase might equally be applied to him. Even perhaps more pertinently, for Sandwich was minutely observant of things which Pepys did not much notice. He took regular observations of the movement of the heavenly bodies and sent them back to Pepys's colleague, Lord Brouncker, the President of the Royal Society. He was deeply interested in all forms of agronomy and set down all the information he could acquire about crops, yields and methods of production as well as systems of land tenure. Industry and commerce were of course of overriding interest and lent themselves more readily to statistical analysis. Everything to do with the armed forces was sought out with a professional eye and ear. And as the inheritor of a famous house which he was extending and embellishing he was keenly interested in the fittings and adornments of the mansions owned by a richer, more magnificent aristocracy than that of England. Such things were scrutinized and recorded with an exactitude of measurement and drawing for a craftsman to copy.

The breadth of inquiry would nowadays incur the deprecation of dilettantism. Yet everything Sandwich did he did in a thorough and seamanlike fashion. John Evelyn's copy of the great Spanish work on agriculture, first published in 1513 and still reprinted and used in the nineteenth century, Herrera's *Obra de Agricultura* bears his inscription 'Given me by my Lord Sandwich at his returne from his Amassaye out of Spaine, afterwards unhappily perishing in the last war with the Dutch, his ship set on fire.'[1] It was with Evelyn as the leading member of the Georgical Committee of the Royal Society that Sandwich corresponded about the gardens and villas that he described in his journals, supplying 'draughts of places, fountaines and engines for ye irrigation and refresh-

1. Now in the British Library. I owe this and most of what immediately follows to Marjorie Grice-Hutchinson. 'Some Spanish contributions to the Early History of the Royal Society' *Notes and Records of the Royal Society* 42, no. 2 (1988).

ing of their plantations'. It was to Evelyn that he described the *sembrador*, or drill-plough invented by a Carinthian gentleman, an anticipation of that constructed by Jethro Tull in the next century. Sandwich brought one back and exhibited it at Gresham College in 1670. But perhaps the most remarkable scientific achievement of his embassy was the translation of a highly technical work on metallurgy written by a man who had been a parish priest in Potosi, the great silver-mining town in Peru and published in Spain in 1640. Sandwich's translation *The Art of Metals* was published in 1670. In this as in his astronomical and mechanical interests he shared the acquirements of Don Juan, Philip IV's illegitimate son, whose military and political reputation made him, in Sandwich's time, a potential rival to the unimpressive circle of grandees and favourites whose bickerings and intrigues passed for the policy of a great European power. They enjoyed, too, a common skill in music, both playing on the bass and the treble viol. In September 1667 at the Buen Retiro, that echoing monument to the ruined aspirations of Olivares from which, as its historians have written, Don Juan made 'his sporadic, curiously indecisive bid for power',[1] they played two suites by William Lawes, followed by 'short light Ayres composed in Flanders'. 'He playes (and will have others doe so) very soft' noted the ambassador, 'loves light ayres best and goes still forward on, never playes ye same thing twice.'

To us, as no doubt to Sandwich himself, the musical, artistic, social, scientific incidents to his mission are much more interesting than the mission itself. Nothing is deader than dead diplomatic history. The one step forward, two steps back of a negotiation, artificially prolonged as one or other party sees, or thinks it sees, a further point to be gained, lose what halting life they once had when the results have been known and taken for granted for three hundred years. In the present case an exception might be made for the vivid, unusual treatment of Sir Keith Feiling's *British Foreign Policy 1660–1672*. What scholarship of a high order can do to make dry bones live is done there.

Essentially Sandwich's mission was to renew the Anglo-Spanish commercial treaty which had been made void by Cromwell's declaration of war and the retention by Charles II's government of the usurper's conquests of Jamaica and Dunkirk (now sold to Spain's arch-enemy). This

1. J.H. Elliott and Jonathan Brown *A Palace for a King* (1980) p. 239.

was complicated by Fanshawe's botched endeavours which the English government refused to ratify and by the Anglo-Portuguese marriage which outraged Spanish claims to sovereignty over Portugal and her overseas possessions. It was therefore absolutely necessary that Spain should be made to accept the existence of the Kingdom of Portugal and to conclude the thirty years war of which both countries were heartily sick with a treaty made 'de Rey a Rey', a phrase which Sandwich must have heard echoing in sleep. There were a number of subsidiary objectives: the gaining of at least a limited admission to the jealously guarded trade of the Indies: the return of the treasures of Charles I's collections purchased at their dispersal by the Commonwealth: the support, perhaps the co-operation, of Spain against the Barbary corsairs and, in the same cause, the cessation of Spanish assistance to the warlike Moorish leaders who made Tangier such a precarious and expensive possession. All these objectives were to be seen, only too starkly, in the context of England's dangerous isolation in a war against Holland and France.

Sandwich embarked at Spithead at the beginning of March 1666. Among his ample retinue were his son Sydney and the man who was to be the right hand of his embassy, William Godolphin. Godolphin, a scion of the great Cornish Royalist family whose members rose to prominence in the age of the last Stuarts, was a particular protégé of Arlington's. He shared with his patron an early academic distinction at Christ Church, Oxford, soon followed by a successful posting at Madrid, where he was ultimately to succeed Sandwich as ambassador. Like Arlington, too, he was to end his career under the cloud of allegiance, in his case at last openly avowed, to the Roman Catholic Church. Sandwich and Godolphin clearly liked and trusted each other from the start, a fact which certainly fortified the good relations already existing between the ambassador and the Secretary of State.

The voyage revived Sandwich's professionalism as a sea officer. He made his own pilotage chart of the Bay of Corunna. He encouraged a member of his suite, John Werden who was later to become Secretary to the Duke of York by whose recommendation he had entered Sandwich's service in the summer of 1665, to make drawings of Cape Ortegal and its offshore rocks. Preparations for their reception by the Spanish authorities were dilatory and inadequate to the point of discourtesy. While they were still at anchor in the bay a sailor who had been Sandwich's coxswain

Coruña, the English squadron

in the *Prince* died suddenly in the night. He had been perfectly well the day before and had spoken to his old commander on deck but was 'said to have putt himself into a great feaver with Brandy and to have had blowes on his head'. Not the least of the hazards of going to sea was the wild intemperance of the seamen.

At last on March 17th, nearly a week after they had dropped anchor in the bay, they went ashore, after some heart-searching whether the 'country Quinto' offered was consonant 'with the respect and dignity requisite'. Sandwich was the least pompous of men, chatting, as we have seen, with a petty officer who had served with him. But he recognized that personal style must give place to the character of the King's representative. The accommodation was, in fact, poor. 'Beds few and bad.' But the provision of fish and flesh and, especially, the wine of Aribadavia was excellent.

Inadequate as their accommodation was, the arrangements for the journey to Madrid were non-existent. Werden was sent ahead to obtain the necessary documentation and the still more necessary pack animals and whatever might be provided in the way of coaches or litters. After a month he returned with the necessary passes and the promise of two mules and a coach for the ambassador himself but nothing for his retinue or his goods. At least a hundred mules would be needed. Who was going to pay for them? By diplomatic custom the host should conduct an ambassador to the quarters assigned him. Sandwich was faced with the first of an interminable series of questions in which the demands of status and those of getting on with the job seemed irreconcilable. He protested. 'The opinion my Master and other ministers in England . . . might have that I did overtamely receive ye dishonor and inconvenience I resolved to resent it.' But having made his point he made his prep-arations. On April 27th he set out for Madrid and covered eight miles before nightfall.

The first part of the journey was through very difficult, stony, moun-tainous country. Its poverty was appalling: 'My Goods and servants lay in ye open ayre . . . a very barren country, mountainous and heath with short furrs and very rarely a patch sowed with corn.' Even at their slow pace the scene changed quickly. On the 29th they were in Lugo, a walled town 'most pleasantly situate . . . fertile country for 7 or 8 miles round'. It was celebrated as the only town in Galicia never to fall into the hands of the Moors 'and for this reason they keepe ye Holy Sacrament alwaies exposed in a Glasse offertory upon ye High Altar beleeving by ye vertue of yt ye Towne was soe preserved (they shift ye wafer every 8 dayes to prevent corruption)'. The parenthetical note is as characteristic as the absence of censorious Protestantism, shocked at these manifestations of Papist superstition. The miracle of a pendulum that was set in motion during the celebration of mass by the ringing of a bell in the steeple he found susceptible of a natural explanation. But he does here allow himself a comment: 'It seemes to mee a light thing that god should worke a miracle at any time ye priest pleases to Gratify ye curiosity of Spectators.'

From Lugo they began to climb the range of hills that divide Galicia from Leon, a road of narrow and dangerous precipices, over which carriages and mules sometimes fell '. . . some of ye Trunkes tumbled a furlong without stopp and one mule laden with Trunkes tumbled over 7 or 8 tymes together and yet had noe hurt considerable but beinge helped up againe proceeded with her load'. Sandwich noted, and drew, the thatched beehive houses without chimneys or windows: he even drew a device for keeping 'ye oleo pott out of harmes way . . . that ye dogg and catt cannot gett in theire heads to lique ye oleo'. The practical man and the statistician were not numbed by the 'mighty high mountaines on either side of us Terrible with Craggy and loose rockes'.

By May 4th they had emerged from the mountains into 'a delicate plaine countrey full of pleasant cornefields.' At 'Mancanares (soe called from ye number of Apple Trees, which yet wee would thinke very few to deserve to denominate ye place) we dined under a Tree in ye high way by a spring syde.' They received much hospitality from ecclesiastics: sweetmeats and snowed wine from a convent of nuns; 'partridges, henns, bacon and kidds' from the Bishop of Astorga, a decrepit walled town with a great castle falling into decay. 'It looks like a Custard on ye outside, not one house being suffered to be built, without ye walls.' The Cathedral however was very splendid 'very fine iron work painted and gilded and very fine musicians in ye Quire'.

A few miles further on the harsh conditions he had experienced in crossing the mountains took their toll. He was laid up with a fever for four or five days. When he 'adventured though not with much health to goe forward' he was rewarded by the highway 'all growinge with camomile and tomilio and tyme, which gave an excellent smell and vineyards all along'. The wine of Balderes, their next post 'is ye best in all these parts, a deepe red and of excellent body and tast'. By now they were covering well over twenty miles a day. It was a prosperous country, the houses built of clay bricks dried in the sun, many of them containing very good rooms. At Rio Seco he lay in a great nobleman's palace, conducted to it by the magistrates 'with ye Hoy boyes before them (as theire custome is)'. The town thrived on importing baize and cloth from England and Holland via Bilbao and distributing it all over Spain.

On May 11th he reached Valladolid 'a most noble Cittye, seated in a bottome by ye Brave and pleasant river Pisurgus . . . and planted with most pleasant Trees all alonge even unto ye waters edge, a pleasanter view I have never seene'. He was met by the Corregidor with three coaches and shewn over the great palace built by the Duke of Lerma, which Philip II had bought and adorned with magnificent pictures, most of which had now been removed to Madrid. Sandwich was most impressed by the Tiltyard and by 'a roome built on purpose for Comedies, 53 yards long, 17 broad, 9 high, wherein King Charles ye 1st of England was entertained'. The ecclesiastical establishment, which included the fabulously rich Convent of San Pablo, numbered 20 Nunneries, 60 Friaries, 3 Hospitals and 14 Parish Churches besides 'chappells and hermitages many'.

But the real attraction was the King's Garden. '24 box borders and 5 fountaines, 4 in ye angles and one in the middle.' These were fed by a water-tower twenty feet high which Sandwich drew together with a diagram of 'ye Ingenio which raises the water from the river' (see p. 162). The remains of the picture collection were also on show here: 'One Titian rarely good, 5 or 6 Bassanos and other fine thinges of unknowne handes. Out of this garden King Charles ye 1st of England carried away 2 statues as bigg as ye life of Cain killinge Abell.' Valladolid might easily have been preferred to Madrid as the capital city. It contained thirty houses belonging to Grandees of Spain. Its only faint shortcoming was that though surrounded by vineyards its wine was, as Sandwich politely put it, 'not to be praised'.

Two days' travel, much of it through great pine forests, brought him to the seat of his opposite number, 'the Conde de Molina, now Spanish ambassador in London'. His two great houses were all but derelict 'made use of for shearing of sheep whereof he makes a great revenue'. His wool was reputed the best in Spain and was exported through Bilbao for the English and Dutch markets and through Alicante for Venice. Soon the road began to climb the Guadaramas 'very stonny and troublesome, the countrey round about Hideous with scraggy mountaines of stone, though not very high'. On May 17th he caught his first view of the Escorial and of Madrid about twelve miles away. Next day he was officially welcomed by Fanshawe and Southwell, his Lisbon colleague, at the royal palace of El Pardo. From there the Master of Ceremonies, Don Alonso Antonio de Paz, conducted him with an abundance of coaches the six miles into the city. A 'very noble house' belonging to the Marquis of Colares had been prepared for him, together with another very good one for his train. The total distance from Corunna, he noted, amounted to 354 miles.

Sandwich's first two days of business were devoted to discussion with Fanshawe and Southwell, who was equally concerned in clearing up the

Irrigation of the royal gardens at Valladolid (see p. 160)

confusion into which the kindly but hopelessly unbusinesslike Fanshawe had plunged England's relations with both Spain and Portugal. Although the home government had decided on Fanshawe's recall even before Sandwich was offered the post of Ambassador Extraordinary – which in itself permitted the hope that the ambassador resident would be allowed to remain – it had not warned him of this. Embarrassingly for both parties Sandwich had been entrusted with his letter of revocation. While he was still in Corunna one of his staff, Sir Charles Harbord, had been approached by Fanshawe's nephew Lionel for enlightenment on this sensitive point. No answer had been sent. But as soon as Sandwich set out on his journey to Madrid he received a direct enquiry from Fanshawe himself. He wanted to know because his wife was about to set out for England and if he were to be recalled he would keep her with him and thus 'make his returne more cheape and comfortable'. Sandwich gave no official answer but his prevarication could hardly have encouraged false hopes. Now he delivered the King's letter in which the crushing blow was softened by some kind words from his royal master.

Fanshawe, true to form, took his disappointment like a gentleman. His wife, equally true to form, took it like a Fury. The venom that she was to spit at the name of Sandwich even long after he had been killed in action was not for an instant concealed. It is almost justified by her husband's nobility and generosity of spirit. Although overwhelmed with debt and disappointed now of the enormous sum that the Spanish government had promised him (and which he ought never to have contemplated accepting) he gave his successor and the whole diplomatic world 'a noble Treate and collation' to celebrate the King's birthday on May 29th. Almost immediately afterwards he took to his bed with a fever, no doubt brought on by the winter journey to and from Lisbon. It was soon evident that he would not recover. The Queen Regent, much under the influence of her confessor, a tactless Austrian who had begun life as a cavalry officer, sent two Dukes to convert him to the True Faith. Lady Fanshawe indignantly repulsed them. The dying man seems to have indicated to his chaplain that he would like to take leave of his successor. Sandwich gives a moving account of their interview:

> I found him in a Dieing condition, as soone as he saw mee he lifted his hands upwards 2 or 3 tymes (havinge not spoke of an houre before) to signify he was goinge to heaven and then strivinge to speake said this was ye end of this world and said I submitt, I submitt . . .

Apparently the missionary Dukes returned to the charge as Lady Fanshawe stepped in from the adjoining room to protest. Sandwich took his leave and later that night Sir Richard died.

The new ambassador honoured his memory by showing his widow, in the teeth of her scurrilities, that chivalry which her husband had made his rule of life. He purchased her coach and horses and such furniture as she wished to be rid of. He arranged an escort for her journey and for a frigate to meet her and her husband's embalmed body at Bilbao. She left Madrid on June 28th by which time Sandwich was already deep in his new duties.

XV

Ambassador at Madrid

To a man as observant as Sandwich his new station offered a wide field. Apart from the customs and character of the Spaniards which never ceased to interest him, apart too from the everyday phenomena of life in the warm climate of southern Europe, there was the diplomatic dimension. The kind of business and the way in which it was done were both very different from anything he had experienced, even in appointments such as those to the Sound or at Dunkirk under the Protectorate, or to Lisbon and Tangier and the Barbary ports under Charles II. In all those cases, although he had diplomatic responsibilities, he derived them from his command of a formidable fighting force. '*Ultima ratio regum*', the slogan that Louis XIV embossed on his guns, defined his position in those contexts. He had lived, or at any rate had been based, in his own flagship. He had not been beholden, in small things or large, to the power to whom he was accredited.

In the world of diplomacy proper every act, every detail of ordinary life, seemed susceptible of interpretation as a claim to, or denial of, status. Most obviously was this to be seen in the arrangements made to receive an ambassador. Those at Corunna had been inadequate almost to the point of insult: those at Madrid appeared to promise better things. It was the convention that the host power provided accommodation and entertainment for a strictly limited number of days, after which the ambassador fended for himself. The scale and extent of this welcoming hospitality, like the farewell present (usually a jewel but sometimes plate or even cash) was closely scrutinized and jealously compared with that offered to one's predecessors or colleagues. Sandwich's entertainment by the Queen of Spain ended with supper on May 28th 'which was indeed very handsome, but ye allowance viz. 7000 reals vellon per diem large enough to have afforded better'. Vellon was the debased coinage, of varying value, which, like the inflated currencies of our day, needed up-to-the-minute reference to an agreed standard, usually the gold coins long familiar as pieces of eight. In this case Sandwich calculated that at 17 reals vellon to a piece of eight the actual value was 411.764 pieces. His journal is full of tables for making such calculations, varying from region to region as well as from date to date, for which he sometimes but not always gives the source. Money necessarily provided the yardstick against which hospitality and leaving presents or other ceremonial gifts were instantly measured. Sandwich clearly felt at home with such calculations as with every purely mathematical operation.

The other ubiquitous indicator of diplomatic standing, which had to be read with the care with which a gardener or a sportsman now watches a barometer, was where and how a visitor was received or sent on his way. On June 22nd 'I went to visite ye Conde de Castriglio (Presidente de Castile) a very old man who putt himself upon his bed to receive mee, because immediately representing ye King's person he gives ye chaire to none – neither doth he revisite . . .' Sandwich had to decide whether or not this was acceptable: clearly he was not sure: 'Nevertheless I did think it was fittinge to doe it at this tyme . . . the Queen ruling by consent of a Junto whereof this Earle was ye Chiefe and also Cheife in ye Council of State and ye principall man in point of faction and dependances as well as place and a great enimy of ye Duque of Medinaes (in which one respect it was for mee to sweeten him that he might not in ye English businesse oppose only to thwart ye other) . . . and to salve ye other punctilios I suppose ye age of ye man pretext sufficient for him to receive mee in his bed.' Ruminating afterwards he remembered that Clarendon as Lord Chancellor never returned visits to any minister. He was still further fortified by a member of his staff discovering a precedent: when Clarendon and Cottington as ambassadors of the exiled Charles II visited Castrillio in 1650 they 'gave him ye place'.

'Salving ye punctilios' and yet not compromising the objectives of his mission by insisting on the status due to the representative of the King of England – how were they to be reconciled? It was, as Sandwich must have known in his heart, to square the circle. Either way his enemies

Drawing (and valuation) of the jewel presented by the Queen Regent to Godolphin in December 1667 on the ratification of the Anglo-Spanish Treaty. The portrait in the centre is that of her son, Charles II

could find means to disparage him. But a man who had fought it out yard arm to yard arm with Obdam was not going to lose any sleep over what the Duke of Buckingham or William Coventry might be going to say.

The last of the perpetual hazards of diplomatic life, still as sensitive a topic in the twentieth as it was in the seventeenth century, was immunity. The area immediately surrounding the embassy was in the phrase of the day, within the barriers. But how valid were they? Did they afford refuge and asylum to Spanish subjects and foreigners or only to the ambassador's train? And was any such right proof against the arbitrary authority that the government so easily resorted to? Was it proof against the Inquisition? Here again it was not so much a matter of establishing a clear line of demarcation but of judging how far in any given situation it was politic to go. Pilotage, not navigation, was the necessary art.

A great part of a diplomat's time, then as now, was occupied by exchanging civilities and, if possible, information with other members of the *corps diplomatique*. Fanshawe had supplied him with a complete list, in Latin, of all those resident in Madrid. It seems to have been a great freemasonry. All of them had a common interest in resisting the high-handed interference and not infrequent extortion of the civil and ecclesi-astical authorities. All of them found the government to which they were accredited dilatory and ineffective to the point of imbecility. All of them were professionally interested in international affairs and all of them loved gossip. So strong was the fellow-feeling that both the Dutch and the French ambassadors sent Sandwich warm though necessarily un-official messages of welcome and looked forward to the day when the ending of hostilities with England would enable them to enjoy each other's company.

But though conversations with intelligent and well-informed col-leagues might seem more rewarding than the mixture of ceremony and prevarication that passed for the transaction of business in the highest circles of Spanish government it was there, and there only, that he could bring his mission to a successful conclusion. To take the measure of the men most likely to support or oppose him in the Junto – the small committee properly entitled the Junta de Inglaterra established to con-duct negotiations with him – and the Council of State – the more formal body that advised the Crown on large issues of policy – was therefore essential.

The statesman generally considered most favourably inclined towards friendship with England, the Duke of Medina de las Torres, had been pushed to the sidelines the previous autumn on the death of Philip IV. None the less it was to call on him in the great palace, built by his kinsman and patron Olivares, the Buen Retiro, that Fanshawe took Sandwich and Godolphin on May 25th, within a few days of their arrival. The Duke was very civil and gave them the news that the French fleet commanded by the Duke of Beaufort 'was gone by for ye English channel to joyne with ye Dutch'. It was similar intelligence, reported from other sources, that led the government of Charles II to detach a large part of the English fleet under Rupert to watch Beaufort's movements, and thus to open the way to Monck's fighting the Dutch on disastrously unequal terms, the so-called Battle of the Four Days which raged from June 1st to the 4th. Sandwich of course knew nothing of the division of the fleet or of the reasons for it. A brilliant new study[1] suggests very strongly that it was the fear that Beaufort would embark troops from a French Atlantic port for a descent on Ireland, and only secondarily the prevention of his reinforcing de Ruyter, that prompted this much-criticized decision. Sandwich noted the information, which seemed to be confirmed by an intercepted despatch of Beaufort's which he saw three days later, in which Beaufort expressed the intention of making for Belleisle to await advice 'of how he will joyne with ye Dutch, makinge noe question to curb the Pride of these Islanders'. The addition of an inexperienced French force of uncertain quality to a Dutch fleet always handicapped by bitter personal feuds and inveterate provincial rivalry probably did not seem to him so very terrible.

In any case the Duke and he seem at once to have established good relations which on the whole they continued to enjoy throughout Sandwich's mission. They met frequently, often at the Buen Retiro of whose gardens and pleasure houses Sandwich made a number of sketches and scale drawings. He records the presence there of camels as beasts of burden: 'their Load ordinarily 60 arrobas [i.e. 15 cwt.] and more many tymes ... They are kept with less charge than a horse and eate less.' Their only disadvantage for general use was that they themselves were considered good eating by the population at large and could not just be turned out and left.

The Duke's protégé and diplomatic man of business, variously called Don Patricio d'Omuledi or Sir Patrick Muledi, was in almost daily contact with the ambassador who describes him as

> An Irishman borne (of no splendid extraction that I have heard of), educated at a Jesuit college in Germany, attached to the Duke ... who sent him to London with £50,000 to bribe the ministers: generally believed that he embezzled it and bought himself a house

1. Frank L. Fox *A Distant Storm: The Four Days Battle of 1666* (1994).

Draught of view from the Portugal Lodge at the Buen Retiro by Sir Charles
Harbord with Sandwich's legend, and below, a watercolour of the Portugal Lodge

and land near Tunnbridge in Kent ... the Conde de Molina [Spanish ambassador in London] had written over that ye ministers of England had received none of ye money (and Truly I beleeve none had for the King at his [Muledi's] first coming over gave us warning at ye Junto that such a sum was come over, and declared his severe displeasure that anybody should receive a penny of it.

My Lord Chancellor and my Lord Arlington gave commission. when I came that ye matter should be examined to ye bottom in Spayn and ye scandall cleered ... that nothing was placed among ye English ministers. But I have heard indeed that Mr O'neale,[1] Groom of ye Bedchamber, did receive 4 or 5000 li of it and that his lady since his death paid it backe).

The Spanish authorities at once instituted an inquiry on his return but Muledi, in a double defence that would have won the admiration of the Artful Dodger, refused to compromise the people he paid it to by saying who they were and claimed that in so far as he had committed an offence it came under the jurisdiction of the King of England.

Six months later Sandwich was given an itemized account of Muledi's expenditures while resident in England. These amounted to 53,000 pieces of eight, including lavish presents to Lady Castlemaine as well as ministers and secretaries. The wife of the Speaker received a Flanders cabinet. Muledi later denied this and presented Sandwich with a more modest account.[2] Sandwich's original informant was his own ex-prisoner from Cromwellian days, the Marquis de Baides, now grown to man's estate. Baides clearly thought Muledi a rogue and estimated that he had spent '200,000 pieces of eight on his last stay in England which was not above 4 months'. He had called on Sandwich within a week of his arrival, the first Spanish nobleman unconnected with the government to do so, and supplied him with a valuable, because independent, assessment of the men with whom he would have to deal. He did not think much of Medina de las Torres.[3] Later, on November 23rd, he gave Sandwich a graphic account of his abject behaviour when confronted with evidence of his having taken bribes, weeping before the Queen and her confessor.

1. Daniel O'Neale or O'Neile, one of the companions of Charles II's exile.
2. The list (in Spanish) is preserved in the Journal iii ff. 365–9. Muledi's figures are to be found *ibid.* f. 810.
3. For a modern assessment of this figure see R.A. Stradling *Historical Journal* 19, I (1976) pp. 1–31.

Peñaranda, the most effective member of the Junto, was Medina de las Torres' sworn enemy. Sandwich had been warned against him as a pensioner of France: but his inclination towards France probably had its origins in his conviction, shared by many Spaniards, that the Austrian Habsburg connexion was malignant to the true interests of his country. This put him at odds with the Queen's confessor and chief confidant, Nithard the Austrian ex-cornet of horse, who aimed at and soon achieved the succession to the office of Inquisitor-General, a position of extraordinary wealth and power. Peñaranda and Sandwich clearly got on from the start, a start which with all the Spaniards, even with Medina de las Torres, the consistent advocate for twenty years past of an entente with England, was a sticky one. The chorus of disapproval at the non-ratification of Fanshawe's treaty amounted at times to a direct accusation of bad faith. Peñaranda thus appeared the more open and upright in a government where dissimulation was the chief art of politics. As it happened the mere course of events drove him towards Sandwich. By the end of the year the evidence of French aggression was incontrovertible. Peñaranda found himself constantly trying to lure the English ambassador into a full-blooded alliance against France, pointing out to him more than once Queen Elizabeth's determination to prevent the Netherlands passing under hostile control and even quoting Camden's *Annals* in his support.

But for the first few months Peñaranda and Medina de las Torres united in exploiting what seemed to them a position of moral superiority. England had broken faith: England was virtually bankrupted by a war which she was, even in her own estimation, now not likely to win: England's restored monarchy was, according to the Spanish ambassador's reports, slumping disastrously in public favour. Now was the moment to turn the screw and force her to abandon her championship of the Kingdom of Portugal, which was not a kingdom but a fief of the Spanish crown. Until that point was conceded there would be no hope of a Commercial Treaty, let alone access to supplies of Campeche wood or the markets of Spanish America.

Sandwich met these high assertions with courteous obduracy. His instructions did not permit him to give way either on the renegotiation of the Commercial Treaty or on the recognition of Portugal as an independent kingdom. He had, indeed, little to offer. He was not prepared to discuss the surrender of Tangier, an extension of English sea power deeply disturbing to Spain. He was not going to return the Cromwellian conquest of Jamaica, unless he received a tempting cash offer. A sum was mentioned by way of a feeler but dismissed with the contempt it deserved. Perhaps the Spaniards were more insulted at having lost it than anxious to have it back. For the moment there was nothing for the ambassador to do but learn his way about the government to which he was accredited so that when an initiative became possible he would know how to make the most of it. For the rest there was the whole of Spanish life to learn about, there was intelligence of every kind, particularly economic, naval and military to be obtained. There were interests and individuals to protect in the proper enjoyment of their rights and there was a regular correspondence with Tangier, that early and precarious experiment in Crown colonization, on which the ambassador was briefed to report once he had achieved the objectives set him in Madrid. And of course there were the stellar observations to be made for the Royal Society.

Although diplomatically there was nothing to be done, that did not mean that an infinity of time could not be spent doing it. A junto consisting of Peñaranda, the Confessor and Medina de las Torres (here given his grander title of Duke of San Lucar) had been appointed to treat with Sandwich as early as June 9th and it was rare for more than two days to pass without a message or a meeting with one or other of its members, endlessly repeating the same points which the ambassador patiently recorded, usually in his own hand. On the 20th he was officially received at Court. He gives a charming sketch of the little King whose terrible physical afflictions, the consequence of Habsburg inbreeding, have been more generally remarked:

> He is a very fine child about 4 yeares of age. The multitude of company in ye roome discomposed him that he cried and said que se vayan, que se vayan Todos. [Make them go away, make them all go away.]

The sudden touch of nature is the more poignant in the middle of the stifling formality. A further refinement of this is recorded in a visit paid a fortnight later to the Cardinal of Aragon. Sandwich hesitated over the punctilios of place and hand conferred 'by his spirituality . . . ye religion of England havinge no dependance on Rome'. But he was also Archbishop of Toledo and a member both of the Council of State and of the Junto. 'He received me very civilly, tooke ye uppermost chaire but pulled it alonge towards ye doore. I did myne ye like; when I went out of ye doore he gave me ye right hand and I presently shifted to ye other side of him at ye stairs he went down 2 or 3 stepps and I would not stirr till he came up againe.' It sounds like a music-hall turn. They might be there yet.

Fortunately the aridities of diplomatic life were not all that Madrid had to offer. '3 or 4 days before Ashwednesday all ye people are full of liberty and extravagance, throwing eggs at one another in ye streetes and women of ye best quality and virtue walking up and down ye streetes abusing people but being tapada [masked] and nobody must take notice . . . in private conversation free to an excesse . . . among ye reste they suffer ye men to thrust small caraway comfitts downe their breasts and backs in great quantity and springle one another with squirts of sweete water.' The abandoned behaviour of Carnival time was, one gathers, the outward sign of a sexual licentiousness that Sandwich noted without moral censure or sympathetic approval.

> The General Vice of Spaine is unchastnesse to which ye climate disposes very much and also very longe custom. I have been told that K.Ph.4° askinge his favorite Olivares (The Conde Duke) if it were true that soe many of ye weomen of Madrid were whores as he had heard reported. Thereunto ye Conde Duke replied all of them were whores except two viz: ye Queene because she could not for want of opportunity and his owne wife who was soe old that she was past it.

His observations of the relations between the sexes are generally more subtle, as for instance in his story of the lover courting his mistress at the window, a favourite and characteristic Spanish form of amour, who, hearing that she was to be let blood had his own blood let in sympathy and died as a result.

Like his cousin in London he observed and enjoyed street life. Great ladies pay all their visits in chairs 'and ye man that carries ye foremost goes uncovered but ye Hindmost covered'. On March 1st, the Feast of St Angel, that is the Guardian Angel of everybody, the whole world goes abroad in coaches. On the Segovian bridge there is a traffic jam of six or seven hundred coaches that is not cleared till ten at night.

The other great *concours d'elegance* was on St Ann's Day, July 16th, 'which is ye last day of ye publique passeo in ye river, where there were many coaches to-day, 500 or 600 or more.' The Manzanares, though most of its bed was dry and firm enough for this spectacle, still provided enough water for some very restricted bathing:

> . . . about 11 o'clock after ye sunn had well warmed the water and there was noe ayre and I had a tent pitched in ye water to keepe mee from ye sunn. The water . . . runns swift but very shallow, not usually above ancle deepe . . . And ye water runns triclinge in little veins through ye sand, soe that ye river shews like ye highway about Theobalds (in England) where ye water runns triclinge alonge ye Gravell so that when we bath wee are feine to digg a place deepe enough to cover ones body. An houre before I went into ye water I used to drinke Choccolatti and as soone as ever I came out of ye water (wherein I stayed ½ an houre or an houre) I Drunke some allicant wine or other good strong wine of ye Countrey and eate a Biscotch or two with it and an houre after I went to dinner.
>
> The Temper of ye water was very pleasant, not cold but fresh at first steppinge in and after seemed warme.
>
> They hold it necessary to putt ones head often under water to refresh it and keepe ye vapors from flieinge thither.

It was in the middle of this month of July that he moved to the house that the Fanshawes had occupied, the Siete Chimeneas (the seven chimneys). The house and garden were a continual pleasure. He admired the doors and hinges and made scale drawings of them (see opposite), no doubt with a view to improvements at Hinchingbrooke (in this connexion his log of outgoing letters shows that he wrote to 'Mr Pratt', the architect who was just finishing off Clarendon House, in May 1667). He measured everything measurable. Some of the rooms were seventeen feet high, better suited to the heats of a Madrid summer than the climate of the East Midlands. The 'cleare way' of the admired doors – presumably the space exposed by opening them – was 99 inches high by 47.2 broad.

After St John's Day, June 24th, Madrid adopted a hot weather routine. Great use was made of shutters, curtains, cool drinks, fans and – suggestive epicureanism – cool smells. Floors were watered at regular intervals, 'balcons open about an inch for fresh ayre to enter in at.' 'They tie their

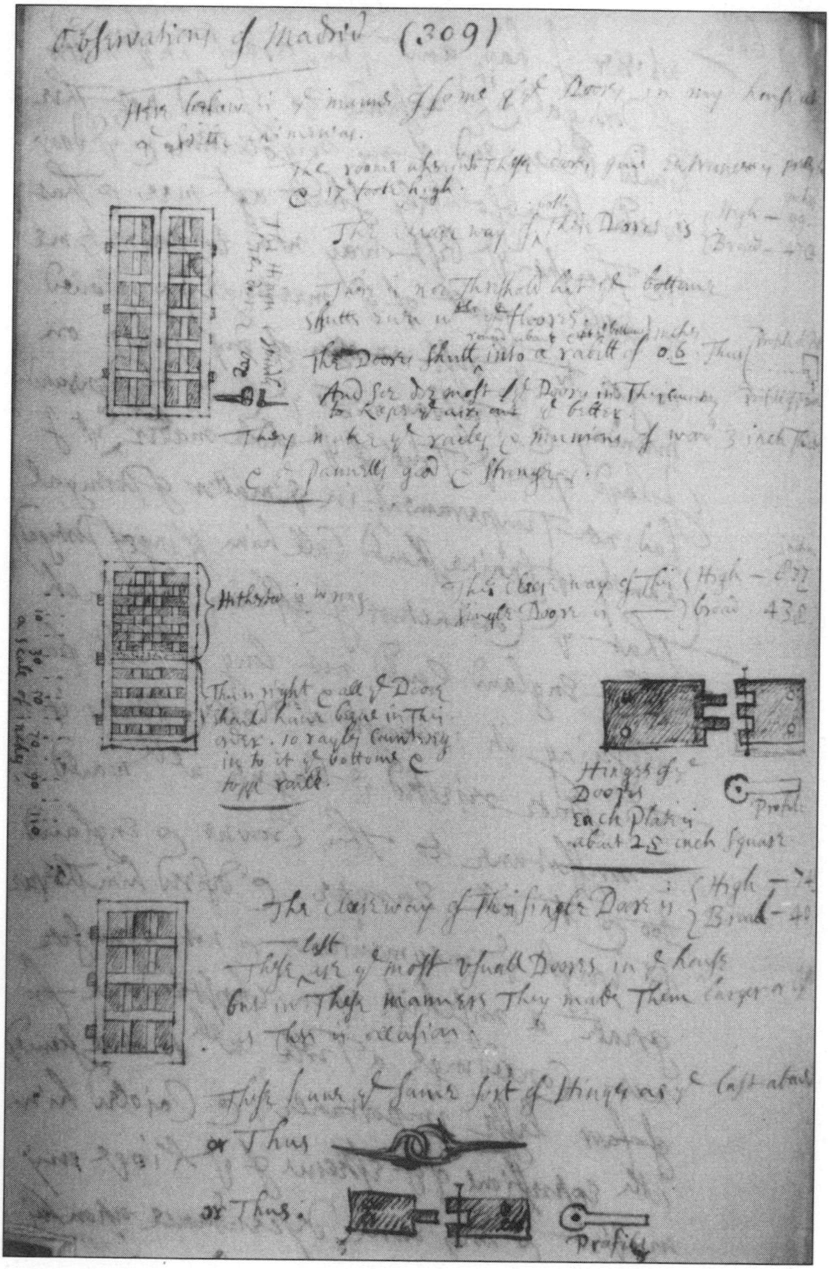
Observations of Madrid (309)

The Doores shutt into a rabbit of 0.6 Thus

Hinges of ye Doores
each Plate is
about 2½ inch square

Profile

The cleare way of this single Doore is { High — 7.4 / Broad — 4.0

These are ye most usuall Doores in ye house
but in These manners They make Them larger as
there is occasion.

These have ye same sort of Hinges as ye last above

or Thus

or Thus.

Profile

haire back behind their heads and lie soe bare-headed all night men and women ... after sunsett they sett all doores and windows wide open untill they sleepe and then they shutt them, holding it dangerous to sleepe if an uncertaine aire should suddenly arise and strike them (for ye ayres are exceeding subtile and piercing and often strike men lame of one side or kills them).'

Sandwich was perhaps wise to err on the side of credulity in matters of health and diet. Although only forty he had become corpulent. But he did not conceal from himself, as no doubt he did from his hosts, his opinion that the Spaniards were a superstitious lot. He reports without comment the spontaneous ringing 'of ye greate bell of Velilla 3 dayes together and ye clapper struck on that side next to France whence they conjecture some greate mischief is imminent over this countrey.' He was surprised by the prevalence of a belief in witchcraft in the most exalted circles. He was even told that Don Luis de Haro, Philip IV's minister who negotiated the Treaty of the Pyrenees in 1659, had practised it. 'But scince I have discussed with one Dammian who is housekeeper of ye Buen Retiro who served neere ye person of Don Luis and was intimately knowinge most of his concernments to whom I give full creditt ... [he] assures me that Don Luis was a great contemner of sorcerie and astrologicall predictions.'

Far from regarding himself as a superior person Sandwich entered enthusiastically into Spanish life. On 30th May 1667 he records: 'This day I first wore ye Gollillio [the ruff] after the Spanish fashion.' And he never ceases to admire the quality and ingenuity of Spanish workman-ship, whether it be in the design of a chair or of a *brasero* that used charcoal made from olive stones to heat a room (see p. 178). He is quick to acknowledge Spanish superiority in so common a craft as that of the blacksmith: '... when a shoe is forged they afterwards hamer it cold exceedingly well into its right shape which makes ye shoes much more strong and durable.' After driving in the nails they 'make a mann take up ye contrary legg of ye horse ... soe with all the weight of the horse standing upon ye foote they clinch ye points of ye nayles which seems a better way to make ye shoe sitt close and fast.' His observation is by no means uncritical. A plough is described as 'bunglingly made' like those he had seen used in Hertfordshire (a drawing of the hammer is on p. 179).

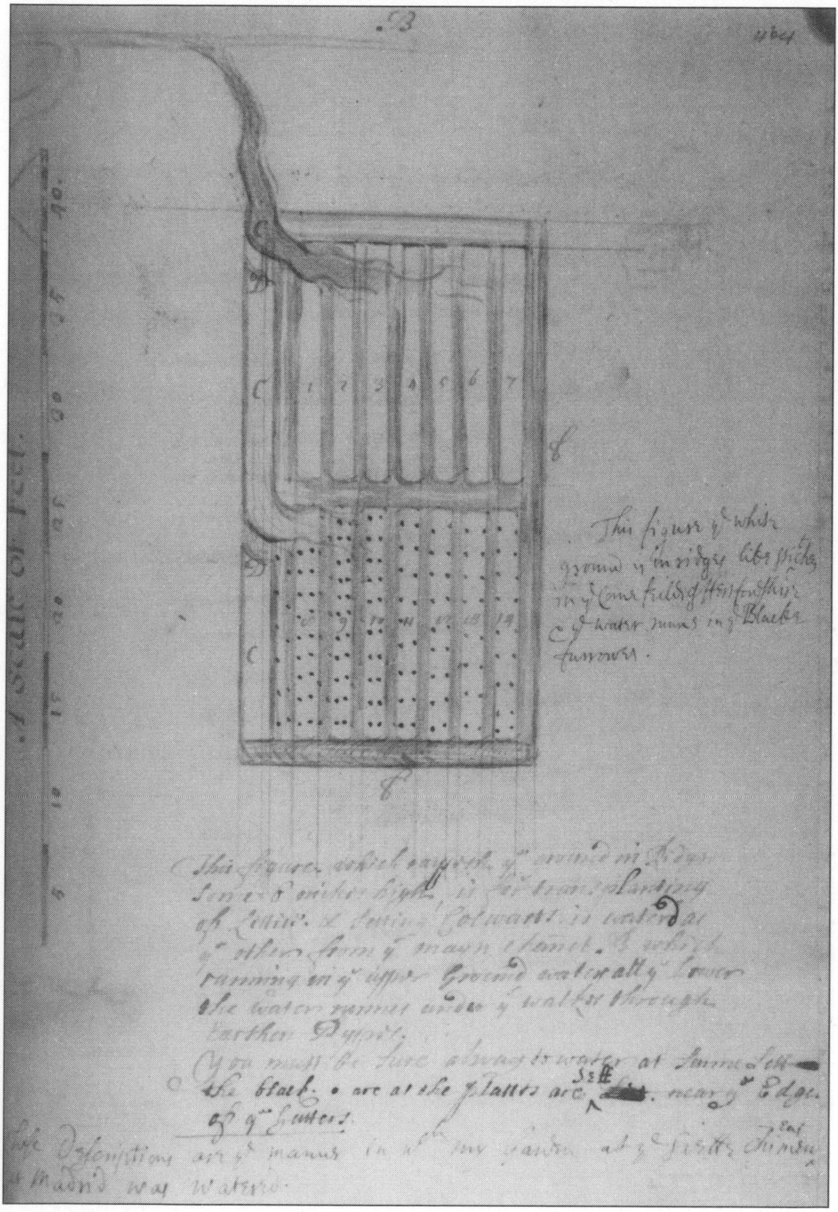

Watering plan of the embassy garden at the Siete Chimeneas

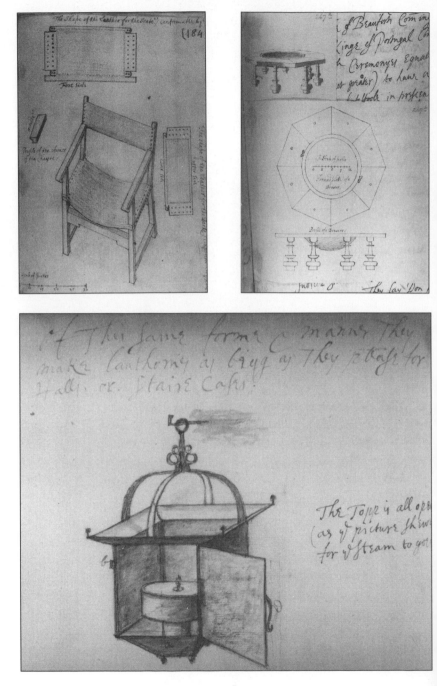

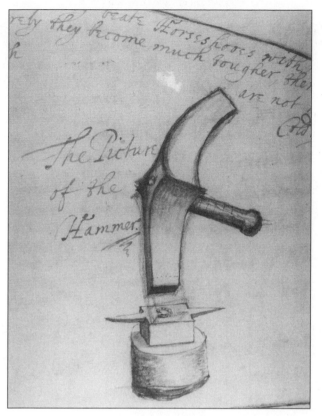

It is hard to imagine the well-bred litterateur Fanshawe deigning to notice such banalities: still less his predecessors in the Madrid embassy Arlington or Clarendon. Arlington would have been equally, if not more, expert in the nuances of language and social intercourse but he was too intent on his own precarious claims to gentility to notice what grooms and blacksmiths were up to. Clarendon simply snorted with contempt at anything Spanish, wildly asserting that so simple a convenience as a chimney was unknown in Spain. One wonders if he ever noticed the embassy's address. Sandwich certainly understood, and accepted, the social stratification of his time. But he did not romanticize it. Rather he was interested in its manifestations and their bearing on the world he lived in. On 8th February 1667 he learned from the Marquis of Baides the refinement of precedence among the noble families of Spain who could lay claim to the blood royal:

1 The Duke of Medina Celi 'truly and legitimately'.
2 The Duke of Cordona 'not legitimately – but not spurious in ye worst degree, the mother beinge a single woman (and I thinke ye Kinge too).
3 The Amirante, Duke of Medina de Rio Seco 'but both by ye mother's side and ye King's too, married people'

Such gradations of bastardy were not applied to the offspring of Sandwich's employer.

The relation between noble birth and liability to legal punishment disclosed further dissimilarities. On 4th February 1667 Sandwich describes (and illustrates above – schematically not realistically), the garrotting of 'a Biscayner (a Hidalgo for soe every Biscayner esteemes himself to be) ... for having counterfeited ye Queen and Councell's hands to an order for a moderate summ of money.' Although the man had taken sanctuary and claimed the privilege of the Church 'yett ye officers of the towne gott hold of him and did execute him' notwithstanding the protests of the Nuncio. Garrotting was 'granted him as a Biscayner and a gentleman, otherwise he should have been hanged upon a Gallows but yett because his offence was base he had not ye favor to have his throat cutt.'

Privilege, as such a case showed, had its own carefully modulated penal code. But its enforcement was capricious. The Nuncio, a mere papal agent, had been defied. But what if the jurisdiction of the Inquisitor General had been involved? Or if the offender had been of higher rank? In November of the same year Sandwich tells the story of Don Antonio de Toledo, son to the Duke of Alva, who made advances to an actress, which she politely declined on the grounds that she was betrothed to a fellow member of her company. Don Antonio instantly had him murdered. 'This Comedian was a very gracefull man upon ye Theatre, spake excellently well and with generous action. He was formerly a Jesuit and expelled theire Society for misdemeanour; the fathers of ye Company say it was a just judgement of God upon him, for having taken upon him soe ungodly a trade, havinge heretofore beene one of them.' The actress herself was imprisoned 'but she dares not tell for feare of beinge killed afterwards or her face carbonadoed'.

The way in which this story is told clearly implies the narrator's censure. But it is rare that Sandwich sits in judgment on what he records or describes. This ex-Cromwellian, brought up by a severe Puritan father, is a true citizen of the world. Other people's way of doing things is what interests him. The importance attached to modes of address leads him to recount a quarrel, in the house of a bishop, between the Duke of Aveiro and a Portuguese Count who also laid claim to that title. The Portuguese persisted in addressing his fellow guest as Sennorio and not Excellencia. The Duke rudely pushed him away. The Count boxed his ears. Both men drew their swords but the Bishop interposed and they were placed under house arrest. An even nicer point of style, according to an Italian priest, had been violated by the recently created Cardinal Montalto. After investiture Cardinals by custom leave off Crowns or Coronets from their arms, substituting the Cardinal's hat and strings 'and also to write his firme with his owne sirname (whereby he is created Cardinal). The Duke of Montalto in his congratulatory letter to ye Pope and Cardinals scince his creation Cardinall has used his seale of armes with a Ducall Crowne on ye Topp and had written his name El Cardenal Duque de Montalto, whereas it should have been El Cardenal Luis Moncada. And hereupon ye Pope hath excommunicated him and fined him 10,000 ducats plate. The sentence will upon his reformation be easily taken off and ye fine too.'

All this, like the observation of the heavenly bodies, had no direct relevance to the objects of his mission. The gathering of naval, military and commercial intelligence was part of his business. The consuls at Seville, Cadiz, Malaga and, less frequently, the north-western ports informed him of the movements and fortunes of English ships and English merchants and mariners and a stream of letters from Tangier reported not only the necessities of the garrison and the fluctuations of the constant war between the Moorish chieftains Taffiletti and Gailan, but also the movements of shipping in the Straits. Sandwich early established cordial relations with the Duke of Veraguas, the admiral commanding the squadron that escorted the outward bound and met the home-coming *flotas*, who claimed descent from Columbus. He formed a high opinion of him and of the force he commanded – thirty good ships, some of sixty guns. There were, Sandwich was told on 8th June 1666 when the West Indies *flota* was expected, 'at least 30 sayle of Algiers men-of-war in ye sea waiting to robb them'.

Naval and military men were doubtless flattered by the unpretending affability of an ambassador who had himself a distinguished record as a commander. For his part Sandwich does not seem to have been overmuch impressed by the Generals. Caracena was old and crabbed. Marsin, though younger and abler, was regarded as not altogether trustworthy. He was not a Spaniard by birth, but a condottiere who owed most of his success and his considerable wealth to the patronage of the great Condé who had himself returned to the service of France in which, some thought, his disciple might once again join him. The soldier from whom Sandwich learned most was a Scotsman, Sir William Cascar, serving on the Portuguese frontier as Caracena's Major-General. He was an enormous man, six foot six, intelligent and well-bred. His account of that interminable war was disillusioned. The military authorities, especially in Madrid, were through and through corrupt. The campaigning season – only April and May – was too short to achieve anything. In fact the war was a racket on both sides. 'The Greate Kindred and alliance they have one with another. And ye benefitt ye Portuguese that are here reape from havinge ye pensions from this Kinge . . .' In February 1667 he supplied Sandwich with a pay list of all ranks in the Spanish service. He thought Don Juan 'ye principall and indeed ye only Captaine they have at this day in Spayn' though he commended Marsin, then second in command in Flanders. Of contemporary soldiers generally he admired Lorraine, Wrangel and Turenne 'but above all He prefers ye Prince of Condé in all points.' It is noticeable that Sandwich who had served with two of these men volunteers no opinion of his own.

Cascar's intelligence seems to have been reliable and his judgment vindicated by events. Unlike his chief Caracena he was convinced from the start that the French would attack in Flanders when it suited them and both he and the Marquis of Baides reported some grisly scenes of the punishment of fortress commanders with whom they had been tampering. In March 1667 he reported that the building of a new fort 'on ye point of old Gibraltar over against ye new' had been ordered by the Council of War. No doubt this was intended as a reply to Tangier. In the following month the English consul at Malaga reported that the Governor of Gibraltar had refused water and shelter to two Tangier vessels forced into the bay by stress of weather.

In June on his way back to join his regiment at Badajoz Cascar got into serious trouble with the Spanish authorities. He quarrelled with a Flemish captain over the purchase of a horse and wounded him in a duel. A few hours later the Fleming was found murdered and robbed. The magistrates at Talavera de la Reyna at once arrested Cascar and his servants, whom they tortured to give evidence against their master. Caracena sent a letter from Badajoz ordering Cascar's release, who at once took refuge in the Madrid embassy until his pardon or his passport should be guaranteed. The unfortunate servants were still at the magistrates' mercy and could not be expected to hold out. Caracena once again sent letters, this time securing the release of the servants. But as soon as Cascar had returned to Badajoz, Caracena broke his promise and imprisoned them all again. This time Cascar made his escape and took sanctuary in a convent. The affair was at last cleared up. At the end of December 1667, when the Spanish authorities had at last empowered Sandwich to go to Lisbon on their behalf to negotiate the Peace Treaty, Cascar, restored to his rank, was charged with the necessary staff work.

Cascar's case was by no means the first incident involving diplomatic protection and immunity. On 26th September 1666 Sandwich recorded:

This night Dennis one of my footmen was killed in ye streete by a shott from an Alguazill, my footman rudely persuing 4 Alguazills through ye streetes upon a rumor that they came through our barriers with Theire Rodds exalted, which by custom they ought not to do.

A sense of proportion is discernible in this sad note of a life thrown away in the maintenance of status and privilege. It is clear that the ambassador, had he been on the spot, would have restrained the zeal of his servant. A year later, in the face of provocation, he showed his usual calmness. A hundred officers of the Inquisition entered within the barriers to make arrests: 'The case was somewhat troublesome to mee because my embassy is from a Prince that ownes not ye power of ye Pope.' The men countered by claiming that 'they did exercise the same authority in ye King of Spayne's own Pallace and ye Barriers of all other Embassadors . . . And for them to be but hindred from doinge theire office untill to-morrow morning (which I pressed them unto) would be such a thing as had not been knowne in Spayne . . . but that they might be civill to mee they desired I would send a person to shew them ye Houses for which I was concerned and they would not disturb them.

'Soe I considered ye noise this matter would make in Towne if I should contest it and that upon a very ungracious subject Here. And theire askinge leave and civility made it to be noe determination of any right and did in substance secure ye Neighbors that I was concerned to protect.'

In the end they seized 'some twenty-one or more persons suspected for Jewes, most (if not all) of ye Portugall nation . . . and carried them away to ye Inquisition Prison.'

Sandwich's attitude, it may be felt, stands at the opposite end of the scale from that of Lord Palmerston in the case of Don Pacifico. Yet perhaps both men would have approved each other's actions on the grounds that politics – a term that comprehends diplomacy and war – is the art of the possible. Sandwich had not sent away the Inquisition with a flea in its ear because he knew that if he did he would be roundly defeated. But he did not let them walk over him and asserted at least a limited authority. Three days later, on September 9th, he heard from the consul at Cadiz that he had been 'thrown into ye Common Jayl and Dungeon' by the governor, the Duke of Medina Celi, for disrespect in making a journey without having first obtained his permission. A month later the Madrid authorities confiscated meat and wine from the Embassy suppliers 'my dispensero and my bottellaria' – a regular method of bringing pressure on diplomats as Sandwich discovered from the Venetian and the Dutch ambassadors. All these infringements were duly reported to whichever member of the Junto with whom Sandwich next had dealings but he never pressed for instant remedy, preferring to wait until he was on a seller's market.

That required patience. For months the Spaniards went on huffing and puffing about the unratified treaty. And then the true impact of the Four Days Battle, which had at first been celebrated as a victory by both English and Dutch ambassadors with illuminations and fireworks, shook the reputation of English sea-power and depreciated the value of an English alliance. It was a defeat: but a defeat that reflected more credit on the courage and tactical resourcefulness of the English, fighting on disadvantageous terms, than some more famous victories. As its latest and best historian points out the much-admired English opening manoeuvre on the second day of the battle, the approach in line abreast turning together into line ahead so as to present their broadsides to the enemy, was 'originally devised by the Earl of Sandwich in February 1665. This was probably its first use in action.'[1] The French observer on board the Dutch flagship, the Comte de Guiche, who records it was evidently impressed. Sandwich himself however cannot at this stage have known of his vicarious contribution to the hardest-fought of all battles in the age of sail.

The French, with their usual thoroughness, were exploiting England's disarray. In Madrid their ambassador the Bishop of Embrun was, according to Muledi, carrying all before him. On August 31st Sandwich wrote a long and careful summary of the position to Clarendon. The Spaniards, he thought, might well be inclining to a treaty with France 'soe greatly is this nation corrupted in understanding and military vertue'. In Lisbon he saw their hand behind his colleague Sir Robert Southwell's sudden and unwelcome arrival in Madrid in the second half of September, nominally to assist in mediating a peace between Portugal and Spain but probably manoeuvred into it by the Portuguese so as to have him out of

1. Frank L. Fox. *A Distant Storm* (1994).

the way while they did a deal with France. There was, of course, Southwell's own ambition to grab any credit that might be going:

> He ought not to have come hither at all – havinge noe caracter nor creditt here . . . I am apt to thinke . . . that he himselfe excogitated and contrived this errand, being youthfull and Hott in his persuits and of little experience.

Negative and frustrating though his professional life was for the first twelve months of his mission it at least gave scope for those powers of observation which are so profoundly characteristic. The Council Chamber, used on alternate days by the Council of State and the Council of War, was twenty-four yards long by eleven broad and in summer hung round with copies of Rubens. There were no chairs at the Council Table but benches with backs to them running the full length of the table on both sides, cushioned in silk. A less formal conference sometimes took place in 'ye Consejo de Italia (a roome on ye West side of ye Palace that hath ye pleasantest vista upon ye river of Mancanares both wayes that ever I saw in view of ye Escurial, ye Segovian bridge and ye Casa del Campo and many lovely feilds and villages and ye mountains of Guadarama)'. There was, he noticed 'a window covered with fine calico high up in the wall for ye King to hear debates undiscovered'. It was in this room that the ambassador was received on 15th May 1667 after the Spaniards had at last signed the Commercial Treaty, the first of Sandwich's objectives. It had been a matter of waiting for the wind to change. Everyone in Madrid, including the English ambassador, regarded the signing of a peace between England and the United Provinces as almost certain which would leave France free to pursue her designs in the Netherlands. Fear of France led even the traditionally pro-French Peñaranda to contemplate an Anglo-Spanish alliance.

In fact the Dutch had a card up their sleeve. Annoyed by the English reversal of the Four Days Battle by their victory, a bare seven weeks later, in the St James's Day Fight and its sequel, the burning of a great part of their merchant fleet in the anchorage of the Vly, they inflicted the most humiliating defeat ever suffered by the Royal Navy, the virtually unopposed destruction of its major units at their moorings in the Medway. This proved fatal to the already troubled ministry of Clarendon. The raid took place early in June 1667. Clarendon was dismissed at the end of August. By Christmas he was an exile in France.

This was both a political and a personal blow to Sandwich. He was clearly identified as a Clarendonian and the Chancellor's overthrow was a triumph for his own enemy and rival in naval affairs, Sir William Coventry. It was Clarendon who had stood by him when the knives were out for him over the Prize Goods and the disappointments of the summer campaign of 1665. On the personal side Clarendon's letters to him and the character he was to give him in his autobiography show a warmth and an esteem generally reserved for the companions of his young manhood or of his long exile. The connexion between them was at that moment in the process of being strengthened by marriage. On 20th March 1667 Sandwich had been approached by two fellow Clarendonians, Anglesey and Carteret, proposing a match between his eldest son, Hinchingbrooke, and Lady Anne Boyle, a daughter of the Earl of Burlington, to whose elder daughter Clarendon's son Laurence was already married. The negotiation prospered and the wedding eventually took place in January 1668 while Sandwich was still abroad. It is noticeable that Pepys was not included in the small group of friends and advisers whom, together with his wife and his father-in-law, Sandwich entrusted with the conduct of the affair. Pepys had, as he himself later admitted, been a neglectful correspondent at a time when his patron stood in need of all the political intelligence he could get and which Pepys was supremely qualified to supply. It is from this period, not from the Great Letter of Reproof, that the breach between the two men opened.

It was fortunate for the ambassador that he had always been on good terms with Arlington, who as Secretary of State was the minister with whom he had to deal. Arlington's own position was strengthened by Clarendon's fall in which indeed he had played no little part. Without the least tincture of greatness he was a sober, shrewd, capable Secretary of State, provided that he was not required to back his own good judgment by a political courage he perhaps did not possess. On the eve of the Medway fiasco both he and William Coventry had written to Sandwich by the same post. Coventry affected confidence: 'His Majesty continues his resolution of making ye warr by small parties and not by great fleets. We believe the Dutch fleet abroad by this time, with which they intend to make this Rhodomontade, and I hope that is all they will be able to doe.' Arlington's tone is less breezy: 'The Dutch . . . are very positive and insolent, valuing themselves upon the protection of France and their own strength at sea, so superior to ours . . . a fleet of near 80 ships . . . Colonel Dolman is aboard.' Dolman was an English political refugee who had been attainted of treason for not surrendering himself. Arlington alone among ministers seems to have sensed the danger that threatened.

Sandwich's other strength was that things at last were moving his way in Madrid. The treaty he had signed in May had, after more than the usual vicissitudes of the posts between England and Spain, been ratified. On November 14th there had been a ceremonial exchange of the ratifications. Peñaranda had raised again the advantages to be gained from an Anglo-Spanish alliance. Medina de las Torres had discussed the possibility of admitting England to the trade of New Spain, excluding the Philippines to which no entry could be considered. Muledi hinted that there was a real possibility of obtaining the monopoly of Campeche wood, the essential raw material for the best dyestuffs. The French ambassador who had lamely apologized for leading the government up the garden path had been sent packing, albeit with the present of a jewel valued at £1500. Most important of all the Council had all but decided to empower Sandwich to go to Lisbon on their behalf and negotiate the peace on terms which they would confide to him but would not admit to their enemy until they were sure they would be accepted.

Sandwich had learned the lesson that his cousin was later to enunciate: 'vizt to bee most Slow to beleeve what we most wish should bee true'. He knew that there was a party in the Council that were toying with the idea of entrusting the mediation of the treaty to the Papacy, thus escaping the concessions that England was likely to exact for her good offices. He understood how dangerous a precedent it would be for Spain to acknowledge Portuguese claims to independent sovereignty: the particularism of the Peninsula was disruptive enough, to say nothing of Spanish possessions in Italy and the Netherlands. And then there was the paralysis of the will to govern, the habitual avoidance of decisions until external (and hostile) pressures took them instead. The whole process was a sort of self-hypnosis: 'The ministers of this Court who much insist upon forme (even to ye destruction of ye substance oftentymes).' It was Louis XIV who in the end would do his business for him.

In fact he had already done it. The flagrant breach of faith involved in his unprovoked invasion of the Spanish Netherlands in May had flabbergasted the government and outraged public opinion. By November the tide had turned for action. That Sandwich was really going to be sent to Lisbon was evident from the number of aristocrats with claims to Portuguese titles and estates who privately approached him to promote their interests. On Christmas Eve he received his passports. On Christmas Day he extracted the cash payment, the *ayuda da costa* of 4000 pistoles promised him by the government. He left half of it behind to defray the costs of the embassy in his absence and at two o'clock he took coach for Portugal.

XVI

Journey to Lisbon

=====

THE JOURNEY TO LISBON was a much grander affair than the introduction to Spanish travel recorded in the *Journal* for the spring of 1666.
Then Sandwich had been uncertain of his reception and the host government had taken care not to put him at his ease. Now he was entrusted
with the interests of Spain as well as those of his own master in a
negotiation that must, if successful, bring longed for relief to the country
to which he was going. All that could be done to smooth his path would
be done. Even though his route lay over harsh, inhospitable country and
mid-winter was not the season to choose for traversing it, so observant,
so enjoying, a traveller might expect a great deal of pleasure and interest
from the experience.

The tone in which the ambassador records his impressions is that of
a ship's log. Like Commodore Trunnion in *Peregrine Pickle* he uses
nautical terms to describe distance and direction and, most unusually in
a seventeenth-century journal, he records time with a scientist's exactitude. 'At 7.51 wee had on our larbord beame a furlong of, a Grange
belonging to ye Jeronim Convent of ye Escuriall, where they have powers
of Horje y Cachillo (i.e. hanging and cutting ye throate).' That churchmen should possess these alarming privileges struck him as curious
enough to be noted. His knowledge of Spanish life was of course much
greater than on his previous journey. And he had added to it by finding
out all he could about the country he was now to visit, especially about
its military strength. Sir William Cascar who had once again come to
see him at Madrid on December 14th gave him up-to-date intelligence
as to the numbers of Spanish and Portuguese troops, together with their

foreign mercenaries, on the frontier. According to him Schomberg, a great soldier lent to the Portuguese by Louis XIV, commanded a force of about 1800, horse and foot included. Of these the English contingent, mostly Sandwich's old comrades-in-arms from Cromwell's army, amounted to about 300 horse and 500 foot. They were so badly paid that they had been making approaches to Caracena about changing sides.

As to the Portuguese forces in general Sandwich had already obtained a minutely detailed account of their regular establishment from an English officer, Captain Shannon, on whom he makes the following note:

'Adjutant-Generall of ye English Party in Portugall, a Pretty Intelligent Soldier But not preferred as he desires & risen from a low beginning and soe one must allow graines in giving Creditt to this paper, where he speakes of Generalls & officers that may have disobliged him, or commends or censures such a forme of discipline as is against his Particular Interest or Preferring Gentlemen etc.'

To which he adds the further note:

'This Poore Gentleman, Captain Shannon was after this tyme viz. in May 1668 killed at Lisbon in a Duell by Colonel Moore, Colonel of an English regiment of Infanterie in that country.'

The suite he took with him was proportionate to the weight of the undertaking. Werden, Moore and Windebank rated at 18 reals per diem, would look after the details of the negotiation and the observances proper to an English ambassador (Moore was his chaplain). Five gentlemen at 12 reals., including his master of the horse, would attend to appearances and entertainment. Three English pages, among them Sir Winston Churchill's eldest son, Winston,[1] and two Spaniards at 9 reals a day each would support the dignity of the embassage.

Sandwich did not stay even to eat his own Christmas dinner but bowled off in his coach at two o'clock in the afternoon of Christmas Day – his Christmas Day but not that of the Spaniards who had adopted the New Style calendar and had celebrated the feast ten days earlier. He

---

1. From Sandwich's letters to Sir Winston it is clear that he had found a place for his son but his Christian name is not mentioned. I conclude that it was Winston because he was the right age and was killed, as Sandwich was, at the battle of Solebay in 1672, serving in his first commission as Lieutenant of the *Fairfax*, an appointment one might reasonably ascribe to Sandwich's recommendation.

kept up a good pace: 'I judge all along this journey (where it is not specially said to ye Contrary) that 3 miles English an houre is a good estimate of ye way wee have made.' He was generally on the road by seven, sometimes earlier, and gave his animals a good rest of two hours while he had dinner in the middle of the day. Their route followed that of the present main road through Talavera de la Reyna and Truxillo to Badajoz. The country pleased him, particularly as they drew near to Talavera 'a most lovely country of corn fields (plowed plaine without any sorte of ridges and furrows) vineyards and abundance of olive trees'. He noticed the abundance of castles. 'I suppose in ye Moores tyme to keepe ye Country in obedience ... forme generally square with round towers at each corner, high square keep.' But the buildings he was most impressed by, even when they were semi-ruinous, were the bridges. That over the Alberche outside Talavera was in such a state 'wooden Plankes very ruggedly layd over which a Coach may be guided by the hands of men but cannot be drawn over by Cattell'. The river was so shallow that he saved time by having his coach driven through it while he walked over the bridge which had stone piers for twenty-three arches. The bridge in the town itself spanning the Tagus was a magnificent structure for once not exactly measured ('I was told it was above 100 arches and I beleeve could not be of less than 70. The Tagus hereabouts is in many places 20 fathome deepe'). The grandest of all was that at Badajoz. '650 yards in length 400 whereof is over ye cleare water. 28 large arches of a delicate fabrique.' It was not mere size that impressed. At a narrower point of the Tagus between Navall morall and Cavaysejo they crossed by 'ye finest stone bridge of 2 arches that I ever saw'. He stopped to draw it as well as to measure it. He had an eye too for antiquities and drew the 'most famous Bridge' of Merida, a largely Roman structure topped by modern work, and spent a morning walking about the town to admire its other Roman remains.

Churches and houses were noticed, but more cursorily. Pages were devoted to patient attempts to make mathematical sense of local weights and measures which manifestly belonged to a pre-scientific age. Prices, taxes, church dues, excise and suchlike were more easily assimilated. Farming and wine-growing, trade, manufactures, social and economic intelligence of all kinds he clearly found of absorbing interest. Talavera specialized in the manufacture of earthenware 'coated in white mettle,

The bridge at Merida

a composition of Tinn, Lead and Barrilla (a plant whose burnt residue is brought by mule from Valencia and Murcia) the tinn and lead from England by Bilbao ... exceeding strong and will not splitt with hott liquor'. But its real wealth was in woollens. Eight master workmen each employed about fifty men. The ownership of the sheep – about 14 or 15,000 – was a monopoly of a convent of Jeronimite Friars 'who are held mighty rich in estates and rents'.

At Oropeza, a little further on, the local wines are 'excellent strong'. One, grown at Freznedosa, is so powerful that it will last for twenty-five years. Presumably it was kept in cask (with the consequent loss through seepage) since cork was not yet employed though readily available. In fact on the very next day, December 30th, Sandwich notes that they passed through a wood of cork oaks 'whose barke they now strippe of ye Trees, that are old, to benefit ye Trees and also to use ye Corke for firing.'

A landowner naturally assesses the potentialities of the country he is passing through. If, like Sandwich, he has passed his early manhood in campaigning he is likely to notice features that would make it defensible or invite an attack. Similarly a man whose political consciousness has been roused by civil war and *coups d'état* is aware that public order and the institutions that maintain it are not immutable facts but social phenomena varying from time to time and from place to place. Sandwich does not seem to have shared his cousin Pepys's intellectual interest in politics but both were keen observers of what was going on round them. He noted the differing balance of aristocratic, ecclesiastical and bureaucratic power in the towns he stayed in, recording with particular approval the enterprise of the inhabitants of Naval morall who had bought the privilege 'of not having a single hidalgo in the towne, who doe not pay taxes equally with ye vezinos and doe besides oppresse them in divers occasions'.

Like most travellers he took particular notice of the victuals and drink provided. Local noblemen such as the Conde de Oropeza entertained him lavishly, partly no doubt because he was the authorized representative of Spanish interests but also perhaps because his mission offered the best chance of ending a ruinous and unwinnable war. After he had arrived in Lisbon Sandwich recorded:

> I am told . . . that ye warr of Portugal one yeare with another as it was now managed of later yeeres . . . cost Spayn 4 million [patacoons] a yeare. And that yeare that Don Luis de Haro went with Intention to conquer Portugal it cost 27 million.

As he neared the frontier he saw more and more evidence of the misery inflicted, fields left uncultivated, towns 'decayed halfe in halfe since ye warr with Portugall'. It was in such a town on New Year's Eve that he saw the first orange and lemon trees growing in a garden.

The great flocks of sheep that came for winter feed and the hogs that were fattened on the acorns of the plains round Truxillo preserved it as an island of comparative prosperity. The Corregidor made them a generous present of hens, gammons, six dozen sausages, six gallons of wine and six boxes of preserved fruits. There were even cork mats in the bedrooms 'by ye side of ye beds whereby they keepe theire feete cleanly and from ye ground.' The Bishop of Placentia paid them a visit 'a brave Joviall fatt man, a good schollar, and hath about 70,000 ducats a yeare cleare to himself.' Milton, no doubt, would have pointed out how easy it was to be Joviall and fatt with such endowments. But the absence of anti-Papist or even anti-clerical bias is one of Sandwich's most striking characteristics.

By now they were in a military zone. Leaving Truxillo they were met 'in a ruinous village formerly great . . . Their houses were exceedinge neate on ye Inside' by a cavalry escort. 'Here ye 12 Artillery mules of ye King were putt into my 2 coaches (without any Person riding on ye backs of ye mules and with Bells on them as they use to draw in ye Traine of Artillerye . . .' At the much ruined town of Miajada they found '60 clericos in ye Towne . . . and but one church. These men soe many of them turne priests to enjoy ye priviledge of not quartering soldiers . . . here upon ye Raya [boundary line] where ye Army is lodged and continuall passinge up and downe.' At Merida, the Roman Imperial stronghold whose remains Sandwich admired, the authorities put on a show, coming out to meet him with two gold maces borne by serjeants with 'red Bonnets round (like ye Scotch ones) and red Gowns of Velvet'. Fresh fish and melons were presented, together with a Latin guidebook to the antiquities. Sandwich admired them as well as the ten great ovens of seven yards diameter in which was baked the ammunition bread for the Army of Badajoz.

At Badajoz itself 'a poore towne' he was received with full military honours. He was met there by Henry Sheeres, a member of his staff whom he had sent on ahead to Lisbon whence he was bearing letters together with a letter of welcome from the Governor of the Portuguese province of the Alentejo. He was also overtaken by a despatch from Werden in Madrid. Both informants were full of the proceedings against Clarendon and it was here that Sandwich heard of his flight. He heard too that the Earl of Burlington, with whom he was negotiating the marriage of his heir, had taken possession of Clarendon House in right of mortgage. It was at moments such as this that the gossip of the Whitehall world with which in earlier days Pepys had supplied him would have been appreciated. But none came.

To enable the ambassador to cross their lines the Governors of Badajoz and of Elvas declared a twenty-four hour cessation of arms within a twelve mile radius of each garrison. The hand-over took place at a rivulet to which the Spanish Maestro de Campo conducted Sandwich in his own coach. On the other side of the brook he was received by the Governor of Elvas 'as civill a gentleman as I have mett with and a greate lover of ye English professing much kindnesse to mee'. He was escorted by 11 battalions of horse (about 700 men) 'which all gave us a volley of shott and ye 3 last Battalions were ye English horse who gave us 2 vollys of Shott and Shouted after ye English fashion.'

Elvas contrasted favourably with Badajoz. 'This Towne is one of ye most regular Compleate fortifications of Europe, all ye Bastions and forts and curtains built of freestone layd in Morter as high as ye Parapett and then ye Parapett breast high of earth.' It was supplied by a 'noble Aqueduct of about a mile – it hath 400 arches and in some places it is 4 arches high one above the other. At highest we judge it 52 yards.' It stood in 'a good flatt country, uncultivated because of the warr untill we came within a league of Yelvas where it was plowed and planted with Olive Trees ye best of ye kind in all Spayn and most excellent oyle.' Sandwich was installed in the Bishop's house 'an excellent good one' and provided with 'ye Noblest Supper (drest in ye French mode) that I have seene.' All the English officers were invited and they sat down thirty or more at his table.

The three-day journey to the little port of Aldea Gallega on the opposite side of the Tagus estuary from Lisbon presented none of the hazards of travel in Spain. Although undertaken at so uninviting a season 'all this journey wee had curious sunnshine weather and noe raine except a little sprincklinge in ye night at Talavera nor one breath of wind' until they met the fresh northerly breeze coming off the sea as they approached the coast. As usual the ambassador noticed how the chimneys were constructed to avoid smoking and informed himself of the system of land tenure and of the rotation of crops. But the country was uninteresting, the last part, near the coast, barren or marshy. Two royal barges awaited him at Aldea Gallega and the crossing gave him a fine view of Lisbon 'and Beline Castle and ye Almada and all that bay'.

It was the twelfth of January, St Vincent's Day, the patron saint of Lisbon, a great feast there. Sandwich landed 'at 10.15 . . . right against ye Church of St Vincent below ye Church of St Paul at Buena Vista'. He was met at the waterside by Consul Maynard and conducted 'through the ye Placa Mayor unto the house of ye Duke of Aveiro . . . very Nobly furnisht for mee and very Noble entertainment provided for mee at ye King's chardge'. Sir Robert Southwell, the resident ambassador, had been waiting for him on foot in the Placa Mayor until invited into Sandwich's coach. This show of submission was rapidly abandoned. Southwell was furious at being upstaged in a diplomatic negotiation in which he had promised himself the principal role. But the business and pleasure of Lisbon require a chapter to themselves.

XVII

A Peace Achieved

THE POLITICAL and diplomatic hazards of the Lisbon scene were such as might have been devised by a librettist intent on dramatic confrontations at every turn with a proper scorn for common sense or probability. To start at the top the King was mad, bad and physically repulsive. He had recently been married to a French princess, an important success for Louis XIV's policy of supporting the Portuguese in their war against Spain. Were it ended, as Schomberg pointed out to Sandwich, it would enable the Spaniards to move a sizeable part of their forces to Catalonia and present a direct threat to France. Schomberg also 'fully expressed his opinion of ye folly and incapacity of ye King for Government or for matrimony'.

In both these functions his brother Dom Pedro was in the process of supplanting him. Within a week of arriving in Lisbon Sandwich attended a meeting of the Cortes at which the nobles, some four hundred of them, and the ninety-year-old Bishop of Targa, apparently the sole representative of his order, swore fealty one by one to Dom Pedro as Governor of the Realm. The deposition of the King, the annulment of his marriage and the wedding of the Queen to Dom Pedro were to follow in short order.

How far did this change affect Sandwich's chances of success? The nobility were by no means united in recognizing the necessity, obvious to all disinterested observers, of ending a war that had dragged on for twenty-six years. Some of them had positions or interests that would be threatened by a peace. Some were in receipt of French pensions. And France was making the running. The Queen was French. The French ambassador, the Marquis de St Romain, was a forceful and well-supplied advocate of his master's interests. Besides a number of nobles he had bribed the one important representative of what passed for popular opinion in seventeenth-century Lisbon, the *juiz do povo* or mayor. A litter-maker by trade he had been elected on the widest franchise by the populace who were themselves passionate for ending the war, the financial burdens of which fell largely on them. Southwell had openly tried to enlist his support, a move which Schomberg deplored as conduct unbecoming a foreign envoy. Bribery and confidential discussion were admissible: embroiling oneself in the brawling of street politics was not. Anyway it was counter-productive. Southwell ended by threatening legal action against the man and was only restrained by Sandwich's firm veto.

Schomberg was the man from whom Sandwich obtained the best intelligence and for whose judgment he seems to have had the highest respect. He had been on sick leave when Sandwich stayed the night at his headquarters at Estremos but he was one of the first to call on him after his arrival in Lisbon – 'Count Shomberg (Generall of ye Stranger forces in Portugal) and allied to mee by his mother.' The relationship was of the kind savoured by connoisseurs of genealogy such as Sir Walter Elliott or the late Earl Mountbatten. Schomberg's mother was Anne, second daughter of Edward Sutton, fifth Lord Dudley. The Suttons were connected with the Mountagus through the marriage between Agnes Dudley and Thomas Mountagu which had taken place in or before September 1485.[1] Anne Sutton had been brought up with the Princess Elizabeth, the Winter Queen, and it was as her Lady in Waiting that she met and married the young nobleman who was a member of the Palatine Court. She died giving birth to her distinguished son, to be followed a few months later by his father. The disasters that overtook the Palatine family only three years afterwards made the upbringing of this well-connected orphan even more cosmopolitan than his lineage. He spent a great part of his boyhood in England with his mother's relations. He studied for two years at the University of Leyden, subsequently serving in the Dutch and Swedish armies before embarking on a career in the French army that was to culminate after Sandwich's death in a Marshal's baton. A lifelong Protestant he left France on the

---

1. G.E.C. *Complete Peerage* IX, Appendix D.

Revocation of the Edict of Nantes, was William III's Second-in-Command in the invasion of England in 1688 and, honoured by a Dukedom and the Order of the Garter, was killed two years later at the Battle of the Boyne. He was a man of cultivation and great humility, conspicuous among the successful commanders of his day for the care he took of his troops.

Ten years older than Sandwich he was to outlive him by nearly twenty. Yet in spite of the difference of life-span, both in time and place, the two men had much in common and from Sandwich's account of their conversations seem to have been aware of it. There was a professionalism, a detachment in their approach to the responsibilities with which they were charged as well as unspoken assumptions of what was, and what was not, tolerable behaviour. They were, diplomatically, on opposite sides of the fence. Schomberg, in the French interest, advised delay in negotiation so that the proposed terms of the peace could be approved by Paris. Sandwich knew that the Protean slipperiness of both the Portuguese and the Spanish governments requested the nailing down of an agreement at the earliest possible moment. He was inflexible in pressing ahead. The French ambassador, St Romain, took a threatening overbearing line. Sandwich must know that the King of England had been making confidential overtures to Louis XIV which had been so far kindly entertained. Louis would be deeply displeased if his Portuguese ally, so liberally supported, were to make peace with Spain without reference to him entirely on the initiative, and guarantee, of England. According to Sandwich's subsequent account, written on his return to Madrid, St Romain, when he saw that he was likely to be outmanoeuvred, planned to have him assassinated.

Schomberg would have been horrified. The two men exchanged opinions and information in a spirit of freedom and friendship. The French army, it appeared, was not so regularly paid as was generally believed. For the last year's service they had only had six months' pay. As for the war in the Peninsula the Spaniards were 'better at standing well in their defence than in advancing and attacquing an enimie. That ye Hott weather and difficultie of victualls was ye greatest enimies an army had to contend with in all these countries.' The Portuguese army was badly officered, partly because promotion was by rule, not merit, and partly because the gentry were too idle. He rated Wrangel 'ye greatest

Captain of Europe and most universall for horse and foote and sea service'. He admired the generalship of Condé, La Ferté and Turenne, his old master, but reckoned them incapacitated by ill-health – 'full of Gout'. After Sandwich had pulled off the Treaty and thus brought the war to an end Schomberg talked of future possibilities. The Portuguese had been very generous and had awarded him a pension equivalent to his full pay while on active service. On his return to France he had a right to expect the Governorship of a Province or to be made Marshal of France '(wh. having beene a Generall abroade is his due if he serve as a soldier in France) or to have some greate charge in ye Court of France without which a greate person cannot live handsomely there'. Failing such offers he would withdraw to Liège 'and looke aboute him a while and see how affaires doe goe in ye world'. He was perfectly ready to enter the service of Charles II and to buy land in England and settle his family there. He spoke particularly of buying Dudley Castle, the ancient seat of his mother's family.

Relations with this widely experienced, well-bred foreigner were much easier than with his own pushful young compatriot, Sir Robert Southwell. Quick in the uptake Southwell saw at once that Sandwich would not have made the journey to Lisbon in the depths of winter (for all that it had turned out unexpectedly mild) unless he had been authorized by the Spanish government to concede recognition of the Kingdom of Portugal – to deal 'de Rey a Rey'. Everything else that mattered had already been settled by Fanshawe's treaty of two years earlier. It was all over bar the shouting. The important point was to secure the credit for this achievement.

Southwell from the first took a high line. He was the minister accredited to the Court: he had initiated and developed the negotiations in conjunction with Fanshawe before Sandwich had appeared on the scene: he insisted on being present at the Convent of St Eloi where the contracting parties were to meet. Sandwich, it may be guessed, was not unprepared for all this. He had already been embarrassed and annoyed by Southwell's unauthorized, uninvited, unannounced descent on his embassy in Madrid and what he had felt then he felt now with rising anger. He refused absolutely: '. . . beinge come interested in an affaire of that weight that I had laid aside all my owne passions and affections or thoughts of my owne glory and found myself oblidged in conscience to carry on ye affaire whatever became of these'. He distinguished between his two capacities '(1) as managing ye mediation of my master (2) as a person that had obtained some credit in ye court of Spayn'.

Sandwich's position was indeed to an unusual degree personal. He was the honest broker authorized by Spain, not Spain's representative with powers to negotiate on her behalf. These had been entrusted to two Spanish noblemen held prisoner in Lisbon, the Marquess de Carpio and Don Añelo de Guzman. Carpio had actually been captured on the battlefield and, since Spain and Portugal were still at war and had signed no truce, was still in Portuguese eyes their property and thus disabled from dealing with them as an equal. Sandwich solved this procedural problem by obtaining Carpio's temporary release on parole into his ambassadorial protection. This gave Southwell an opening. He had visited the two and made friends with them. He now engaged them to press for his admission to the negotiating table. Sandwich answered suavely 'that I was much ashamed to see their Excellencies troubled with our Domesticall affaires, which I thought wee ourselves could terminate'. But his feelings towards Southwell can be imagined. 'I saw no good pretence for it, he havinge nothinge to do in the affaire, the Commission from the King of Portugall being to those Lords to treate with mee and the Marquis of Carpio, and noe mention of Sir Robert's name; soe that I believe the Lords would have refused to admitt him ... Besides his qualitie is so much inferior to every one there, that it would have been very hard to adjust a place for him amongst us, where he should sitt. Moreover I conceive it against practise and not honourable for mee to admitt it.'

In diplomacy as in sea fighting Sandwich was a formalist. Negotiators, like men-of-war, took station in the line according to the guns they carried. An English earldom was at least the equivalent of a Spanish marquisate. Baronets and knights were mere fireships and hired merchantmen. Precedence in seating at the conference table and in signing its product was apt to be more anxious work than the substance of the treaty. As Henry Coventry had wittily remarked of the negotiations at Breda a few months earlier, only Gresham College could 'make a room and a table where everyone should have the right hand and be furthest from the door'.[1] So much for 'qualitie'. The 'practise' Sandwich was

1. Quot. Feiling *British Foreign Policy 1660–1672*, 220.

invoking was the status of an Ambassador Extraordinary (which he enjoyed) as opposed to that of a mere Resident Envoy (which Southwell was). In a rage Southwell declared his intention of returning to London at once. 'I answered him that he had better take up resolutions upon pacate consideration and not in passion.' What would the King and the Secretary of State say if Sandwich were to die or be suddenly disabled and the regular ambassador was found to have gone off in a huff? For the moment Sir Robert was pacified 'and soe we parted very friendly and He invited my sonn Sydney and all ye other comrades etc to a supper at his lodging'. But on the following day, January 27th, he wrote a formal letter announcing his intention of taking passage for England in the frigate *Reserve* which was then in Lisbon homeward bound.

Dealing with a turbulent colleague had not distracted Sandwich from his real business. The first meeting at St Eloi, at which commissions had been read and the order for Carpio's liberty granted, had taken place on January 25th. On the 28th all the main points had been agreed except the possession of Ceuta, once thought of as an alternative to Gibraltar or Tangier as a naval base on the Straits. Sandwich persuaded the Portuguese to relinquish it. Intent on securing his objective he bore down all opposition to obtain a further session three days later on Saturday afternoon at four o'clock. Suddenly everything was agreed: engrossment of the treaty was scheduled for the Monday 'and soe wee embraced each other'.

On Monday February 3rd everyone assembled for the signing, always a moment for the pyrotechnics of protocol. Sure enough the first rocket was fired off by the senior Portuguese plenipotentiary, the Duke of Cadaval. As the only Duke present – or so he thought – he proposed to sign, with a fine flourish, 'O Duque'. But this was fiercely resented by the Marquis of Carpio, who had, it seems, ducal claims of his own should he care to exert them. *He* would sign under the style of El Duque Duque. Other bangs and flashes at once followed. It took all Sandwich's courtesy and firmness to reconcile everybody to sign only by their full proper names, omitting their titles. And against all the hazards of unreason, self-importance and corruption the Treaty was signed. Four days later it was on its way to England aboard the *Reserve*, together with a packet of letters from Sandwich and the person of Sir Robert Southwell. He was able to draw the Secretary of State's attention to the fact that Sandwich had brought shame on the majesty of England by signing the Treaty below Carpio.

That mine, however, was not to be sprung until Sandwich returned to England. For the moment he was free to enjoy the pleasures of Lisbon and to prepare for his return to Madrid by a route that would enable him to see new parts of Spain. Lisbon itself he knew from previous visits. But there were new and old friends. The Swedish Resident who called on him was the brother-in-law of 'Mon^sr Frizendorp (who was Resident of Sweden in England in Cromwell's tyme and a little after, my kind freind and very able minister of State)'. Sweden naturally favoured Sandwich's efforts as likely to result in the discomfiture of the French. The Swedish nation, he said, was 'very opiniatre' in their religion, which explained Queen Christina's mother having changed from the Calvinism in which she had been brought up to the Lutheranism into which she had married. He did not express, or Sandwich did not record, the effect of this stiffness on Christina's own submission to the See of Rome. He paid several calls on a daughter of the Duke of Medina Sidonia, Donna Maria, a nun at the Alcantara. She told him of the secret conversion of 'my cosen Mr Ed. Mountagu, sonn of Ed. Lord Mountagu of Boughton, who was after killed at Bergen'. Clarendon, it will be remembered, had speculated about this in his letter of condolence. Apparently it had taken place when he was in Rome at the age of 18 or 19 and the Pope had so far interested himself in the matter as to give him his personal leave to conceal and deny his change of religious allegiance. Donna Maria claimed to have heard this from Edward himself when he came to Lisbon in Sandwich's retinue on the voyage that brought over the Queen to England.

As usual Sandwich admired, and measured, buildings, particularly the Convent of S. Vicente '. . . hath beene 80 yeares a building and will cost 20 more to finish it'. As usual he was always ready to learn about military matters, such as the ammunition bread baked in the great ovens he had seen on the frontier: 'Excellent good wheate bread and served them in every 3 or 4 dayes. If there be occasion to march then they cutt ye loaves in halfe and bake them hard againe and then it will keepe 3 or 4 months or more.' Victualling was the beginning and the end of military operations since there was no such thing as Free Quarter, 'for ye Landlords and Countrey people have scarce anything to keepe themselves with all and are very curious of their horses and theire woomen . . . They all agree that this country does not admitt a campania of above 6 weekes and that a towne that can hold out above 6 weekes is impregnable.' Misery and military incompetence, the eternal verities of warfare, were, except when Schomberg was directing operations, ever present. An English officer gave Sandwich an account of a cattle raid carried out from Elvas a few days earlier. 'A Sunday and all the clownes at Mass but they came out and shott.' To some effect it appears 'there was never so sadd an action done since warr was knowne'. 20,000 cattle were abandoned and the price of this futility was a large number of casualties. No wonder that when Sandwich returned to Madrid he was met with rejoicings on both sides of the frontier.

Other material for observation was provided by a comet with a particularly interesting tail: 'I beleeve very neere the body of it . . . it looked like ye first comett which I saw at Portsmouth 3 yeares scince, ye streame beinge like a birchen beesome' and by an *auto-da-fé* on his last Sunday in Lisbon at which two men and one woman were burnt alive. No comment or description is offered. To commemorate the success of the conference Sandwich wished to present his portrait to the Convent of St Eloi. He sat for it, apparently only for one day, February 25th.

> One Feliciano drew it, a Picture to ye knees in a vest (ye then habitt of England) and ye Hatt in ye right hand hanging streight downe: it was an extraordinary like Picture.

There were other presents to be given and received. Already he had sent sweetmeats to his wife and son, whose wedding to Lady Anne Boyle had been reported in the newspapers dated January 13th. He now sent off two hogsheads of 'Barr o Barr' wine (made near Lisbon and reputed to stand a round voyage to Brazil) and 'a chest with two pots of silk flowers very curious given mee by Donna Maria'. The Prince (Dom Pedro) gave him 18,000 cruzados of 400 reals and the populace honoured him with luminarios and dancing in the streets. At noon on March 5th he embarked for Aldea Gallega, seen off by the Marquis de Carpio and the English community (Southwell by then had landed in England). The grateful representatives of the Portuguese government had taken official leave of him on the preceding day.

XVIII

The Last of Madrid

SINCE THERE WAS no great urgency about returning to Madrid Sandwich could allow himself a detour or two. He made a loop to the south of the road to Estremos and Badajoz so as to spend a day at Evora 'the best city after Lisbon and the best wine'. Like every visitor he was struck with the beauty of its situation on a hill 'in ye midst of a lovely valley full of corne and wine'. He admired the Roman remains, particularly of a fine Corinthian colonnade now put to unworthy use and he was intrigued to find among the inhabitants a superstitious expectation of the return of King Sebastian 'to governe them with righteousness and to conquer much of ye worlde'. He was received with 'excessive demonstrations of Joy by dancing in mascarade all alonge ye towne as I wente to my lodging – and in my yard doing feates on horseback like ye Moores'.

At Estremos and Elvas his reception was almost as rapturous though tempered by the discipline of military ceremonial. At Elvas he was shown the vast water cistern filled by the aqueduct he had previously admired. It was always kept full and, with walls five feet thick, held enough for 10,000 men for a year. Crossing the frontier he found cheerfulness breaking into those sombre towns through which he had passed on his outward journey. There were signs of spring: 'All along this country and in Portugall wee had storkes building in ye Steeples of most of ye Townes and sparagus pickt out of ye cornfields as it was produced by nature . . . a little bitter but mee thought of reasonable biggness and pretty good.' After Talavera de la Reyna he turned off his route in order to see two of the greatest sights of Spain, Toledo and Aranjuez.

Toledo he was to revisit in the heats of summer on the last of his journeys. On this occasion he devoted the whole of his time to the cathedral. He entered by the West Gate 'called ye Gate de Pardon because our blessed Lady when she descended from heaven into ye church entred in at this Gate'. It was only opened on the greatest festivals and holy days and this was Maundy Thursday. Sandwich made a point of touching the place where she put her foot.

On Good Friday he came to Aranjuez 'where I saw a Drove of Camells of about 150 feedinge. They drive them home every night for feare of wolves and also for feare of theeves who will kill them to eat.' He was struck by the beauty of the landscape and by its unusual Englishness.

'The Elm walkes at Aranjuez (the most famous I beleeve in all ye world) high tall Trees of 34 yards kept stript up to ye topp. The Trees are much too thicke sett (not about 5 yards asunder in each rowe) which makes them I beleeve decay soe much as they doe. These (and all other Elmes in Spain) brought by Ph. 2nd out of England and propagated from them'. The Englishness of the scene was emphasized by 'Greate rookeries of rookes and jackdaws just such as we have in England and fallow deer'. The fountains of Aranjuez (see p. 215) were admiringly described and measured, one of which had been presented by the Pope to the Duke of Terra Nova when he was ambassador in Rome.

'It was ye end of ye Holy tyme when I was at Aranjuez when ye Custome is after ye Resurrection on Easter Day morninge to throw about Hallelujahs in ye Church which ye people catch as they can whereof 2 are here inserted.' And so they are: printed sheets, one with a cut of the Virgin and the other of Santa Casilda. On the evening of Easter Day he arrived thankfully back at Madrid.

Congratulations were in order. He was received in audience by the King and Queen 'and ye Queene spake many sentences but with my best attention I could not distinguish what her Majesty said'. But clearly their burden was complimentary. On April 6th he wrote to England for a ship to meet him in a month's time. What sort of leaving present might he hope for? A veteran English resident told him that Cottington, co-ambassador with Clarendon seventeen years earlier, had been 'gratified with some 6 Habitts which were then esteemed worth 3000 ducatts (now not worth above 1500) each. My Lord ye Earl of Bristoll was gratified with 40,000 pieces of eight when he was Embassador in Spayn.' These sums presumably represented the nadir and the zenith of relations between the two Crowns.

But the procrastination that had been part of life since he had stepped ashore at Corunna was not finished yet. On April 24th he noted that he had still had no instructions from England and both the Spaniards and the Portuguese were giving disquieting signs of mutual distrust. A stream of informative letters from Consul Maynard in Lisbon kept him abreast of developments there. The deposition of the King had been followed by the expected marriage of his Queen to his brother Dom Pedro but this was highly unpopular. The ministers with whom Sandwich had treated were threatened with violence in papers scattered in the streets of Lisbon. The Marquis of Carpio, returning to Spain, had been detained at Elvas until the Portuguese towns specified in the treaty had been handed over by the Spaniards. What underlay this was the deep suspicion that France and Spain were about to do a deal at Portugal's expense 'and then ye Marquis must returne to be a prisoner which indeed he hath great reason to provide against, having suffered in that kind 5 or 6 yeares in as bad a condition as a Felon at Newgate'.

On the Spanish side someone had got wind of the negotiations leading up to the Secret Treaty of Dover. On April 25th Sandwich noted:

'About this tyme here hath been a report (which I beleeve not to be true) that ye King of England should be going about to master his Parliament and make himself absolute by force of Armes and That England should againe embrace ye Roman Catholique religion. That ye King of France should help ye [King of] England with an army and that ye Pope gives ye 3rd part of ecclesiastical revenues of France to ye french King to contribute towards ye chardge (that 3rd part They say is 5m. of Doblons p. ann).'

Sandwich seems to have interpreted the rumour as yet another symptom of the unquenchable Spanish suspicion of English actions and motives, especially when they appeared friendly.

It was something of an anticlimax to be left hanging about after pulling off so considerable a coup. But Sandwich knew, none better, how to conceal disappointment and ruffled feelings. He continued to go through the ambassadorial motions as though everything was proceeding according to plan. He took official leave of the King and Queen towards the end of April although he had still no date of departure in prospect. He raised again the question of recovering King Charles I's pictures, or as many of them as the Spaniards might be ready to part with. He went to see a number of the most famous paintings in the city and at the Escorial and had drawings taken of some. The Escorial 'truly did excel ye expectation I had of it both for magnificence, elegancy and cost. I certainly Believe ye whole world hath nothing that comes neere to equall it.' Amongst its treasures were a cup presented on the occasion of the Nativity by one of the Magi, and one of the vessels employed at the wedding at Cana 'of whytish substance as hard as stone'. He was presented with a book by the King's principal keeper 'of ye manner of hunting and taking game in Spayn'. The walks of the Escorial contained 10,000 fallow deer and 3000 red deer. But deer were not much esteemed. Wild boar was preferred for meat.

Another summer was coming round. On May Day, the feast of the Soltilla 'where in ye meddow to ye East of ye Bridge of Toledo most of ye coaches in towne – about 1000 – meet in ye Passeo ... when they first beginn to water ye Passeo of ye old Prado to lay ye dust that it does not incommode ye coaches'. At last letters from England suggested that he was not going to be left in Madrid for ever. Most valued of all was a note from the King, written on February 12th but not received until the end of April, congratulating him on the Anglo-Spanish treaty and wishing him success in his negotiations at Lisbon:

> You know my humour does not much carry me to write with my owne hand, else you had heard from me long ago to thank you for the good treaty you made in Spaine, so much to my honour.

It was a handsome compliment, and timely. In Arlington's letter, written on April 13th, congratulating him on his achievement at Lisbon, the temperature drops sharply:

> I would I could tell you there were in everybody else ye same value and esteeme of you as there is in mee, then you would be happier and better beloved than ye effects of these last dayes past shew you to bee in some mens opinions. I leave it to your friends to explain this better to you and will onely add that it is impossible for any servant to be more oblidged to a master then you are to his Matie who still persists to have ye same value and kindnesse for you that he hath ever profest ...

Clarendon's fall could not have left the position of so close a political ally as Sandwich unaffected. His journal records, without comment, the

'A beast of a very strange shape' drawn by Ferrer at the Casa del Campo
in May 1668

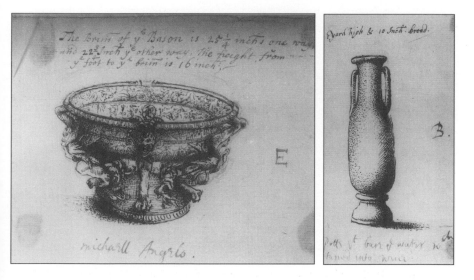

Basin designed by Michelangelo, and right, the water pot from Cana

news of his old friend's misfortunes. On May 20th he inserts two accounts of the assault on him at Evreux, one a letter from Sir John Trevor in Paris to Arlington dated April 18th. Another, again from Paris dated May 6th, summarizes a letter from Clarendon to Sandwich's cousin the Abbot. In Parliament the miscarriages of the Dutch War were being harshly scrutinized. Articles of impeachment had been brought against Sir William Penn for his conduct as Sandwich's Vice-Admiral in 1665. Creed, once Pepys's jealous rival in the days when Mountagu was General at Sea, sent him a copy of them. But Pepys himself remained silent except for a letter of congratulation on the Lisbon treaty. A number of friends urged him to hasten his return. The Commons were in an ugly mood. With so inveterate an enemy as the Duke of Buckingham prominent in the new administration Sandwich might easily be thrown to the lions. Arlington might profess, might even feel, goodwill towards him but pliancy was the beginning and the end of his politics. The steadfastness of the King was his best surety but it would be pushing one's luck to rely too much on that.

The condition of his domestic finances was another powerful incentive to head for home. In Madrid he was constantly embarrassed for money, constantly requesting the urgent payment of accounts which were met with the usual official blend of effusive understanding and evasion of responsibility. But lack of funds does not seem to have cramped his style. With Lady Sandwich this was not the case. She cut down expenses with a self-denying rigour that was not in her husband's character. But even so debts mounted and she could see no end to it. To her natural affectionate longing to be reunited with her husband was added the conviction that only he could take the steps necessary to bring their affairs on to an even keel.

Sandwich himself was no less anxious to be gone. A man of strong family affections he wanted above all to be with his wife and children and to enjoy again the house and estate in which he took such pride. He had done all he came to do and precious little thanks he had got for it. On May 24th

> Ruminating with my selfe ye slender requitall this court hath made mee for all my good services viz: makinge ye peace with England after Sir R. Fanshawe's was blasted and procuring ye King my master to desert Portugal.

Makinge ye peace with Portugall in ye face of ye league with France with perill of my life (which was consulted by Mr. St. Roman to be ye onely meanes to hinder it) at a tyme when I had warrant enough to have returned to England and not have medled with it in ye Hazard of my reputation and family if it had ill succeeded. And thinking opportunity was not to be lost to see if I could gett any thing more out of this Court whiles present I determined to goe and declare my resentment to ye Count Pennaranda and left him the paper which followes . . . desiring him to consider as my friend and patron my case and to advise mee . . . The which with greate Courtesye he undertook to do.

The result seems to have been surprisingly satisfactory. The King and Queen had already presented him with their portraits 'as bigg as life and very like' by the chief Court Painter Herrera. Sandwich had mentioned the very large sum promised to his predecessor Fanshawe and the by no means inconsiderable present to 'ye French ambassador, ye Archbishop of Ambrun. Though he went away declaring warr and that (as was thought) unhandsomely too.' It now appeared that his own *douceur* was to be 70,000 pieces of eight. It is not clear whether he received the whole of this sum but whatever he got left him no reason to complain. In addition the Queen presented his wife with a jewel worth 8000 ducats (of which he made a drawing) and another of equal value for himself. Peñaranda had evidently shewn Sandwich's paper of complaint to his colleagues on the Council of State which embarrassed the ambassador. 'I did intend [it] onely for his private eye.' What would the Duke of Medina las Torres think of his having approached his great rival? 'I made a shuffling excuse to ye Duke for passing him by.' The Duke took no offence. In reminiscent mood he told him how, as a young man, he had been engaged to the daughter of the Duke of Medina Sidonia which Olivares, the all-powerful favourite, broke off for him to marry his own daughter and then arranged for the jilted girl to marry the Duke of Braganza, with the result that she became Queen of Portugal. Old men forget. The fully documented account of Olivares's elaborate strategy for the marriage of his daughter given in J.H. Elliott's definitive biography hardly admits the possibility of the least degree of truth in this intriguing story.[1]

1. J.H. Elliott. *The Count Duke of Olivares* (1986) 116–7.

Jewel for Lady Sandwich

Inevitably there were a number of loose ends as the ambassador prepared to hand over to John Werden as chargé d'affaires. His repeated and persistent attempts to gain an entry for England into the trade of the Spanish Empire had yielded a great deal of useful information and a cautious not entirely negative response. But the piratical activities of the English Governor of Jamaica, Sir Thomas Modyford, had outraged the ministers in Madrid and given them every excuse for recoiling. As to King Charles I's pictures which he raised again only three days before he finally departed 'they told mee it was under consideration'. He had, however, succeeded in some of his minor representations. He had managed to get a Jerseyman out of the prison of the Inquisition. He had pursued through the Imperial Ambassador the rights of Prince Rupert to a small payment due for past services to the Court of Vienna. Such are the tasks that fall to the lot of an ambassador.

There were farewell calls to be paid, some of which yielded interesting information. The Marquis de Fuentes, recently returned from his embassy in Paris gave a lucid account of the bitter faction at that court between Colbert and Condé on the one hand and Turenne, Le Tellier and Louvois on the other. Lionne, he said, was supreme in foreign affairs but meddled neither with money nor the army. His description of Louis XIV emphasized characteristics not unlike Sandwich's, his thoroughness, conspicuous in 'ye craft mechanicall things and ye prise of victualls or armes'. The Marquis was about to marry a lady 'reported universally to have beene of a blemished fame, almost to a publicke profession' and, somewhat to Sandwich's surprise, sent to ask his consent to the union. This, it turned out, was a Spanish courtesy to which the correct reciprocation was to drop in 'improviso' instead of giving notice of an intention to call. For all his fluency in Spanish and his uninhibited readiness to understand and not to censure, Sandwich never made the mistake of believing himself at home there. Only six weeks before he left he set down a report of the arrest and immediate garrotting of a gentleman who was clearly one of the Inquisitor-General's agents. He assigns three possible reasons. The man might have been slightly mad and therefore dangerous. He might have been the author of a scurrilous libel on the Queen. He might have been party to some other guilty secret. Sandwich set down, in his own hand, the evidence of various sources, none properly identified, and in the absence of conclusive evidence draws no conclusion. But it is obvious that he was shocked at the fact. He had not gone native.

The years at the Madrid embassy had widened his horizons and enriched his perceptions. His admiration for Spanish arts, particularly in gardens and landscape and their adornment with fountains and sculptures, his recognition of the intellectual quality of Spanish civilization, notably in those departments such as mathematics that were congenial to him, are abundantly evident in his journal. Before he left he arranged to correspond 'about mathematicall and Philosophicall experiments' with an Italian bishop in the Viceroyalty of Naples, gracefully acknowledging the primacy of that country in such matters 'riconosciendola per Madre di tutte les Scienze'. He brought back in his journal a series of tables for a ready reckoner devised by the Jesuits of Madrid on the same principles as Napier's bones. And like his cousin and the other Fellows of the Royal Society he retained a sceptical but not altogether dismissive curiosity about magic. At his last meeting with Sir William Cascar that grizzled veteran gave him two recipes, especially useful in the military profession, for making a man 'shott and stickefree'. Wearing the dried after-birth of a man-child under one's armpit was one way and certainly simpler than the other:

'To find out a white serpent (which most commonly is had under a Hazell nutt Tree) and take him on any Thursday morning before sunrise and eate some of his flesh any way either raw, boiled or rosted and this will make a man shott and sticke free and proof against anything but a Cannon Bullett.'

The many-sidedness of Sandwich's curiosity did not lead him to forget that his business was with politics and trade. A fortnight before he left, the King and Queen celebrated the Peace Treaty in which he had been instrumental by processing in their coaches through the streets of Madrid. '. . . Greate demonstrations of joy (but I heard few cry vive as ye King's coach passed by). This was ye first time ye King or ye Queen hath beene abroad out of ye Palace since ye Death of King Ph.4°.' He used his own powers of observation as well as the excellent contacts he had developed. He was to apply them to the commercial and economic life of the country through which he passed on his journey to Cadiz where he was to take ship for Tangier.

His last visit on his very last day was to the graves of the members of his mission in the garden of the Siete Chimeneas (one of the powerful inducements to a deathbed conversion to Catholicism was that it was the only way of securing burial in consecrated ground). There was the footman killed in the first days of the affray with the alguazills. There was his chaplain, Mr Moore, 'a learned man, an excellent preacher, of a very good life, and very civill and discreete' who had died of a fever only seven weeks earlier. There was a head cook, a musician, the man who looked after the linen, an interpreter, two pages and a postal agent. The ambassador was not too grand to notice and appreciate them.

Fountain of Hercules in the garden at Aranjuez

The fountain of Nuestra Señora de los Afligidos in Madrid

215

The manner how y King waters y
young walkes of Elmes in y Buen Retiro
& elsewher also y Thus.
The Ground hauinge a descent, They
open a small trench from y Toppe of y
hill to y bottome in y line it selfe
wherring Trees are planted. & round
about y foote of each Tree They open y
Ground about a handfull deepe & some
4 foote Diametre (to Hold a Convenient
Proposition of water to refresh y tree)
Then w th the braÿ four They lett in y water
at y Toppe of y Trench w ch presently
runns to y bottome & fills y round Pitt. 1. when y
gardiner w th his Hour goes upward & closes y East
y lower side of y round Pitt. 2. & after y
filled goes & stopps y lower side of y round Pitt 3
& so Proceeds upwards untill y whole rowe
be supplied w th water.

opposit of y hill

6
5
4
3
2
1

foote 15 ft th

Watering plan for the walks of young elms in the Buen Retiro

216

XIX

Return Journey

=≈≈≈

AT THE HEIGHT OF SUMMER a wise traveller waited for the end of the day. It was half-past seven in the evening of July 10th that Sandwich set out from Madrid. As before he employs the language of navigation and laid off a course south-east by south which brought him at eleven o'clock to a village where he lodged. At midnight a terrible storm broke 'a greate blessinge to us in these Dogg dayes to coole ye ayre, lay ye Dust and make our journey much more fresh and wholesome'. He employed the pause to record in his own hand the local methods of vinification, two pages on the subject, besides exact measurements of the great casks, even down to the thickness of the pipestaves, which were made of pine, while the hoops that bound them together were of poplar.

He stopped a day at Toledo where he lodged in a silk merchant's house, no doubt the better to find out about the chief manufacture of the city. The statistics of the trade are duly recorded. Here as in many other Spanish towns he found that people preferred to drink the river water to the rain collected in cisterns which was used for washing. Like their wine it was more palatable if kept for six months or more. A six-hour journey brought him to Mora. Here he had an interesting conversation with a friar who had been surgeon to the garrison at Oran, where the tentacles of the Inquisition did not reach. Jews were tolerated there and had their synagogue, acting as 'ye Brokers betweene them [the Spaniards] and ye Moores'. Indeed some of the neighbouring Moors were allowed to raise cavalry for their own protection, swearing fealty to Spain. Mora was the centre of wine production for the region 'most of it white and excellent good'.

Wine was the main crop of the poor country he was passing through. At Consuegra in the month of May before the river dried up the capture of tortoises was a useful subsidiary. The breaking of the shells from which the baby tortoise emerged was believed to result from an intent paternal stare: 'only ye force of his eyes looking upon them hatches them'. The flesh '*poco aspero*' was disdained even by the poor. The wine, all red, was kept in vats and earthenware vessels (cuevas and tinajas), the best for as much as eight or ten years. The great pine hogsheads were not used in La Mancha.

It was here that Sandwich saw 'the first windmill that I remember to have seen in Spayn. The Greate Lords that have ye watermills will not suffer windmills, allthough they make their tenants goe 7 or 8 leagues to grind their corne (as they do round about Toledo to that towne)'. The poverty of the land made for a very primitive agriculture, evident in the methods of winnowing corn and in the absence of barns or stacks. Harrowing was effected by hurdles set with sharp flints. A cultural detour was made to the house of Quevedo – 'they say he was a man of very shaying splay leggs and an ugly face and deformed nose'. Such is literary fame.

La Mancha left behind they entered 'ye sierra morena, which are one of the most famous çierras of Spayn running quite along from sea to sea from ye side of Badajoz unto Valentia'. It was well-timbered and sheltered a number of highwaymen as well as an abundance of wild life, 'wolves foxes, Beares of a Dunn Color (but noe lions, tiger or pards)'. There was little vineyard or arable but what wine there was at St Estephan was good. 'The white is somewhat of tast like ye Arribadabia wine of Gallicia but stronger excellent wine.' The silk factory there had a wheel for winding the silk of which his companion Harbord made a drawing. Honey and wax were the mainstay of the economy. Between two and three thousand beehives made of cork were managed by smoking the bees with rosemary smoke. It seems strange that so knowledgeable a man should be imperfectly informed on so ancient a craft as bee-keeping but we read 'In a swarme if they house not ye Master Bee that Hive will come to noe profitt and ye Bees will not worke.' A good naturalist he records the wild plants and trees with their Spanish names including 'a most high-smelling plant of ye species of thyme – the Spanish call it Polèo – a very picquant tast, a Hott herbe . . . to warme ye stomach'.

Changing course to west-south-west and still travelling by night – it was so dark that they had to halt for four hours for moonrise – they came to Linaris, the site of the best lead mines in Spain. Shot was manufactured by heating the metal and dropping it through a kind of colander (drawn by Sandwich) as indeed it continued to be as late as the war of 1939–1945 in the Shot Tower near Waterloo Bridge. The industry was in the hands of 300 registered proprietors who had the right to dig where they liked but had to pay for the damage they caused in addition to the royalties payable to the Crown. Output was generally in the range of 80,000 to 100,000 quintals per annum but 'when ye Prise runns low they forebear working and then some years they make not above 40,000 quintals'. The eddies of a more advanced economy were beginning to stir: but Sandwich noted 'Although this Towne be in Andalusia yet ye bras money [vellon] goe here and all over ye Country untill you come neere ye Sea Coast where foreign merchants Traffique and There onely silver and Gold passes.'

Moving almost due west in twenty miles they found themselves in a rich landscape: 'ye Bravest view of olive trees that ever I saw in a Country'. Annual production amounted to nearly 3000 tons, much of it exported to Madrid and other parts of Castile. Not much corn was grown but there was plenty of wine 'very stronge and sweetish of taste both white and red. Very little beefe is eaten in Castile, nor milke or cheese or butter of cows is used.' Oxen were bred for draught and tillage. In the town of Andujar the inhabitants would drink no water other than that of the Guadalquivir and very good it was. The town was large 'a good Plaça and a very fine building 3 storyes high upon pillars, all open to ye plaça to sitt and behold ye torrearing . . .'

On the way to Cordoba Sandwich turned off to visit Carpio. It had been the seat of Don Luis de Haro, the skilful mediocrity who had endeavoured to repair the calamitous failures of his more ambitious uncle Olivares in the conduct of affairs under Philip IV. His architectural projects were correspondingly modest when compared with the Buen Retiro, so much admired by Sandwich. 'He hath layd foundations of a greate house in a Square round about that old Tower but died before it was brought to any perfection; He hath built a chappell and Pantheon here which I saw [his body and others of his kindred were shortly to be brought from Madrid] . . . his Ancestors conquered ye place from ye hands of ye Moores (as they say)'. The titles and places inherited by his son, here set out in detail and their emoluments converted to sterling, yielded the huge annual income of £20,676. Great latifundia of this kind could provide capital for engineering.

'Here is a Greate Ingenio to raise water out of ye river Guadalquivir to water a greate quantity of Grounds employed to Gardening uses and herbage. It is antique, built by Don Diego Lopez de Haro A.D. 1568. It is by 3 greate waterwheeles of 14 yards Diameter that workes in ye nature of an Anoria. They worke perpetually and cost in repaires 2000 ducats a yeare and advance ye Ground in profitt 4000 ducats a yeare.'

Sandwich reached Cordoba next day, July 25th. Among the wonders of the cathedral he observed that one of Mahomet's banners preserved in a chapel was 'much like a horse colors used in England'. The silk industry and the oranges growing in the streets impressed him. 'And here we mett with a fresh breeze in ye nights at S.W. which I gesse to be ye influence of ye western ocean.' The journey to Cadiz by the fine walled town of Exija was through a land rich in corn and wine and oil and textile factories. The single and double taffetas were reputed the best in Spain. On the 27th he noted 'at 8 o'clocke this nighte I had passed my 43rd yeare of age'.

Next day at the hill-top town of Carmona he was met by two messengers from the *Greenwich* frigate which had come in to Cadiz on the 26th, having sailed from the Downs on June 13th, calling at Lisbon on July 7th to land Sir Robert Southwell returning to his embassy. The huge postbag they brought included letters from family and relations, from ministers and officials, from the East India Company, from the Duke of York and the King but nothing from Samuel Pepys. The Duke of York congratulated him on the treaty between Spain and Portugal. The King set out at large the terms on which he was to inquire into the affairs of Tangier. Arlington fired the first shot in the salvo prepared by Southwell. He warned him that he would be 'severely chidden' on his return for allowing Carpio to sign above him. Ruvigny, the French ambassador in London, had told the King that Sandwich always gave Carpio 'the good place and the right hand in all meetings and visits at Lisbon'.

This touched Sandwich on the raw. The feeling that he had been treated basely and ungratefully hardened into conviction. His reputation was being, in his own verb, 'exposed'. He devoted several pages to the

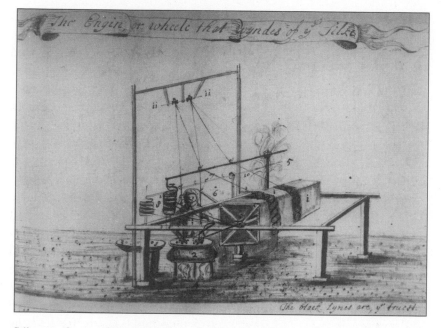

Silk manufacture. The drawing was made by Harbord at St Estephan in July 1668

analysis of precedence in diplomatic affairs, citing the elaborate courtesy shewn to each other by Henry VIII and Francis I. He defended his own towards the Marquis of Carpio because he was his prisoner and thus by definition incapable of any pretence to honour 'And I beleive the Marquis of Carpio will be found better to deserve blame for treating unfree and under ye Protection of another Prince.' If it came to procedural hair-splitting Sandwich could hold his own. But perhaps what really annoyed him was to have good breeding mistaken for weakness.

At sunrise on the 29th he entered Seville after a night journey of twenty miles. 'In ye time of K. Ferdinand & Isabell shipps of 800 Tonn from ye Indies came up to ye key at Sevill, now a vessell of 200 scarce hath water enough.' Although it had lost its primacy as a port it was still the centre of administration and trade. In Malaga, Cadiz and San Lucar English sales, including Newfoundland fish, amounted to £1m a year. 'The English merchants make their returnes home again in West India commodities, chiefly in Verinaes tobacco (formerly) Cuchineale logwood and Indigo but most principally now in peeces of eight . . . ¼ part of this

Sandwich's own annotated drawing for the most common contrivance for irrigation

goes hence in ready monye for ye Canarye to ballance that Trade. A greate prejudice to England ... They say our Colchester bayes is ye best English commodity in Spayn (if it be not adulterated which of late yeares it hath been but is mended againe). The Dutch have of late yeares outtraded us in light stuff and fine to ye eye ... English merchants complain that ye English take not care enough to make ye English manufacture faire to ye eye.' English merchants, it appeared made all their payments in gold. The exchange rate between gold and silver was set out and the movements of the two metals discussed.

The Alcazar is succinctly described: 'a very Noble Pallace Anciently of ye Moorish Kings but most magnificently and richly repaired by K. Pedro el Cruel and ye Emp. Carl. 5° and ye most elaborate carved work that ever I saw (beyond any of H. 8 of England though somewhat of that strayn)'. A cousin of Catherine of Braganza's, the Marquis de Villa Manriquez, presented him with a document dated 1648 dealing with Portuguese history and the claimants to the throne and expounding the prophecies of Bandarra, the source of the cult of King Sebastian and the expectation of his victorious return which Sandwich had come across at Evora on his way back from Lisbon.

'They drink much Lucena wine here but ye best wine I tasted ... came from ye Topp of ye Sierra Morena, a wine not so strong and Hott as lucena though strong enough and of an amber color.' At Xeres, two days' journey away, there was 'The best Sacke in Spaine and abundance of it.' The Corregidor 'and many of the Cheife Senors of this towne mett mee in their coaches a mile out of ye towne ... The most civill usage I have found in any citty of Spaine.' England, Ireland and Scotland between them drank one-fifth of the total production, with Cadiz itself and the King's fleet accounting for another fifth each. 'Lucena wine will not beare the sea. Xeres beares ye sea ye best of any in the world.' Water kept in cask aboard ship rapidly became so disgusting that it could only be swallowed if mixed with beverage wine, as Sandwich knew from experience. The Corregidor, oddly enough, came from Navarre and stoutly maintained the supremacy of the wine called Per Alta, especially if it were more than three years old (at which age Xeres became undrinkable 'soe stronge that it is like Hott water'). According to him it was the habitual choice both of Don Luis de Haro and 'ye olde K. of France Lewis 13.'

On August 4th on the bridge at Sirase which divided the galley harbour of Cadiz from the moorings of the ocean-going ships Sandwich was met by Consul Westcomb at the head of the English merchant community in their coaches. They carried him off to a neighbouring Quinta 'to refresh with fruits and chocolatti' and then into the city where he at once took to his bed. 'My greate infirmities occasioned in my journey oblidged mee to ye Quickest and easiest putting an end thereunto as I did.' For a very fat man in very hot weather so long a journey, even if the travel were largely by night, must have been exhausting. While he was convalescent he took down a circumstantial account given him by 'an English merchant of Good Creditt' of the betrayal to the Spaniards of Cromwell's secret instructions to Blake in the early summer of 1655.

The villain of the piece was Henry Rumbold, a Royalist wine-merchant in Cadiz who was in partnership with Secretary Thurloe's brother-in-law, a connexion which would nowadays attract the attentions of the security services. The Duke of Medina Caeli, then General commanding the coast of Andalusia, had been informed by Madrid of Cromwell's probably hostile intentions. The fleet for New Spain was on the point of sailing from Cadiz, off which Blake was cruising, and the returning plate fleet was expected at no distant date. Had Cromwell given Blake a free hand to attack as and when opportunity offered? Or was he to await some colourable pretext? The Duke sent for Rumbold and asked him to find out. Rumbold managed to get aboard the flagship, probably in the ordinary way of business as Blake's letters at this time complain urgently of the shortage of liquor which threatened the sea-keeping capacity of the fleet. Once aboard 'Mr Rumbold pretends ye fearefullnesse of ye English merchants in Spayn of theire persons and estates in case of a rupture between England and Spayn ... promises reward to ye Generall's secretary (wch was, as I thinke, Mr Hempson) to lett him know ye Contents of ye Generall's new orders. The Secretary was prevailed with to be consenting, but was not possest of ye letter, but it lay in ye Gen$^{ll's}$ cabin upon ye table in ye State Room.' The Secretary then enlisted the help of 'Mr James Wilson (a broken merchant then on board Blake that died this last yeare at Tanger)'. They managed to slip into the great cabin while Blake was doing the honours of the ship to a visiting Dutch admiral and Rumbold took down the letter at their dictation. The key clause was that Blake was 'by no meanes to beginn a warr but if he mett with any Spanish shipps that were goinge to or cominge from ye Indias that he should then take or destroy them.'

Medina Caeli at once sent the copied letter to Madrid:

by this accident ye new orders of Blake were discovered to ye Spanish Court in 20 days after they were issued out at Whitehall. Ye Duke stopps ye goinge out of ye New Spayn fleete (which were impatient of demurrage and would certainly in a day or two have gone out to sea having confidence ye English would not have broke with them and this was the cause ye fleete of warr was immediately sett out under Don Pablo de Contreras with orders not to beginn with Blake, knowing ye uncertainty of Blake's instructions would in likelihood restraine him from falling first upon them (as indeed it did notwithstanding ye advice of his councell of warr to fight ye Spaniard.) . . . The ambiguity lay in that ye Spanish fleete was neither going to nor from ye Indias but expecting ye arrivall of ye Galleons to conduct safe into theire Port.

This action of Rumbold's was of infinite ill consequence to England and was ye occasion of much fame and creditt to ye Duke of Medina Caeli . . .

There are several points of particular personal interest about Sandwich's long transcription of this recital, made, as he observed, 'for my owne curiosity. Beinge Then of ye Protectors Councell I preserve ye memory of it.' The first is that he misdates the episode to 1656, when he himself was serving as Blake's joint General at Sea, instead of 1655, when he was indeed a member of the Council of State and had written, at the time, a vivid account of the meeting at which Oliver had pressed his policy of war with Spain against the objections of Lambert (see p. 36). Here he enlarges upon that earlier version:

. . . Cromwell chose it as beinge necessary to have some enimye to employ ye many shipps, which ye late Dutch warr had brought into use, against and to spend unquiett spirits by land forces. The french was too dangerous a neighbor to make an enimye of as ye case stood, for he was neere allied to ye King of England and strong in monye and forces being now ye rising power of Europe and soe able to Helpe him and Trouble Cromwell. The Spaniard was decaying in power . . . besides ye native sloath of their councells and entreprises, an enimye hated of ye English of old and ye returne of their Indias rich, an enimye ye English had always prevailed against and gotten by their sea warrs. Besides ye Gratifying ye zealous persons in England that have ill will to Spayn upon ye notion of his being ye Support of ye Papacye and ye power that they thinke ye Scripture Prophesyes point at as to be taken away in order to ye fall of ye Pope.

Of the minor characters in the story James Wilson seems to have been acting as an Admiralty agent at Cadiz in September 1654,[1] and might well have been aboard the flagship at the date specified. Hempson's name, tentatively inserted by Sandwich, is probably a mistake. He seems to have been a banker at Cadiz who could remit payments to Leghorn.[2] Henry Rumbold's part in the story is very much in character and is supported by his own claims, rewarded after the Restoration by his appointment as Consul at Cadiz until his return to England in 1663. Apparently he used his partnership with Thurloe's brother-in-law as cover for the source of his intelligence. His elder brother was one of the chief Royalist secret agents in England. Especially interesting is the fact that in Sandwich's eyes Rumbold, now highly regarded and richly rewarded for his ultra-Royalism, is a traitor to his country.

Some accounts of Rumbold's career credit him with supplying the English forces at Tangier with provisions from Cadiz during the embarrassing interlude between its cession to England and the arrival of Lord Peterborough, the new Governor, together with his troops. Since Sandwich was himself the Commander in Chief on the spot throughout this difficult period when the old Portuguese Governor, disavowing the orders of his own government, was breathing fire and slaughter it is odd that the name rang no bell. There is no mention of him in the admittedly terse passages of the journal dealing with this period though there are several references to vessels crossing over to Cadiz for provisions. No doubt Sandwich had other things to think of more important than the name of his purveyor.

The Duke of Medina Caeli, still in office as Governor of the coast, was huffy and incivil, partly, Sandwich thought, because he had refused access to the ambassador's son Sydney when he called on him a year earlier. But both the Duke of Veraguas 'Admiral and Generall of ye fleete for ye guard of ye coast and ye true Heire of Columbus' and the son of General Pablo de Contreras mentioned above made up for the Governor's discourtesy. On August 11th Sandwich went aboard the *Greenwich* frigate, exchanged salutes with the city and with a Dutch Rear-Admiral in the port, and sailed for Tangier. Though not a great distance there was a strong levanter blowing so that they could not

1. *Letters of Robert Blake* ed. J.R. Powell (1937), 315.
2. *ibid.* 314.

weather Cape Spartel (or Cape Sprat as the English seamen generally called it) and had to beat out to sea. It was the morning of the 14th before they came to an anchor in Tangier road.

The levant wind dominated Tangier. 'They say many tymes it blowes 4 or 6 weekes together and never make reconing of it by dayes.' Unlike Cadiz, on the opposite shore, where it blew for odd numbers of days, 1, 3, 5, etc. making 'exceedinge hott weather. At Cadiz one Doctor was of opinion one should goe out and gape to receive it into one's mouth, as doing much good to ye body and drieing up humors but at Tangier . . . the old Portuguese Priest told me they held it to encrease humidity in ye body, and that it was observed in pestelentiall tymes that 2 for one died in a levant wind.' Whatever its medical effects it certainly played the devil with navigation and even with boat-work, making it impossible for vessels in the roadstead to take on stores or water for days together.

Sandwich's brief was wisely drawn to encourage him to report on every aspect of the colony; military, naval, commercial, political, administrative. It would be hard to think of any servant of Charles II's government equally qualified to do so. Tangier presented two central problems, the first practical, the second constitutional: the enormously ambitious project of constructing an artificial harbour 'the Mole' in deep fiercely tidal waters, lashed as we have seen by winds of exceptional violence; and the reconciliation of the military and commercial interests of the colony, which had reached a state of open hostility. Defence against a native population who lived for, and by, war as well as against the possibility of sea-borne assault by a European power had been from the beginning the first essential. This had led easily to arbitrary military control of every aspect of life with the usual concomitant of corruption and oppression. To correct this the Government at home had issued a new charter, incorporating Tangier as a free city encouraging merchants to settle and trade there. This was to be publicly read and the new régime inaugurated by Sandwich with fitting ceremony. To honour the occasion he wore his Garter robes, a heroic gesture given the temperature at that time of year.

The theses and antitheses of imperialism had blossomed early in Tangier. The Blimps of the military party were openly opposed by a forward-looking merchant and his even more forward-looking wife, Mr and Mrs Bland. Mrs Bland, one suspects, was the better man of the two. Pepys

Detail of a large drawing of the construction of the mole at Tangier

had been much impressed by her commercial acumen in the sailcloth
business 'Above all things pleased to hear Mrs Bland talk like a merchant
in her husband's business very well, and it seems she do understand it
and perform a great deal.' 'Fain to admire the knowledge and experience

of Mrs Bland, who I think as good a merchant as her husband.'[1] The Blands had emigrated to Tangier and had prospered. 'A merchant that has built more than any of them, and lives in better port' noted Sandwich. He was the Mayor-elect under the new charter but before it came into force the military Governor, Colonel Norwood, convened a hastily rigged court which at a trial bristling with irregularities convicted Bland of fraudulent practices. Sandwich indicated in no uncertain terms that those involved would find themselves in very hot water, at which 'theire stomachs came downe'. In the military hierarchy he outranked Norwood.

The resident whose advice he listened to most closely was a Genoese merchant, Don Carlos Soltrano, 'a rich man and a witty man'. Soltrano urged the importance of peace and free trade with the Moors, instead of the sporadic warfare that the English had inherited from their predecessors. He had been elected to the new Common Council but two aldermen of the Old Guard had challenged his right to sit. 'They would have noe Papists and Don Carlos something too quicke replied that if they desired not his company he cared not to stand.' Sandwich pointed out to them the importance of admitting Strangers ('ye King had made them freemen as well as ye others') and ordered them to put matters right before he sailed.

Soltrano also advised Sandwich on the building of the mole, recommending the method employed by his native city of lowering chests filled with rubble or cement. Although the Genoese were the acknowledged experts (Sandwich had discussed the technique with their Resident at Madrid) the scale and nature of the Tangier enterprise was of an altogether different order, the equivalent in its day of the Channel Tunnel or the Golden Gate bridge. Nothing like it had been attempted. The journal is full of scale drawings and details of costs. The manhandling of stones was assisted by 'Major Taylor's engine', a kind of four-wheeled cart, but that seems to have been the limit of mechanical ingenuity. From a complete nominal list of all the workers on the mole it is clear that a high proportion were either Spaniards or Italian or Portuguese. But obviously with a large garrison (1252 common soldiers, 117 Non Commission Officers against a mere 159 'Moldmen' in a poll count carried out by Sandwich) the soldiers provided a convenient labour

1. *Diary* 31st December 1662, 8 September 1664.

force. Since according to Sandwich's calculations a private soldier's pay, net of all deductions, amounted to £3 per annum they were understandably ready to supplement it at the rate of 14 pence per diem offered them by Sir Hugh Cholmley, the contractor and architect. This in turn offered a natural opportunity to corruption. 'This was begunn in Lord Teviot's tyme who . . . having a mind to gett money to Gratify his Major (Major Knight) invented a way to snipp 3^d a day of it from ye soldier under pretence it should be layd out for repayring ye soldiers quarters but indeed little or none was that way disposed but all went into ye Major's pocket . . . This Thinge continued . . . and ye present Lt. Govr has proclaimed that noe soldier shall voluntarily work at ye Mold unless he pay 3^d to the King.'

Nothing is clearer from Sandwich's account of Tangier than his dislike and distrust of military rule. It is the more noteworthy since his own distinguished career as an officer in the fighting services might have been expected to predispose him in its favour. But on all the questions on which he had to rule he came down firmly on the side of civil authority and citizens' rights.

How practicable, one wonders, was Soltrano's advice to cultivate peaceful relations with the Moors? The advantages to a European garrison often hanging on by its eyebrows are obvious enough. But what might the Moors expect to get out of it? Warfare, it appears, was their way of life, whether against European settlers or against each other. When Sandwich had first visited Tangier the local chieftain who was carrying all before him was a man variously referred to as Gailan or Guyland. In the years that followed his supremacy had been undermined by a base-born son of an earlier ruler, usually referred to by Sandwich and his correspondents as Taffiletti. In fact this was, as Sandwich seems to have found out, a territorial title deriving from the oasis of Tafilet to the south of the Atlas Mountains and his real name was Muley Rexid. He had all the marks of a successful military leader, ruthless, efficient and honest. To these he added the personal fearlessness and inflexibility of Muslim fundamentalism 'for he is alwaies first in action and saies that he cannot live one minute shorter than what God has promised him and that if he could he would not'. His personal bodyguard consisted of '3000 Blackes of Guinea' and he had already conquered Fez and Tetuan. The whole of Morocco seemed about to fall to him 'They say he promises to take in ye Christian Guarrisons.' When Sandwich arrived an envoy from the Governor of Tetuan was discussing the exchange of prisoners with Norwood. Sandwich recognized him as 'one La Roche, a Moore that was Secretary with Gayland and with mee on board my shipp 7 yeares ago when I was in this bay and first possessed Tanger'. His late employer, Gayland, was closely besieged in Arzila, on the coast, from where bids for English support and especially English munitions arrived at frequent intervals. Sandwich was too shrewd to recommend their acceptance.

It is easy to see now, with more than three centuries of hindsight, that the whole Tangier venture was a rash imperialist speculation. But are not all speculations rash until justified by success? Both Cromwell and Sandwich himself had investigated alternatives, including Gibraltar which in the end turned out a far better bet. But Tangier was obtainable without a war and without the violation of what passed for international law, not that that was an item much valued in the calculation of policy. Tangier, in short, was cheap. But what about the cost of building the mole, without which it could not serve the purpose designed for it? Then, as now, the Government listened to the experts and then, as now, the experts, like the rest of us, proved fallible. The scepticism of the man of affairs was well expressed by Pepys at the signing of the contract for its building by the Commission of which he was a member: 'a thing I did with a very ill will, because a thing which I did not at all understand, nor any or few of the whole board.'[1]

Sandwich was personally and politically committed to making a go of Tangier. His Cromwellian as much as his Clarendonian antecedents made him one of the founding fathers. In any case he had not been asked to report on the feasibility of this experiment but on its practical working. 'Cogitations ... of Thinges to be considered in order to ye making Tanger Thrive' he wrote in his *Journal* as he sailed, at last, for home on August 29th. The thoroughness of them would soon weary the reader. 'Shovells good 498 Shovells ould 2' is a fair specimen: even pick-axe handles and spindles for wheelbarrows were accounted for. But he still saw the wood for the trees: 'The new charter and suppressing ye military tyranny there I thinke hath done much for ye Inhabitants Gusto.'

1. *Diary* 30th March 1663.

Drawing of the picture over the high altar in the church at Tangier

XX

The Blessings of the Land

=====❦❦❦=====

IT WAS MID-SEPTEMBER when the *Greenwich* came to an anchor in
Mounts Bay. Sandwich noted with professional displeasure that they had
anchored too close in shore. Had the east-by-south wind that was in
their teeth freshened to a southerly gale 'we had ridd upon life and
death'. He sent his son Sydney and one of his gentlemen on ahead to
give news of his arrival but decided to go round with the ship to Spithead
rather than face the rigours of another long journey by land. Cornwall
was *terra incognita* to him. As in Spain he noted the facts about tin mining
and the pilchard fishery and was shocked by the barbarous violence of
a hurling match between two neighbouring villages. Throwing one's
opponents down mine shafts was just part of the fun.

At noon on September 28th the ship anchored at Spithead. The
Governor of Portsmouth came on board, accompanied by Colonel
Norton, son-in-law of Sandwich's old comrade-in-arms Sir John Lawson, who was to entertain him at his house at Southwick nearby. As an
ambassador returning on the successful conclusion of an important mission did he expect a rather grander reception? Or was he more exhausted
than his insatiable curiosity suggests? At any rate for two days he did
nothing except take minute measurements of Colonel Norton's garden
and notes on what it cost. (£45 per annum plus house and diet for the
gardener and his man. For which he found everything down to weeders,
seeds, plants etc. and everything well kept.) He was short of money and
had instructed Sydney to raise £2000 on the security of his friends.
Pepys, when applied to, grudgingly and guiltily came across with a draft
for £500 'the rather because I have been remiss in writing to him during

this voyage – more than ever I did in my life, and more indeed then was fit for me'.[1] The money was followed next day, October 1st, by Pepys in person, accompanied by Sandwich's two elder sons together with two coaches and six horses to take him to London. The longed-for reunion between husband and wife must have taken place there since he stayed a week in the capital before setting out for Hinchingbrooke, a journey which conveniently enabled him to present his humble duty to the King who was staying at Audley End.

That first week in October was employed in taking the necessary soundings, public and private. Where did he stand with the new administration known as the Cabal? Where did it stand with itself? Who's in, who's out? Was he looked on as a Commander whose prudence and professionalism compared well with the narrowly avoided disaster of the Four Days Battle and the national humiliation of the Medway, or were his irregularities over the Prize Goods to make him a scapegoat for a war which had brought nothing about? Was he to be congratulated for achieving two important treaties or rapped over the knuckles for not having made enough fuss about precedence? Was he, in a word, successful and on his way to be rich, or written down and likely to be distrained on for debt? There were substantial grounds for either view. For months past Lady Sandwich and a number of his friends had pressed him to return and defend himself against the Parliamentary inquiry into the various miscarriages of the war. Some of them such as Pepys's old rival for the position of right-hand man, John Creed, had tempered this advice with encouragement. People had been critical of Monck and Rupert's performance and there was a current of feeling – this was in April 1667 – that Sandwich should be recalled from Madrid, not to face a Parliamentary inquiry but to take command of the fleet for the ensuing year.[2]

On one question there was no room for any doubt. His finances, personal and official, were in a parlous state. No wonder Pepys had felt such reluctance to advance him money. As an ambassador extraordinary, an Earl and a Knight of the Garter he had thought it beneath his dignity to stint on his retinue or in his style of life. The government he rep-

1. *Diary* 28th September 1668.
2. Carte MS 223 f. 305.

resented, at its wits' end for money to carry on the war, had responded infrequently and inadequately to his urgent requests. His liberal expenditure had been surcharged by borrowing at a high rate. At home Lady Sandwich had cut every outgoing to the bone, even selling some of the family plate and of the expensive presents sent home by her husband. Getting the accounts of his embassy passed took the best part of a year and even then the figures he had submitted were much reduced.[1] The Wardrobe, that great office with which he had been rewarded at the Restoration, had proved a sad disappointment. The payments to which he was entitled were charged on various Exchequer funds which were always in arrear so that, like the seamen's wages, they could only be realized at a heavy discount. Pepys, a financial realist, estimated the profits in September 1667 at less than £1000 a year. One of the most valuable incidents of the office, the large house and garden in the city, had been destroyed in the Great Fire. Sandwich was probably therefore the gainer when, in 1668, the financial structure was comprehensively reorganized and the Master put on a salary of £2200 a year in place of his extensive but uncertain perquisites. In August 1671 he sold the place to his cousin Ralph Mountagu, younger brother of Edward killed at Bergen.

The only tonic that could restore a debilitated fortune was politics. Here Sandwich's position though vulnerable was not without its hopeful aspects. In the first place the King was as gracious as ever when he received him at Audley End. And in the divisions that were opening up in the ministry there were advantages to be gained by those whom attachment to Clarendon, the fallen Chancellor, had put at risk. Throughout his service abroad Sandwich had maintained close relations, strengthened by intermarriage, with those pillars of the Clarendonian party, the Earl of Burlington and Sir George Carteret. Arlington, the ablest of those now running the government, had been Clarendon's bitter enemy and had shewn signs of displeasure with Sandwich over his refusal to allow Sir Robert Southwell a part in the Treaty of Lisbon. He was now threatened by the manoeuvres of his colleague, the Duke of Buckingham, Sandwich's old enemy. In the thieves' kitchen of Restoration politics both Buckingham and Arlington found themselves at daggers drawn with one of their most formidable allies in overthrowing Clarendon,

1. Details in Harris ii, 162 ff.

Sir William Coventry, who had himself at the same time succeeded in antagonizing both the King and the Duke of York who in their turn had been on far from brotherly terms.

The most lucid and convincing modern interpretation of the political confusion that confronted Sandwich on his return from Madrid is to be found in Chapter 10 of Dr Ronald Hutton's biography of Charles II (1989). Dr Hutton, who has made full use of Sandwich's papers, has with the insight of a historian perceived the gross overestimate of Buckingham's power and importance into which nearly all his contemporaries, except in Dr Hutton's view the King, fell headlong. His worthlessness and irrelevance to any serious purpose have long been obvious. But the power, even if it was only negative, destructive power, ascribed to him at the time is evident in Sandwich's own analysis of the political parties as he saw them in December 1669.[1]

He divides the two parties (or factions as he sometimes more aptly calls them) into those of Buckingham and those of Ormonde, Clarendon's old friend and close confidant. Ormonde's party, he writes, 'consists of the Duke of York's friends, the Church, the old Cavaliers and the Clarendonians'. The new Cavaliers, who supported Buckingham, included such formidable politicians as Sir Thomas Osborne, the future Marquis of Danby and, confusingly, Buckingham's enemy, Sir William Coventry. The reason for this was Coventry's dismissal from the Privy Council and from his position as chief naval adviser to the Duke of York. Coventry as a naval expert was by far the biggest gun that could be brought to bear on his Clarendonian ex-colleagues such as Sir George Carteret and Sandwich himself. The Commission appointed by Parliament to inquire into the suspected mishandling of money voted for the Navy held its sittings at Brooke House. 'Buckingham' wrote Sandwich '(whose greate engine hath beene the Commissioners of Brooke house wherewith he hoped to crush all that joyne not with him and to weaken the other party) to make an essay of the strength of his party and to flesh them in conqueringe, fell upon Sir G. Carteret hoping by his ruine to have made way for that of Ormonds . . .' That faction, not party, was the truer name for what Sandwich was describing is shewn by the re-drawing of the lines caused by the eruption of a long-simmering personal feud between

---

1. Printed in Appendix G in Harris, vol. ii from vol. x of Sandwich's journal.

the two major Clarendonian figures charged with the government of Ireland, Ormond the Lord Lieutenant and Orrery the Lord President of Munster. Orrery was, like Sandwich, an old intimate of Oliver Protector. In addition to that connexion his elder brother the Earl of Burlington was father-in-law to Sandwich's son and heir, Hinchingbrooke. Burlington was also Treasurer of Ireland but was only too happy to leave the discharge of these duties to his much abler and more energetic younger brother.

It is difficult not to be sucked into the current of a narrative once plunged into with such tedious particularity. But the story is well told in the work referred to, and its importance to the understanding of Sandwich is twofold. First, it unmasked the deep mutual hostility that Pepys had always, and at first uneasily, sensed between his patron and the senior colleague he had taken for his model. Sandwich knew that Coventry was out to discredit him and reciprocated wholeheartedly. He drew up a list, a long list in his own hand,[1] 'of some sums of money wch. officers of ye fleete have payd out to Sir Wm Coventry the Duke's secretary, irregularly for their places wch. is supposed not to be a tenth part, if strict enquiry be made how every officer came into ye Navy'. The whole sum amounted to £3732. Restoration politics were not fought by Queensberry rules. Sandwich did not think it necessary to point out that Coventry had himself proposed substituting a regular official salary for the under-the-counter system he had inherited. But he anticipated that defence in his concluding sentence:

> Although He Alledge in Parliament that he hath sold noe places scince ye beginning of ye warr, yct that excuses nothinge scince these men were in ye fleete and continued their places during ye warr whereby ye good discipline of ye fleete was lost and unfitt men in places of Trust.

If there were to be Courts of Inquiry, two could play at that game.

The second insight given by the 'Letter Upon Parties' as he heads it, is that it shows Sandwich's powers of detailed observation applied as rigorously to a world from which he professed to stand aloof as to phenomena which pleased or interested him, whether it be the movement of the heavenly bodies or the economy of rural Spain. One sometimes

1. Journal x, 248–50.

forgets that the man who devotes ten pages of his journal to the different methods of preparing chocolate had sat at the Council Table with Oliver. Sparing in the censorious moral judgments in which his contemporaries revelled – figures as different as Milton and Pepys can hardly get through a page without them – he records

> It was greately observed that all the Clarendonians (even my Lord Cornbury himselfe) was against Orrerye, notwithstandinge the Alliance of Mr Hide[1] with my Lord Burlington and that Lord's freindly defendinge theire father in his adversitye. Upon this ground my Lord Cornbury loses creditt.

Sandwich was surely right in estimating Buckingham's party weaker in the Lords than in the Commons; and even there he thought its strength overestimated, shrewdly observing that it 'onely is stronge when in point of accounts, liberty of conscience, or trade, the Countrey Gentlemen or the Presbiterians joyne with them but they dare not undertake any thing alone'. The movement of parties resembled the pattern of a country dance or an eightsome reel rather than that of the parade ground which we take for granted. Similarly the constitutional limits which have become axiomatic had not yet been set in stone, in particular the privileges and powers of the two houses in relation to each other. Had the Commons a share of the judicial powers allowed to the Lords? Had the Lords the rights of a court of first instance or was its jurisdiction inherently appellate? Had the Lords the right to modify or initiate measures of money supply on which, famously, the Commons based its power? All these questions were soon raised by the Brooke House inquiry, on which, to the fury of the Commons, the Lords asserted a right to hear both the accused and the Commissioners and to pronounce between them. That, and an analogous conflict between the Houses over a dispute between the East India Company and an interloper brought the King, according to Sandwich's information, to the verge of an immediate dissolution.[2]

The King did not in fact dissolve but prorogued Parliament. When it met again the Brooke House Commissioners resumed their inquisition, demanding in an increasingly peremptory tone the production of Sand-

---

1. Clarendon's second son Laurence had married one of Burlington's daughters.
2. On the details of these issues see Ogg *England in the Reign of Charles II* ii, 469–70.

wich's papers concerning the Prize Goods. For as long as he could he fenced and evaded. He had the King's warrant for what he did. He could not be expected to remember the details of affairs so long passed. In July he went to drink the waters at Epsom, pursued relentlessly by the Commissioners' requests. At last, brought to bay, he consulted the Solicitor-General, but his advice proved no match for the inflexible determination of the Commission. In September he sent, by his Master of the Horse, William Ferrer, a letter which the Chairman 'after two or three lofty looks, and wallowings in his Chair' coldly dismissed as inadequate. The Christmas prorogation gave him a breathing space. He was probably aware, as a member of the Lords' Committee appointed to consider the dispute over privilege that exacerbated relations between the two Houses, that the King was going to bring the Brooke House proceedings to a close before any damaging conclusions were reached. It sat for the last time in February 1670 without having seen the papers it had consistently demanded and which Sandwich had in fact preserved. He had got away with it.

Yet the very fact that the slur on his reputation had been kept exposed to view for so unconscionable a time hurt his pride. His successful and prudent command of the fleet had been, he knew, misrepresented by the sneers of his rival Monck who had no use for any naval action in which the scuppers did not run with blood. The imputation of cowardice was as intolerable as it was unjust. The sense of inadequate recognition of his services would have been keener in a vainer man: but even so it smarted. The matter of precedence in signing the Treaty of Lisbon had been accommodated at his first audience with the King at Audley End. Charles's graciousness had been sufficiently advertised to the Council for Buckingham to urge at its meeting that 'all the clamour was come to this; that the King had sent a gentleman his Ambassador, and he had beene civill, and if the King had sent a clown probably some rudeness or other would have beene done'. Perhaps the knowledge that the issue had been raised by Southwell, Arlington's protégé, and that Arlington had taken up a position on it, encouraged Buckingham to this uncharacteristic good sense.

Without ever being one of the King's intimate circle Sandwich was always on easy terms with him. The King, we know from Halifax's character of him, did not love an asking face: and Clarendon explicitly clears Sandwich of this all but defining characteristic of the courtier. Both men were clubbable, well-mannered and percipient. Both were deeply interested in and well informed about naval matters. Both loved discussing their diet and their health. On Christmas Eve 1668 Sandwich recorded the King's advice 'To gett away a cold *viz* Not to supp but to eate a Crust of Bread and Drinke halfe a pint of Good Bourdeaux Clarett Wine and soe goe to bed and then in ye morninge to take a draught of Coffee with a spoonful of Juniper water in it.' Whisky, too, was beginning to come into its own: 'The King now uses Usquebah in ye mornings, mingled half water and 20 dropps of Quacum [? hartshorn] putt in it. Eates noe bread nor other thing till dinner and finds it excellent against flegme.' The Victorian convention that the well-bred did not discuss their ailments would have found no favour in the age of Charles II. Clearly it was a staple of conversation at the Council Board in the intervals of affairs of state. 'Mr Secretary Trevor saies that 5 dropps of distillation of Scurvey grasse taken in 2 spoonfulls of warme mulled sacke in ye morninge when one is up and ready is excellent against ye flegme and Cleers ye Head from fumes.'

The King was ready to employ Sandwich but not to take him into his confidence. Charles II did not like ministers who ventured to disagree with him: he had had more than enough of that with Clarendon. And he certainly would not have expected Sandwich to approve of the policy that was about to culminate in the Secret Treaty of Dover. Sandwich at Madrid had corresponded regularly with his colleague Sir William Temple in the Netherlands and largely shared his ideas, namely that the rising power of France must be contained by European alliances and that England's future lay in developing her maritime and commercial potentialities. Sandwich's special knowledge and experience in this field from Cromwell's time onwards was recognized by his appointment on 5th March 1669 to the Committee for Trade and Plantations, leading a year later (30th July 1670) to the Presidency of a new Commission for the Plantations.

Within the strict limits imposed by the axiomatic assumption that colonies existed for the good of the colonizing power Sandwich brought an open mind and a law-abiding temper to the infancy of empire. He had spent a great deal of time as ambassador in Madrid trying to negotiate a limited admission for English trade to the Spanish possessions in the

Pacific and the Caribbean. He thoroughly disapproved of the bucca-neering over which the English governor of Jamaica, Sir Thomas Mody-ford, had presided. His Journal shows that he was aware of Arlington's double-dealing over this as Secretary of State under Clarendon, sending one letter to Modyford 'reprimanding him sharpely', which was to be shewn to the Spanish ambassador, and another secret letter egging him on. The Duke of Albemarle was Modyford's partner in his privateering enterprises and the Duke of York, as Lord High Admiral, was also an automatic beneficiary (ten per cent of the proceeds: it was this that made Tangier, too, a useful supplement to his income). Against these perquisites of lawlessness Sandwich argued that honest trade, such as he had secured in his treaty, was far more profitable.

On the other hand he never made the mistake of confusing the world as it was with the world as he would have had it be. In February 1669 he noted

'They say ye Pirates that use Jamaica now for theire port whence to prey upon ye Spaniard are 1000 persons already. They say also that there be a sort of men in Hispaniola called Buckaneers or Cowkillers who are not only a numerous body viz: 2000 but accustomed to all hardnesse and exellent at ye use of ye Speare and at small shott. They are a sort of Banditti or Renegades ... from out ye English, French and Spanish plantations (but especially ye French). And they are ready to joyne in any desprate mischievous designe ...' About four years earlier they had offered their services to the English who did not accept. They then applied to the French King 'who has sent a person of great prudence, conduct and quality to them'. England maintained no naval squadron in the West Indies and the military forces were negligible. On 19 July 1671 Sandwich noted of the regiment 'in the Caribee Islands. They have beene in ye W. Indies 4–5 yeares and have not had above 12 months pay from ye King and some clothes.' Early in 1670 Modyford's son, Charles, appeared before the Committee of Trade to give an account of the economy of Jamaica and submitted a proposition of his father's for retaining a thousand of the privateers and ten of their ships in pay for the security of the island. Otherwise, he said, they would go off to the French at Tortuga.

England was still uncertain of her hold in the West Indies. It was only thanks to Harman's victory there over the French and Dutch in 1667, whilst the Breda negotiations were in their final stage, that she retained any of her possessions. At this moment France appeared the most dangerous rival. Sandwich inserted in his journal an account of the French West India Company, created in 1664 'to include Canady, Accadey, Newfoundland as well as Caribee Islands and the whole coast of Guiana from ye River of Amazones to that of Orenock. From N. of Canady to Virginia & Florida with all ye coast of Africa from C. Verde to ye C. of Gd Hope.' It sounds an ambitious undertaking. In January 1670 the Committee received a long and vehement letter from Mr Gold, a considerable Newfoundland merchant. 'Sirs, I have pen in hand and I know not how to cast it aside.' Against the growing French power at sea he urged the plantation of a 'fisher colony' with a Governor and the rest of it. 'All our opinions rann against havinge any Governor or plantinge there. The best remedy against ye French being to beat them out again if ever they attempt to injure us there' noted Sandwich, who then proceeded to analyse the economics of the Newfoundland fishery, for four centuries the prime source of seamen for the Royal Navy.

The trade was the lifeblood of the south-western ports. 'Towns that have a patent and rules to govern ye fishing trade: Weymouth, Melcombe Regis, Southampton, Poole, Lyme, Dartmouth, Exeter, East Looe, Foy, Plimouth, Biddeford, Barstaple, Bristow. Their monopoly of victualling broken into by ye New Englanders. Ye Merchants every yeare take a $\frac{1}{3}$ or $\frac{1}{5}$ new men and soe nurse up men to be mariners. They settle on the Newfoundland coast in combination with ye barbarous people . . . in ye last Dutch warr 1000 stayd there. English catch yearely 300,000 quintals of Codd (or Poore Jack) called Bacaleau at Bilbao where it sells for 38 or 40 Reals per quintal. Anno 1605 250 sayle of shipps employed now 1670 about 80.' The manning ratio was exceptionally high – 2 tons to a man as against 15 or even 20 in most other trades[1] – and the ships ranged from a hundred to three hundred tons.

The relation – symbiosis rather – between trade and seapower was fundamental to Sandwich's conception of the national interest. Tangier was the *locus classicus*. Only by developing its commercial life could it be made to sustain the huge charges of a naval base. Bland, the radical mayor whom Sandwich had supported, had put forward proposals for

---

1. See Ralph Davis *The Rise of the English Shipping Industry* (1962), 58–61.

ships from the Plantations to be allowed to unload there and pay half customs, thus establishing Tangier as an entrepôt. On 20th January 1669 the Commissioners for Trade 'utterly rejected' the suggestion. Sandwich, though he does not say as much, had probably championed Bland. But at least part of his mind would have been predisposed to agree with his colleagues' emphatic rejection. On May 27th in the same year he records a debate at the Council of Trade on a proposal to liberalize admission to membership of the Company of Merchant Adventurers trading to the Eastland (the Baltic). 'It Prooved a consideration of weight and soe was putt off to another meetinge. But I observed 2 maximes in ye Debate which must overrule in this and like cases of Trade.

1. That whatsoever contributes to ye exporting thinges of English Growth or manufacture in greatest quantity is best for England. And it was affirmed by Coll. Birch, that it was soe tho' Cloath shd. abate a 3rd or ½ in Price (but then I suppose it must be understood ye manufacture still preservinge ye same goodnesse and goinge out in as great quantity) because thereby we sh. undersell our neighbours and beate them out of such Trade.

2. That ye larger and more numerous any Trading Co. of merchants is . . . ye more advantage it is to England.

In short, volume of exports was the aim of trade, and regulated corporate organization was the means to achieve it. This was not only the traditional wisdom of the past: it was also the economic doctrine of the most up-to-date monarchy in Europe. Louis XIV's 'Declaration for ye Incouragement of Commerce in general' was full of it: subsidies for building ships of 100 tons and over, mercantile representatives to be elected annually by each province to reside at Court. All this together with the constitution and general brief for the French East India Company takes up ten or twelve pages of the Journal.

What is distinctive about Sandwich is his mathematical approach. As his travels in Spain abundantly demonstrate the obtaining of statistics was his first concern. He does not actually use the word, which was not yet current English, but he was at home with the concept. He was aware, too, that the means for collecting them were sadly deficient. In November 1669 a Committee of the Lords addressed itself to finding out the causes of the decay of rents and internal trade. The Customs Commissioners acknowledged the inadequacy of their information as to the balance of trade. Much never passed through Customs, for example the herring and cod fishery, the foreign earnings of soldiers, sailors and merchants and 'the pocket Trade from France ... (such as laces, points, gloves, ribbands, necklaces, tweezers etc.) ... not driven by merchants that send goods out again but by private pedlars that are paid all in money and picke up ye Gynneys and carry them out of ye Kingdome.'

Similarly when their Lordships a day or two later turned their attention to the rate of Interest, although it was agreed that foreign money must be attracted to London, the best estimate of how much there actually was rested on nothing more than the guesses of various merchants. Holland and Italy both restricted the rate to 4%, the one by the Bank's rules, the other by the laws of the Church. In the absence of accurate information Sandwich opposed doctrinaire reform. In any case he thought supply and demand, not legislation, must determine the matter. He was outvoted on the Committee which recommended lowering the rate from 6% to 4%. But this was overturned in a vote of the whole House 'by neer 20 voices'.

Sandwich's mind never ceased to occupy itself with the great general issues of trade and national wealth but his appointment as President of the new Council for Foreign Plantations in July 1670 concentrated his attention on the colonial aspect of these matters. This involved him once again in military and constitutional affairs. How were these places to be governed and defended? The civil war and the interregnum had left them very much to their own devices which some of them, Massachusetts in particular, were not slow to exploit. The Puritan antecedents of New England had made Parliament, not the King, their favoured cause: and the Regicides who had fled there at the Restoration had eluded the pursuit of a revengeful home government. The Commission which Clarendon had sent out to bring the New England colonies to heel had been openly defied in Boston, a telling augury of the future. Sandwich was alert to the possibility of a declaration of independence with the probable support of the French and reluctant to threaten the use of force, as much from temper as from an appreciation of the difficulties of making it good. As always he started from first-hand evidence not from first principles. His journal is full of information gained from men newly come from North America, notably from Colonel Nicholls, one of Clarendon's commissioners, and Major Rainborough, a scion of that family famous in New England and in the democratic politics of the Parliamentary army. Sandwich was a good listener. His policy was also much influenced by the views of Dr Benjamin Worsley, adviser to the Council, whose opinions on interest rates he had earlier consulted.

The Council met for the first time on 3rd August 1670. Apart from the poet Edmund Waller and the Master of the Mint its membership was undistinguished. Next year, reinforced by John Evelyn, Prince Rupert and one or two other public figures it acquired permanent premises in Lord Bristol's house in Queen St, Lincoln's Inn Fields. Evelyn's *Diary* for the summer of that year shows how serious were the fears of the government that a breach with Massachusetts was imminent. The King, the Lord Keeper and the Secretaries of State attended several of the meetings. It is Evelyn who records on 3rd August 1671 that 'Coll. Midleton being called in assured us they might be curbed by a few of his Majesties 5th rate fregats, to spoile their Trade with the Ilands [the West Indies]; but though of this my L: President was not satisfied, the rest were . . .'

How relations with North America might have developed had Sandwich not been killed in the following year is a matter for speculation. The King obviously valued his judgment. A commission, not a gunboat, was to be sent.[1] Yet Sandwich was just as keen as any of his colleagues on cutting the colonies down to size should their economic development threaten any English domestic interest. New England might easily replace the old country as the supplier of manufactures and raw materials such as fuel to the sugar producers of the West Indies and that would never do.

It was sugar production that thrust Sandwich, against his every inclination, into the thick of a new struggle between the two Houses. Were the planters to be allowed to refine their sugar before exporting it, or was this an industrial interest of the home country that must be protected? The Commons, lobbied by the refiners, hit on the device of imposing a penal excise on all imports of refined sugar, irrespective of their country

1. For an admirable and much fuller account of this and of what follows see Harris ii, 208–236 and Appendix J, 333–337. The proposed commission was overtaken by events.

of origin. The Lords, petitioned by the planters, amended the clause of the Excise Bill. The Commons at once flew into a passion. Their privilege, that of granting money by taxation, was being invaded. Nonsense, bellowed their Lordships, why, in the time of Henry III . . . The point, as we know, was not finally settled until Lloyd George's famous budget two and a half centuries later. Charles II, whose immediate necessities had been met by the down payment on the Secret Treaty of Dover, separated the contestants by prorogation.

Sandwich's role in the affair is not without interest. His official knowledge and responsibility made him the obvious champion of the Lords' position on the immediate cause. Moreover he seems to have had no reservations on the historical and constitutional issues involved. He therefore accepted in principle the management of the Lords' case in the conferences with the Commons. But before agreeing to act he thought it necessary to clear his yard-arm with the King. His revenue was at risk and he had, in Sandwich's eyes, a right to be consulted. Here, surely, sounds the deepest note of his career. Government, whether the King's government, Cromwell's or the Parliament's, must be carried on. Only within that framework could the language of ideology or law have a meaning, as Hobbes had pithily pointed out twenty years earlier. It was an assumption on which he and his intellectually more agile young cousin were agreed.

Pepys and he saw comparatively little of each other in this busy period between the two wars. Both felt at first that Pepys's failure to keep in touch while Sandwich was in Madrid had distanced them from each other. And when they met, and began to talk with some degree of intimacy, it soon became clear that their relation to each other on the scale of public importance, the pecking-order of the government of Charles II, had altered considerably. Sandwich muffed the opportunity offered in presenting his report on Tangier. Pepys muffed nothing. Just how the two men were viewed by their employers was made plain when the Duke of York declined to accept Sandwich's nominee for the post of paymaster at Tangier without first securing Pepys's approval. Here was the world turned upside down!

'This my Lord in great confidence tells me that he doth take very ill from the Duke of York, though nobody knew the meaning of these words but him; and he did take no notice of them, but bit his lip . . . and did seem industrious to let me see that he was glad that the Duke of York and he might come to contend who shall be kindest to me; which I owned as his great love, and so I hope and believe it is – though my Lord did go a little too far in this business, to move it so far without consulting me.'[1]

The very fact that Sandwich should himself have admitted his humiliation to his up and thrusting cousin suggests a move towards the old warmth, as does Pepys's reaction for all its characteristic self-love. He at once invited Sandwich to dinner 'he having never yet eat a bit of my bread' and on his acceptance spared no pains to prepare an entertainment over which he sighs lovingly in the entry for January 23rd. '– one dish after another, but a dish at a time; but all so good, but above all things, the variety of wines, and excellent of their kind, I had for them, and all in so good order.' A rapprochement might well have followed this unforgettable repast. But Pepys's eyesight was giving cause for alarm. He obtained leave from the Navy Office, went for a European tour lasting several months tragically ended by the illness and death of his wife, and then had to face the Brooke House inquisition. This, as we have seen, opened such a breach between Sandwich and Sir William Coventry as to make things extremely awkward for anyone who wanted to remain on good terms with both. And with Sandwich's increasing engagement in government business that had no direct connexion with the navy the professional bond was weakened. Besides the Plantations he was on a number of Committees of the House of Lords. They were both busy men.

All this activity was necessarily London-based. Besides his lodgings at Whitehall Sandwich took the lease of a house in Hampstead and at one moment appears to have had a house in Piccadilly.[2] None of them engaged his interest and affections as Hinchingbrooke did, little though he was able to go there in the last years of his life. It was to Hinchingbrooke that he had gone to enjoy the family life he loved in October 1668. It was there that his first grandchild had been born to Jemima and Philip Carteret, a fine boy as Lady Sandwich had delightedly informed him in a letter of July 1667. It was there a day or two after his arrival,

1. *Diary* 18th January 1669.
2. Journal, x, 350. 28th March 1671 '. . . at Mr Brill's house at Pickadilly (where I lived) . . .'

that he heard of the death of his brother-in-law and fellow Cromwellian, Sir Gilbert Pickering, whom he had preserved from the vengeance of the Cavalier Parliament. It was there, five months later, that he retired to recover from a far heavier blow:

> This morninge [Feb 28] about 9 of ye clocke it pleased God to take unto himselfe my deare sweete daughter Paulina in her 20th yeare of age, beinge yett unmarried – at ye Upper Chelsey in Mrs Becke's house.

If no man is a hypocrite in his pleasures, still less is he in his griefs. No one who was in Pepys's often quoted phrase 'wholly scepticall' in religion could so express himself in his private journal. Pepys, who called at once to condole, found him 'shut up with sorrow'. He left for Hinchingbrooke that day and did not return to London for two months. His deep attachment to all his children is evident from the care with which he preserved their earliest letters and from the active interest he took in their education and health. Since his absence abroad he had acquired a new daughter-in-law who proved as gentle and affectionate as the family into which she had married. Ned, her husband, the eldest son and heir was a steady not very robust young man who would never set the Thames alight. But both contributed to their parents' happiness. 'Dearest scruple' her mother, Lady Burlington called her in a letter preserved among Sandwich's papers in the Bodleian. Her mother-in-law Lady Sandwich, that wise and kindly judge, loved her from the first.

There were four boys of school age or younger. James, the youngest, had been born in 1664. Of the daughters, Anne at the age of eighteen made a good marriage with Sir Richard Edgcumbe of Mount Edgcumbe in Cornwall in January 1671. That month was also marked by the return of 'my sonn Sydney' from the very grand European tour on which he had embarked with a family friend Clement Cotterell nearly two years earlier in May 1669. They had travelled in Germany, Italy and France so that with his experience of Spanish life his father had good grounds for saying that he had 'more liberal breeding than the rest of my younger sons'. He was his father's favourite and, after his father's death, was to marry the great heiress Anne Wortley, of whom Sandwich and his cousin Manchester had been joint-guardians. On Manchester's death in May 1671 Sandwich was left with sole responsibility.

What this entailed in those days before there was either a police force or a Married Women's Property Act to protect so rich a prey, may be seen from his Journal entry for May 29th. As a Knight Companion of the Order he was obliged to attend the Garter service at Windsor. Considering '. . . the Hazard . . . of Havinge violence used to gett her into possession of others whilest the Court and myselfe were out of Towne, beinge not out of feare also lest my owne Kindred to secure their pretensions to her might not unknowne to mee remove her to some obscure place out of my power, in which case I should have suffered deeply in my reputation in the world . . .' he had her sent down to Hinchingbrooke under strong escort. Among the posse were 'my Cosens, Mr Edward and Mr Charles Mountagu' of whom the first may well have been the predatory relation alluded to. He was Manchester's son and had been talked of as a likely suitor.

The death of a great nobleman, a Knight of the Garter, Lord Chamberlain and head of the Mountagu family involved prolonged and expensive funeral rites. The cortège set out from London for the burial at Kimbolton, two days' journey. Sandwich himself travelled in a black coach with six horses. Contingents from Boughton and from Hinchingbrooke met the hearse a few miles short of the church. It was a ceremonial postscript to the distant Civil War phase of Sandwich's career.

Sandwich had evidently been told by his cousin that he was one of his executors. On the day after his death

> Early in ye morning the Earl of Bedford met me at Whitehall (being brother to ye C^{tess}) his L^P Mr Geo. Mountagu and I went into ye Chamber where ye dead L^d lay and opened his cabinet to find his Will which we offered to read in Presence of his C^{tess} but her Ladyship being on her bed in her chamber (wee had not then beene in her L^{ship}'s Chamber but ye E. of Bedford went in and brought us that message from her) excused herself as not being fitt to hear anything of that kind (her L^a sister ye Lady Newport and Mrs Layton onely being in her chamber) but desired we should goe and reade it in ye presence of ye present Earl ye which we did.

He goes on to summarize the contents of the Will from memory and adds 'This will is ill-Drawn and beleeved to be done by ye advise or privitye of noe councell learned . . . all with his L^P's owne hand . . . but no witnesses to it nor any publication of it expressed.' Sandwich's practical curiosity elicited the details of Manchester's finances from his secretary Mr Cooling. The Lord Chamberlain's place was worth £2110 p.a. including board wages of £4 per diem. 'He said my Lord had not much above £2000 p.a. coming in by ye rent of his Lands cleere of charges. And my Lady's jointure abt. £1200. Total £5310. And he thinkes my L^d lived within compass. His table cost not above £30 a weeke wine and all.' As an afterthought, perhaps prompted by reflection on his own liberality, he adds 'And I am told my L^d of Bedford spends noe more.'

It is an instructive glimpse into the life-style of the heads of two great houses that had risen to place and wealth under the Tudors. How different, how very different, from that of Charles II's court. Among the scenes that Sandwich records in his Journal two may be selected. The first took place when the King was being entertained to dinner at the Dutch Embassy in February 1669.

Mr Thos. Killigrew [one of the Grooms of the Bedchamber] beinge merry with wine and speakinge bold raillerie (according to his custome) upon my Lord ye E. of Rochester concerning his keeping his wife in ye Country and not letting her see London, my Ld Rochester beinge irritated thereat was seene to take a Table Knife and secretly putt it into his shash, which one of ye Dutch emb^rs men told to Mr Killigrew whereupon he stood up and told ye King that mischiefe was intended against some body for one was seene to putt up a Knife secretly, and so he beleeved it was against ye King, and beinge asked who they should search he replied they should beginn with ye E. of Roch. and soe they did and found ye Knife; whereupon ye E. of R. rose up and reached his arme as far as Mr K. (who sate within one of him) and gave him a greate box on ye Eare, after which Mr K. rose from Table. The King very angerly called my Ld R. impertinent fellow and bad him be gone and soe he rose also; But a while after Dinner ye D. of Monmouth made my L^d R's peace and brought him to kisse ye King's hand and that same night he waited in ye bedchamber (in his place as Gent.) and ye next morning also. But before Dinner ye K. gave order he should be advised to withdraw from Court and goe into ye Country for a while and soe he did.

Reviewing this unedifying scene, the more disgraceful for having taken place on a state occasion, Sandwich added at a later date:

It seems my Ld R. was advised to absent himselfe some considerable tyme from Court, soe that he resolved to goe over into France ... and arriving at Paris he presented himself at ye Queen Mother (of Engl's) Court and obtained ye favour of Madam [her youngest daughter, Henriette] to bringe him to kisse ye hand of ye K. of France, but when Madam attempted it ye K. told her that he was sorry to refuse a civility to anybody that she presented him, but in this case he was obliged not to admitt into his presence one that had done so great an affront to Matie as my Lord R. had.

Reputation was the only sanction of government, apart from naked force. This incident had tarnished it in the eyes of the two European powers from whom England had most to hope or fear.

The second example, also involving the Killigrew family – this time Thomas's son, Henry – shows how the beau monde of Charles II's England conducted the gallantries on which they prided themselves. Early in May the same year Henry Killigrew, driving out to his country house at Hammersmith in his coach and two was overtaken at Hyde Park Corner by the Countess of Shrewsbury in her coach and six. She was heard to order her pages 'to gett in and goe beate Mr K (some say to kill him).' They pulled him out and set on him leaving him for dead with dangerous wounds in the neck and arm.

The Occasion was ye implacable resentment of that Ladyes of speeches and actions of Mr K's in defamation of her reputation and they say that of late he had shewed about publiquely a paper signed by her (as he affirmed) when they were kind one to another, attesting ye ability of his performance (viz. 34 or 35 tymes in 3 nights).

She Beinge now esteemed ye mistresse of my Ld D. of Buckingham who is in great favor with ye K., and tho' Mr K.'s father was very angry at first and tooke out ye Chief Justice's warrant and searched my Ladyes house (but found her absented) yet ye Prosecution cooles and is sd. nothing of, and young H.K. is like to recover of his wounds. This makes it worthy observation. Beinge a riott of so heinous a nature to all good gov^t.

But the good government that Sandwich prized and wished to serve came low on Charles II's list of priorities.

XXI

The Last Fight

IF SANDWICH'S imperial and colonial concerns took precedence over naval business the two sometimes coincided. On 21st July 1669 a Spanish renegade came to see him with plans for an English-sponsored revolt in the Indies.

> Principally he boasts of his Interest in Chili & Peru. But to this he findinge noe eare lent (my Mr being fast to his faith passed to ye Spaniard) he pretends to help us to discover considerable trade and advantages upon ye Coastes of America downe from Baldivia (ye last Spanish towne in Chili) to ye streights of Magellan and thence againe up as far as ye Rio de Plata in which Tract noe Treaty of State intervenes.

This was backed up by a remarkably comprehensive break-down of the political, financial, administrative, commercial and naval structure of the whole Spanish American empire. On October 19th a twenty-six gun ship accompanied by a pink was sent out to these waters 'for discovery'. Sir John Narbrough's equivocal reception by the Spaniards and the arrest and detention of two of his officers and men in Valdivia has usually been explained as a reprisal for Sir Thomas Modyford's activities in the Caribbean. Whether the Spanish authorities suspected England of accepting the scheme originally proposed, the voyage was not immediately productive, except in improving knowledge of navigation.

As Admiral of the Narrow Seas Sandwich was called on to rule in the matter of Salutes, on which the absurd English claims were to provide a nominal pretext for the Third Dutch War. On 11th June 1669 he was asked for an opinion on what should be required from foreign vessels

coming up the Thames and the Medway. Among the precedents considered at the meeting called 'at ye Robes in ye longe Gallery at Whitehall' three days later was the dispute between Captain Hall 'Admirall
for ye then Usurper' and the Grand Duke of Tuscany at Leghorn in
1651. The consideration of such a precedent shows that he regarded
the matter as a strictly naval one, not as a perquisite of royalty. Sandwich
was as keen as any sea officer that the flag should be respected but
professionalism and common sense were the stars he steered by. The
instructions on the subject issued by the Duke of York as Lord High
Admiral, at once assertive and ambiguous, made such a course difficult.
Sandwich kept an eye on the standing of distinguished sea officers. On
Christmas Day 1669 he noted:

> Today Sr Fretz. Hollis had his co. of foote taken from him (in ye
> Gen[ll's] Regt) upon complaint of ye Duke of York (as is reported)
> of scandalous speeches of Sir Fr. concerning ye Duke of his High-
> ness's behaviour in ye Dutch warr and other vaine boastings and
> overvaluing of himself.

Sir Frescheville Holles was a close associate of Sir Robert Holmes who,
in his turn, was one of Buckingham's followers and therefore to be
reckoned no friend to Sandwich. Yet on 31st March 1671 Sandwich
included in his journal a drawing of a boom defence invented by Sir
Robert Howard which Holles had submitted to him.

Much the most important rival was removed from the scene by the
death of Monck on 3rd January 1670. Monck was the chief, and far the
most important, source of the aspersions on Sandwich's courage in action
which cut so deep. On September 16th the only other survivor of Cromwell's Generals at Sea, Sir William Penn 'with a Gentle and Even Gale,
In much peace, Arrived and Anchored In his Last and best Port'.[1] Still
only in his forties Sandwich was now indisputably the most eminent and
experienced admiral at the disposal of his country.

His only voyage between his return from Tangier and the outbreak
of war in 1672 was to Dunkirk and back to fetch the King's sister,
Henriette, over to England in May 1670. That this was the culmination
of the policy embodied in the Secret Treaty of Dover, signed during her

---

1. Inscription on his monument in St Mary Redcliffe, Bristol.

visit, was of course unknown to Sandwich. It was much more of a diplomatic than a naval occasion. Sandwich took with him Sir Charles
Harbord, his cousin Edward Mountagu, Manchester's son, and Colonel
Lynch, a considerable Jamaica landowner who was soon to be knighted
and sent out to replace the unscrupulous Modyford as Governor. From
the Court were sent Sir Winston Churchill 'an officer of ye Greencloth
. . . to manage ye provisions' and the veteran courtier Lord St Albans.

St Albans, the long-established favourite of Henrietta Maria, regaled
Sandwich with reminiscence of the period immediately following the fall
of Richard Cromwell in 1659. He credited Mazarin with a zeal for the
House of Stuart that few have discerned:

> The Card. offered unto his L^P to send £10,000 to Lockart to pay
> and content his Guarrison of Dunkirk (provided he could be
> inclined to serve ye K^g my Master). Also to send Mr Ralph
> Mountagu into ye Sound to mee to offer mee ye monye, ports and
> other assistance of France in ye like case. Also to offer ye like
> conditions to Henry Cromwell in Ireland and to Scotland. And
> lastly that he would send his fleete from Tolon to Rochel to be neere
> for ye better employment in ye K's restitution. This proposition was
> made known to ye K. my Master but he saies my L^D Cha's interest
> opposing ye K's restitution by ye helpe of ye Q.Mother was the
> cause why that was not accepted.
>
> Moreover he told mee that after ye Treaty at Font Araby ye
> Card. offered to engage ye whole power of France for h. M's
> restitution and meete h.M. any where in person to Discousse about
> it but was of opinion that it would be better not to meet him for
> fear of disgusting ye party in England that was necessary for that
> intention.

Much of this rings true: in particular Clarendon's determination that
come what may Charles II should not be restored to his throne as the
creature of France. And it is easy to believe that Mazarin made large
offers that concealed the small print. Sandwich does not express any
opinion. But he must certainly have known that the approach to himself
had been initiated by Clarendon, St Albans' bitterest enemy, not by the
Cardinal.

The Secret Treaty, for which St Albans and the Queen Mother had
worked so assiduously, was all too soon to bear its sour fruit. Lady
Temple, the wife of Sir William whose correspondence with Sandwich

shows their complete unanimity in advocating a Dutch alliance against French aggression, returning from The Hague in an English yacht met the Dutch fleet at anchor. The English captain, because the yacht was Royal and had the Union flag at her masthead, demanded the honours of the salute. The Dutch admiral courteously acknowledged with seven guns and, because he was a personal friend of Lady Temple, went on board to pay his respects. But he declined to strike his flag and lower his topsail since his orders forbade him. The yacht's captain wisely decided not to take on single-handed the most formidable fleet in the world, and one indeed with which England was at that moment officially allied. For this dereliction of duty he was committed to the Tower and on his release not subsequently employed. Cynicism, it might be thought, could go no further. But that would be to underestimate the policy of Charles II who worked up the incident to a *casus belli*, which, without any declaration of war, was opened by an unprovoked attack on a Dutch convoy coming up Channel in March 1672.

That Sandwich both deplored the policy and despised the shabbiness of its execution is explicitly stated by his friend John Evelyn.[1] But there could be no question of refusing to serve, as he had pointed out, at the very beginning of his naval career, to Lawson's follower, Captain Lyons.[2] More especially was this true because of the imputations made against his own courage. He had, it seems, convinced himself that nothing short of his death in action could wipe his reputation clean. The second Earl of Clarendon recalled in 1694 a conversation in the garden of Lord Burlington's house shortly before Sandwich went to sea in April:

> ... his Lordship then walking with his hands one upon the shoulder of Charles Harbord and the other upon Clem Cotterel's (for his greater ease being then grown somewhat goutish and otherwise unwieldy) told the Company by way of reflection upon the then management of our Sea affairs that though he was then Vice-Admiral of England, and Admiral of the Narrow Seas, yet he knew no more of what was to be done that summer than any one of them ... 'This only I know,' he said, 'that I will die and these two boys (meaning Harbord and Cotterel) will die with me.'[3]

1. *Diary* (ed. de Beer) iii, 618.
2. Above p. 43.
3. MS account dated 27th April 1694 in vol. x of Sandwich's Journal.

A recollection of talk set down after so long an interval is not hard evidence. But the gist of it is strikingly confirmed by Evelyn, writing three days after he had heard of Sandwich's death:

> . . . it was not above a day or two, that going at Whitehall to take my leave of his Lordship (who had his Lodgings in the Privy Gardens) shaking me by the hand bid me *god buy*, he should he thought see me no more, & I saw to my thinking something boading in his Countenance: no says he, they will not have me live: Had I lost a Fleete (meaning on his returne from Bergen, when he took the E. India prise) I should have fared better; but be it as please God; I must do I know not what, to save my reputation . . .

It is more than likely that the proposed arrangements for fighting the first sea power of the age led by the greatest of all sea commanders did not inspire him with confidence. The English were to form their line of battle in conjunction with the French whose quality was unknown and whose experience of fleet action against a first-class power, let alone the Dutch under de Ruyter, was nil. Even in an all-English fleet the primitive state of signalling made communication tricky to say the least. With a foreign ally it would be wide open to disaster. Conceivably Sandwich himself had he been entrusted with the supreme command might by a combination of personal tact and professional skill have found means to minimize the dangers while making the best use of the undoubted superiority in men and guns enjoyed by the Allies. But the Duke of York was once again to be Admiral of the Fleet with the Frenchman, D'Estrées, a land commander with no experience of sea warfare, as Admiral of the White and thus second-in-command. Sandwich was to be Admiral of the Blue with, however, the prudent reservation that if the Duke were to be killed or disabled he, not D'Estrées, should succeed to the chief command. It was not an auspicious structure with which to confront the genius of de Ruyter; and it was the more unsound because D'Estrées was on the worst possible terms with his own second-in-command, the brilliant and experienced sea fighter Duquesne.

As it was the Allied fleet blundered into an action in which they were decisively worsted by an enemy little more than three-quarters of their combined strength. The Duke of York for all his courage in battle 'most pleasant when the great shot are thundering about his ears' was no match for his great opponent. He had had no opportunity to work up the combined fleet but he had not even made sure that his fighting instructions were properly understood by his allies, who as a result became fatally detached from the battle in its opening stages. He had, by some accounts, disregarded Sandwich's advice not to remain at anchor when the wind changed so that the fleet was on a lee shore: and, overconfident, had dismissed Sandwich's misgivings that the enemy might be closer than he thought. De Ruyter knew, none better, how to exploit these mistakes. When he attacked from windward in the early morning of May 28th the Duke's flagship was on the careen, that is partially heeled over, and it was some time before she could be righted and got ready for action.

The wind was a light easterly breeze, or perhaps a little south of east. The Dutch were sighted to the north-east of the Allied fleet, coming on in line abreast. Allied reaction was confused by the fact that the Van or White squadron, commanded by D'Estrées, was the southernmost and Sandwich's squadron, the Blue, the northern. Thus for practical purposes the Rear became the Van, since to engage the Dutch a northerly, or north-eastern course had to be steered. The French, misunderstanding the Duke's signal, set off on a southerly course, doubtless thinking that they were to get to windward of the enemy and then tack once they were clear of an all-too-close, and probably too-little known, lee shore. Though a small but respectable Dutch squadron stood after them to prevent this possibility it did not employ its advantage of the wind to press home an attack. Simply it held them off though not without some brisk action.

This was, however, nothing to the ferocity of the battle between the main body of the Dutch under de Ruyter and van Ghent and the two English squadrons. Here the attack was pressed to the limit and the slaughter on both sides would have satisfied the desiderata of Monck. His surly ghost seems to have troubled Sandwich as, with the assistance of his secretary Valevin, he put on the full dress appropriate to a commander leading his men into battle. 'Now, Val, I must be sacrificed' he is said to have remarked as he left the cabin.[1]

To describe the Battle of Solebay is beyond the scope of the present work. It has in any case been well done by the late R.C. Anderson in

1. Harris ii, 266.

his introduction to the volume he edited for the Navy Records Society *Journals and Narratives of the Third Dutch War* (1946). Among the documents he prints is a letter written by Sandwich's Flag Captain in the *Royal James*, Richard Haddock, who was wounded but survived the battle. This gives us the last first-hand account of the subject of this biography. It was among several accounts required by the Duke of York from those who had been best placed to observe the development of the action. Liberal quotation from it seems the best way of bringing Sandwich's conduct in that last scene before us, though the crash of the guns, the shouts and screams, the foul sights and smells, are necessarily left to the imagination in an official report made by a professional fighting man.

> Upon signal from our scouts of the Dutch fleet's approach (about 4 in the morning, the wind at E. by S.) we immediately put our ship into a fighting posture, brought our cable to the capstan, and heaved apeak of our anchor; which upon firing a gun and loosing fore topsail of your Royal Highness's ship we presently weighed . . . till our anchor was up; which done, we made sail and stood off (stemmed N.E. by N.) with our signal abroad for our squadron to draw into the Line of Battle, which was done as well as the short time we had would permit; and finding ourselves one of the weathermost ships, we bore to leewards till we had brought ourselves in a line; the Vice-Admiral and most of his Division right ahead, the Rear-Admiral and his right astern; only one or two of our Division a little to leeward of us, the *Edgar* and (as I remember) the *Mary Rose*, and they so near us as within call.

Sandwich, it will be remembered, set great store by the line formation and wished to tighten and toughen it by excluding the armed merchantmen with which it was (in his view) weakened and extended. He thus entered his last fight in the tactical disposition that he would have chosen. The Dutch, however, having the wind retained the initiative. They let the van of the Blue squadron under Sir Joseph Jordan sail on without engaging them and then hurled the full weight of their broadsides, supported by fireships, on the outnumbered Centre and Rear. In Haddock's words

> The Dutch squadron, Van Ghent Admiral, attacked us in the Body and Rear very smartly; let our Van go ahead without engaging them for some considerable time as far as I could perceive. We engaged

above an hour very smartly; when the Dutch found they could do no good on us with their men-of-war, they attacked us with two fireships, the first of which we fired with our shot; the second we disabled by shooting down his yards. Some time before I had sent our barge by my Lord Sandwich's command ahead to Sir Joseph Jordan to tack, and with his Division to weather the Dutch that were upon us, and to beat them down to leeward and come to our assistance. Our pinnace I sent likewise to command our ships to come to our assistance, which boat never returned, but were on board several ships, who endeavoured, but could not effect it.

Already Haddock implies a distinction between the Rear under Kempthorne, which in those light airs could not increase speed to overhaul the Centre, and the Van under Jordan who had only to tack to the southward in order to rejoin his hard-pressed Admiral. By coming down to windward of the Dutch they would catch the enemy between two fires and at once relieve Sandwich from the concentration of force that must otherwise soon overwhelm him. In fact Jordan had tacked before Sandwich's barge reached him but instead of rallying to his flag he stood on to the southward where the Duke of York's flagship, the *Prince*, was by this time under fierce attack. That Haddock, for all the grudging acceptance necessarily demanded in a letter to the Duke, never forgave what he saw as a base betrayal is clear from the picture painted for him by Van de Velde in 1672. It shows the *Royal James* with Sandwich's Blue Flag at the main and – here is the nub – the small union flag at the fore. This was the signal for the Van division to tack. It was to fly forever in the picture as a reminder of Jordan's desertion of his chief.[1]

No doubt Jordan had his reasons. His own account of this phase of the battle is not enlightening and seems to represent himself as taking on a considerable part of the Dutch fleet single-handed: '. . . a hot dispute against an Admiral, Vice Admiral and Rear Admiral and 5 or 6 great ships more, with 4 or 5 fireships . . .'[2] The Duke of York was evidently satisfied with his conduct since he promoted him to be his own Vice-Admiral of the Red. But Sandwich was a commander who engaged

---

1. I owe this fascinating detail to the kindness of Mr Frank L. Fox. Michael Robinson in his great catalogue *The Paintings of the Willem Van De Veide* (1990) ii, 578 records the suggestion and traces the history of the picture.
2. *Journals and Narratives* (N.R.S. 1946), 171.

the passionate loyalty of his subordinates and it is not surprising that the officers of his flagship and his division felt as they did. To resume Haddock's account at the crucial point when, after the failure of the fire-ship attack on the *Royal James*, van Brakel, one of the most daring of the Dutch commanders, had succeeded in running his 60-gun ship aboard the bows of the 100-gun flagship and raking her from stem to stern:

> When he had been thwart our hawse some short time, my Lord Sandwich asked me whether it was not our best way to quit ourselves of him, to board him with our men, and take him by force; I gave him my reasons, that it would be very disadvantageous to us. First, that I must have commanded our men from our guns, having then, I believe, betwixt 250 to 300 men killed and wounded; and could not expect but to lose 100 men in taking him. [Her full complement was 800 men.] Secondly, if we had so done, we could not have cut him loose from us, by reason the tide of flood bound him fast thwart our hawse; and thirdly, had we plyed our guns slowly by taking away our men, we had then given cause to the enemy to believe we had been disabled; and consequently more of them would have boarded us, which might possibly have overpressed us: so that my Lord was satisfied with my reasons, and resolved we should fight it out in our defence to the last man, being still in expectation of assistance.
>
> About 9 or 11 o'clock Van Ghent himself finding those his other Flags could do no good upon us, nor that party with them, came up with us himself (we having lost the conduct of our ship). He ranged along our starboard side, gave us a smart volley of small shot, and his broadside, which we returned with our middle and lower tier; our upper guns almost all disabled, the men killed at them; he passed ahead of us in musket shot. [Van Ghent himself was killed in this exchange of fire.]
>
> Some time after, Sir Joseph Jordan (our barge having been with him and gave him my Lord's commands) passed by us to windward very unkindly, with how many followers of his Division I remember not, and took no notice at all of us; which made me call to mind his sayings to your Royal Highness when he received his commission that he would stand betwixt your Royal Highness and danger; which I gave my Lord account of, and did believe by his [i.e. Jordan's] acting yourself might be in his view in greater danger than we, which made my Lord Sandwich answer me, we must do our best to defend ourselves alone.

Near 12 o'clock I was shot in the foot with a small shot, I suppose out of Van Ghent's maintop, which in a short time filled my shoe full of blood, forced me to go down to be dressed; I gave my Lord account of it and resolved up again as soon as possible; when went down I sent up Sir Charles Harbord [Sandwich's young follower who had been commissioned as First Lieutenant of the *Royal James*] and Lt. Mayo to stand by my Lord, and as soon as I came down, remembering the flood was done, sent up to my Lord desiring him to command the ship to an anchor by the stern, which was immediately done, and after brought up, the ship thwart our hawse fell away, and being entangled with our rigging, our men entered her and took her, cut her loose from us, and at my Lord's command returned all on board again; upon which I hearing the ship was loose from us, sent up to my Lord that the cable might be cut and the ship brought to sail afore the wind, and to set our mainsail, which was presently done, and then my Lord sent me his thanks for my advice, and withal to be of good cheer that he doubted not but that we should save our ship; at that time one of our chirurgeons was cutting off the shattered flesh and tendons of my toe; and immediately after we were boarded by that fatal fireship that burnt the noble *Royal James*; which that she may be the last, is the prayers of, Royal Sir, your most dutiful and obedient servant, Richard Haddock. August 25th 1672.

Nothing is more striking in this vivid and moving account than the relations of courtesy and trust, maintained in the tightest of tight corners, between the Admiral and his Flag Captain. Haddock was a fine officer who had begun his service under Blake and ended it as a Commander-in-Chief in the wars of William III, dying as Comptroller of the Navy in the first months of George I. His good opinion, eloquent almost to the point of insubordination to the Duke of York, is one that any sea officer would value. Clearly it had been touch and go with the *Royal James*. As long as the *Groot Hollandia* had been fast across her bowsprit she had lost steerage. Not much of her rigging could still have been standing after the fearful punishment she had undergone, but she had managed to set her mainsail and the wind, now backed to south-east, was on her quarter. But before she could get any way on her that same wind wafted up the lighter fireship under a full spread of canvas. A wooden ship soon became an inferno. She burnt to the waterline. Haddock and his old shipmate Lieutenant Mayo were among the handful of survivors.

Sandwich's prophecy that Charles Harbord and Clement Cotterell would perish with him was fulfilled. He himself had been wounded slightly in the arm and thigh. His companions urged him to jump and swim for it but his bulk and general unwieldiness disinclined him. Perhaps the constricting formality of the clothes he had put on, the caparison of a commander leading his men into battle, further inhibited him. When his body was found in the water thirty miles away nearly a fortnight later he was still wearing his Garter ribbon. He had still been on board when everyone else who could stand had left the ship but the corpse showed no sign of scorching or singeing.

The recognition that had been denied him in life was granted in death. The King, it is true, had consistently shewn a sense of his worth and an appreciation of his services, even if he had not troubled to call his ministers to heel with the sharpness he reserved for any disobliging reflections they might cast on his mistresses. He gave orders that he should be buried in Westminster Abbey with the magnificence of a great public occasion.

The body had been landed at Harwich where it was embalmed and carried to the chapel of the Landguard fort. On June 22nd a despatch vessel, saluted by twenty-one guns from the fort, took the coffin up to Deptford where it lay for several days while the great preparations for the funeral were completed. On July 3rd a procession of state barges led by musicians and heralds set out for Westminster. The funeral barge draped in black velvet with the Earl's coronet on a cushion over the pall was followed by those of the King, the Queen, the Duke of York, the Lord Mayor and the various City Companies. The coffin was carried in procession to Westminster Hall, where another, and grander, procession formed up to attend it for the short journey to the Abbey. Oddly, to our eyes, the newly succeeded Earl of Manchester was Chief Mourner, as head of the family, not Lady Sandwich. Shoals of Mountagues were prominent among the array of Peers and officers of the Order of the Garter but the true and truly reciprocated loyalties of the dead man were faithfully represented by the servants, household officers, chaplains, secretaries and shipmates who walked ahead of the coffin. By its side the bannerols of Mountagu, of Crew and of other families with whom he was connected were carried by old friends; among them Samuel Pepys and the bereaved fathers of the two young friends who in death had not been divided, Sir Charles Cotterell and old Sir Charles Harbord.

Lady Sandwich did not long outlive her husband. She left Hinching-brooke soon after the funeral and went to live near her daughter Anne, who had married Sir Richard Edgcumbe of Mount Edgcumbe, dying in 1674. The grief that had come upon her was superadded to the un-looked-for loss the previous September of her young and much-loved daughter-in-law Lady Hinchingbrooke. Ned, the bereaved husband who succeeded as Second Earl, lived a respectable but undistinguished life, dogged by ill-health. Of the other children one reached the eminence of the Mastership of Trinity, Cambridge and the Deanery of Durham and two more followed the family tradition of the law with modest suc-cess. None of them, not even Sydney, occupied the leading position in the life of their country that their father had achieved with such grace and goodwill.

And what shall be said of him that is not a repetition of what has been said already in these pages? John Evelyn who wrote the best epitaph on his cousin Samuel Pepys may justly claim the last word:

> The Earle of Sandwich, that incomparable person and my particular friend . . . this brave man . . . being an able & experienc'd seaman . . . he allwayes brought of his Majesties ships, without losse, though not without as many markes of true Courage as the stoutest of them; & I am witnesse, that in the late War, [i.e. in 1665] his owne ship was pierced like a Culender; But the businesse was, he was utterly against the War from the beginning, & abhor'd the attacquing of the Smyrna fleete; [the Dutch convoy which Holmes had attacked in the Channel in March without benefit of a Declar-ation of War]. He did not favour the brutish & heady expedition of Clifford at Bergin; nor was he so stupidly furious, & confident as was the D: of Albemarle, who believed he could vanquish the Hollander with one Squadron: My L: Sandwich was prudent as well as Valiant, & allways govern'd his affairs with successe, and little losse, he was for deliberation & reason, they for action & slaughter without either; & for this, whisperd it, as if my L: of Sandwich were not so Gallant, because he was not so rash, & knew how fatal it were to loose a Fleete, such as was that under his Conduct, & for which these very persons would have censurd him on the other side.
>
> This it was which I am confident griev'd him, & made him enter like a Lion, & fight like one too, in the middst of the hottest service,

where the stoutest of the rest, seing him ingagd, & so many ships upon him durst not, or would not, come into his succour, as some of them, whom I know, might have don. Thus this gallant Person perish'd to gratifie the pride & envy, of some I named: & deplorable was the losse, of one of the best accomplish[ed] persons, not onely of this Nation but of any other: He was learned in the Mathematics, in Musique, in Sea affaires, in Political: Had ben divers Embassies, was of a sweete obliging temper; Sober, Chast, infinitly ingenious & a true noble man, an ornament to the Court, & his Prince, nor has he left any that approch his many Virtues behind him . . . I am yet heartily griev'd at this mighty losse, nor do I call it to my thoughts without emotion.[1]

1. Evelyn *Diary* iii 616–619 31st May 1672.

SOURCES,
BIBLIOGRAPHY
AND INDEX

SOURCES AND BIBLIOGRAPHY

I MANUSCRIPT COLLECTIONS

My principal source is Sandwich's Journal, preserved at Mapperton, and the Letters to Ministers in the same archive.

Other collections consulted are

Bodleian Library
    Carte MSS
    Clarendon MSS

British Library
    Additional MSS
    Harleian MSS
    Sloane MSS

References to these will be found in the text. One to which no direct reference is made but is of some curiosity is Harleian MS 1625. It is a short and very complimentary character sketch of Sandwich written in French at Bourg Charente and dated 10th October 1684. From internal evidence it seems to have been written by an Englishman. On f. 8 'ennemi' is spelt 'Enemy' and at the foot of f. 4 'My Lord Mountagu' is interpolated to clarify a possibly ambiguous personal pronoun.

Who wrote it and why? It confirms much that was observed of him by other sources: his good temper and gentleness, his deep domestic affections, the breadth of his interests, his readiness to let bygones be bygones and to address the business in hand: 'Ne perdons point courage: le passé est irrevocable, réglons l'avenir: regardons en avant, *Look forward*'.

Its other marked characteristic is its panegyric tone towards Charles II and James, Duke of York, both of whom are said to have had the highest opinion of Sandwich. One may take leave to doubt this. The Stuart brothers rarely saw eye to eye except in matters of appetite.

II PRINTED BOOKS

Easily the most important for this study has been F.R. Harris *The Life of Edward Mountagu, first Earl of Sandwich* (2 vols. 1912) which is discussed in chapter 1. Each chapter of that work is preceded by its own bibliography.

Next to that must come R.C. Anderson's edition of the first volume of

The Journal of the Earl of Sandwich (Navy Records Society 1929). This, of course, is cited in references in italic, whereas the other nine volumes appear in roman.

Thurloe State Papers: *Clarendon State Papers*: *Calendar of State Papers Domestic*: *Commons Journals*: *Lords Journals*: *Clarke Papers* (Camden Society ed. C.H. Firth vols. 3 & 4). These together with the general histories of S.R. Gardiner and Sir Charles Firth or Clarendon's *History* and *Life* and *Continuation of the Life* hardly need bibliographic specification. The great modern editions of Pepys's *Diary* by R.C. Latham and W. Matthews and of Evelyn's by E.S. de Beer have been of course indispensable since both men were Sandwich's close friends and associates.

The publications of the Navy Records Society have contributed much; notable among them *Fighting Instructions 1530–1816* ed. J.S. Corbett (1905), the *Letters of Robert Blake* ed. J.R. Powell (1937), *Samuel Pepys's Naval Minutes* ed. J.R. Tanner (1925) and *Journals and Narratives of the Third Dutch War* ed. R.C. Anderson (1946). So, too, have various articles in *The Mariner's Mirror* the Journal of the Society for Nautical Research, notably Florence E. Dyer 'Captain Christopher Myngs in the West Indies' xviii (1932): M.L. Baumber 'The Protector's Nephew: Captain Thomas Whetstone in the Mediterranean 1657–9' lii (1966) and in the same volume J.R. Powell 'The Expedition of Blake and Mountagu in 1655'.

In the *Transactions of the Royal Historical Society* N.S. vi (1892) pp. 142–166 Sir Horace Rumbold's 'Notes on the history of the family of Rumbold' confirms much of the story Sandwich heard of the collusion of Henry Rumbold with the Spanish authorities against the English fleet under Blake.

Other modern works besides those directly cited to which I am particularly indebted are

JOHN MORRILL (ed) *Oliver Cromwell and the English Revolution* (1990)

ROY SHERWOOD *The Court of Oliver Cromwell* (1977)

R.A. STRADLING 'A Spanish Statesman of Appeasement: Medina de las Torres 1639–70' *Historical Journal* 19, 1 (1976) pp. 1–31.

Finally I compared the table of prices of food, drink and household necessities given by Sandwich in his Journal at vi, 448 ff. with those compiled by EARL J. HAMILTON for the relevant period in his magisterial *War and Prices in Spain 1651–1800* (1969). The two generally agree to a marked extent and Sandwich supplies some items (e.g. coal, veal, bacon) which are not in Hamilton's table.

INDEX

compiled by Mrs Sarah Ereira